P9-CCW-573

Our Unmet Needs

BOOKS BY CHARLES STANLEY
FROM THOMAS NELSON PUBLISHERS

Enter His Gates
Eternal Security
The Gift of Forgiveness
The Glorious Journey
How to Handle Adversity
How to Keep Your Kids on Your Team
How to Listen to God

The In Touch Study Series
 Advancing Through Adversity
 Becoming Emotionally Whole
 Developing a Servant's Heart
 Developing Inner Strength
 Experiencing Forgiveness
 Listening to God
 Overcoming the Enemy
 Protecting Your Family
 Relying on the Holy Spirit
 Sharing the Gift of Encouragement
 Talking with God
 Understanding Eternal Security
 Understanding Financial Stewardship
 Winning on the Inside

In Touch with God
The Power of the Cross
The Reason for My Hope
The Source of My Strength
Winning the War Within
The Wonderful Spirit-Filled Life

Dunn Public Library
110 E. DIVINE ST.
DUNN, N.C. 28334

WITHDRAWN

Our Unmet Needs

Charles Stanley

OLIVER
NELSON

THOMAS NELSON PUBLISHERS
Nashville

Copyright © 1999 by Charles Stanley

All rights reserved. Written permission must be secured from the publisher to use or reproduce any part of this book, except for brief quotations in critical reviews or articles.

Published in Nashville, Tennessee, by Thomas Nelson, Inc., Publishers.

The Bible version used in this publication is THE NEW KING JAMES VERSION. Copyright © 1979, 1980, 1982, Thomas Nelson, Inc., Publishers.

Library of Congress Cataloging-in-Publication Data

Stanley, Charles F.
    Our unmet needs / Charles Stanley.
        p. cm.
    ISBN 0-7852-6799-9 (repackage)
    ISBN 0-8407-9143-7 (hardcover)
    1. Christian life—Baptist authors. I. Title.
    BV4501.2.S719342 1999
    248.4—dc21

                                                                98-43557
                                                                CIP

Printed in the United States of America
01 02 03 04 05 BVG 5 6 7 8 9 10 11

Contents

My God shall supply all your need according to His riches in glory by Christ Jesus.

—Philippians 4:19

· Introduction ·

The Cry of the World

Do you have unmet needs in your life?

You are not alone! Neediness is a major part of the human condition in our world today.

You can look at any part of the globe, from Afghanistan to Zimbabwe, and you will find unmet needs. People of every social stratum, political persuasion, nation, race, culture, economic condition—and yes, religious affiliation—have unmet needs.

The needs that we face are not only those we find on the external surface of life—economic, social, informational, and political. They are not limited to a prosperity that is defined in economic terms, a satisfaction that is marked by material or physical comfort, or a peace that is externally manifested between individuals, tribes, or nations.

The needs that drive, fuel, and shape all of our external needs are the emotional and spiritual needs that cause us to experience a lack of inner peace with God, others, and ourselves. They are the *real* needs we face as human beings. The deeper, unseen, and vastly more important needs are pervasive in our world, even among those who seem to have no external needs. They are not only *unmet* needs, but needs that are growing ever deeper and broader.

The condition of our lives grows out of the condition of our hearts. It is in the soul and spirit of man that needs are more frequently undefined, unaddressed, and unmet. And this book confronts these emotional and spiritual needs.

If we were able to unravel any of the dire problems that exist in our world today, we would find ourselves arriving at the doorsteps of individual hearts and the unresolved, unmet needs that reside within them. The basic condition of man's heart is one of neediness.

Name just about any problem that plagues our world today and I will point you toward an underlying emotional or spiritual need in the heart of man. Drug abuse. Child abuse. Spouse abuse. Poverty. War. Violence. Crime.

Every one of these areas grows out of emotional and spiritual needs that are first manifested in the heart of one man, one woman, somewhere on this earth. The ripple effect begins with an unmet need in the heart of one person. That person reacts to the circumstances that he believes are related to his unmet need in a way that is unhealthy, ungodly, and ultimately unsatisfactory—perhaps with an outburst of angry words, a drink or use of a drug to attempt to escape the need, a retaliatory measure to the person or situation regarded as responsible for the need, or a grasping for things in a hope of resolving the need. At that point, a trigger has been pulled. What the person does in response to an unmet need causes another person to feel pressure to respond to the behavior at hand. Inevitably unmet needs in that secondary person's life influence attitudes, decisions, and behavior, and so the problem expands and intensifies from person to person until an entire family, neighborhood, community, city, or nation is involved.

Are you willing to face your needs?

Can you define or name at least one need?

If you don't believe you have any needs, this book is not likely to be of much benefit to you because you will fail to see the ways in which God's Word might apply to you. However, if you are willing to define or name at least one need that you know you have, then you have a place to begin in your quest to have that need met. Be honest with yourself. That's the only way the full truth of God's Word can make you whole and, in turn, make you a blessing.

Does God know about your needs? Yes.

Does God care about your needs being met? Yes.

Does God have a provision for meeting your needs? Yes.

How can you identify your real needs and experience God's total provision for your neediness? That is the foremost question we will explore in this book.

· 1 ·

What Is Your Need and What Are
You Willing to Do About It?

Do you have a nagging, gnawing feeling that something isn't quite right in your life?

Do you feel overwhelmed by a need you can't meet, a problem you can't solve, or a question you can't answer?

Are you able to identify the real need that underlies your feelings of uneasiness, fear, worry, or restlessness?

As I have asked people about their needs, they often have laughed and responded, "Oh, I have lots of needs!" But when I have pressed for specifics, many have hesitated. They have not been able to pinpoint precisely the true needs in their lives. They have a general feeling of neediness, but they are unable to define their needs or they are unwilling to name their needs.

Is that how you feel about your needs today?

If so, I encourage you to take a look at the following list. These are the top twenty needs that I have routinely encountered in my work as a pastor. Some of these needs overlap and several are closely related to other needs, but this is the way the needs have been expressed to me:

1. Companionship
2. Achievement or success
3. Employment

     4. Love

     5. Health

     6. Sexual relationship

     7. Security

     8. Harmony in relationship(s)

     9. Finances

   10. Basic needs (food, clothing, shelter)

   11. The need to feel needed

   12. Acceptance

   13. Marriage

   14. Forgiveness

   15. Control

   16. Intimacy

   17. Healing past emotions

   18. Victory over sin

   19. Inner peace

   20. Relationship with God

I invite you to review this list and identify the areas in your life in which you feel that something is missing or something might be better. In all likelihood, you will find several areas in which you have an emotional response or a sense of, "I could use more of that."

For most people, "I could use more of that" is a good working definition of need. But is that the definition that God gives to human need?

Needs vs. Desires

As we begin our discussion about need, we must recognize that *need* is not the same as *desire*. All of us have at some point brought to God something that we believed was a need when it truly was only a desire.

A need is something that is *essential* to the fulfillment of God's plan for a person's life. It may be something as simple as the basics of water, food, and shelter. It may be education or training that is required for a person to fulfill God's plans and purposes. It may be a sense of direction so that a person will know more fully what God desires for him. It may be a financial need to meet the expenses that are associated with the work and the family life that God has given to the person.

A desire tends to be something that is not essential but is *enjoyable*. It can be something for which we have a hunger, yearning, wish, hope, or dream. Just because a desire is not essential does not mean that it has no importance to God. Although a desire may not be a requirement for our lives, it is something that is associated with pleasure or joy in our lives. And the truth is that God is in favor of our experiencing pleasure, joy, and yes, even fun in our lives.

Paul wrote to the Romans, "He who did not spare His own Son, but delivered Him up for us all, how shall He not with Him also freely give us all things?" (Rom. 8:32). The good things that God the Father has for Jesus, He has for us!

The idea of desire is not wrong. Too many Christians seem to believe that life should be a tedious, long-faced journey—no laughter, no fun, no pleasure. Their thinking is, *The holier the person, the more serious the person*. What a boring, uncreative, unjoyful way to live!

A person who is walking in obedience to God should have abundant reasons to enjoy life. God desires for His children to have a life overflowing with all things that are good, and certainly laughter, joy, beauty, comfort, creative expression, blessing, love, health, friendships, and adventures can be very good things in our lives.

We cannot conclude in Scripture that God is *for* meeting our needs and *against* meeting our desires. What we can conclude in Scripture is that God promises to meet all of our needs. God does not, however, promise to meet all of our desires.

THE ERROR OF TURNING DESIRES INTO NEEDS

Many people have tricked themselves into turning a desire into a need. Let me give you an example. A person might see something that captures his interest, and he says, "Now that's something I'd really like to have." And then he begins to justify the purchase of that item with reasoning such as this: "Well, I don't drink and I don't gamble and I don't smoke and I don't have any real vices in my life, and after all, the Lord wants me to have some fun and enjoyment in life." And even though the person cannot afford the item, he goes ahead and puts the purchase on a credit card. He ends up in debt, which is not something God desires for us.

Over time, the person might have increasing difficulty paying the minimum payment for the item, and when the struggle gets intense enough, that person might turn to Philippians 4:19 and say to God, "Your Word says that You will supply all my need so, Lord, You see the financial need that I have in my life right now. I ask You to meet that need, and I have faith that You are going to meet it. Now, Lord, I know You don't want my Christian witness to be damaged by my not being able to pay my bills," and on and on the person goes trying to justify to God what he previously had justified to himself.

Such a person has turned a desire into a need in his thinking and in his prayers, but in truth, the problem is with the person's desire.

God is never obligated to meet a desire that we turn into a need. Take a look at your needs right now. Are they genuine needs, or are they needs that have resulted from your foolish pursuit of desires? God is not responsible for answering any prayer request or meeting any need that does not further His plans and purposes for you on this earth.

Is It Wrong to Have Desires?

There is nothing wrong with our having desires as long as they are within the confines of the purpose and will of God for our lives. At times, we have wonderful and genuine desires that God is eager to meet because they are things or relationships that will enhance God's plan for us.

Psalm 34:10 tells us:

The young lions lack and suffer hunger;
But those who seek the LORD shall not lack any good thing.

Note especially that phrase "any good thing." What is a good thing? Something is good if it meets these criteria:

- It is regarded as good in God's eyes.
- It produces a beneficial, helpful, enriching, genuinely satisfying, and eternal benefit in our lives.

Many times we take it upon ourselves to define what is good for us. But do we really know what that is? Only God can see the beginning from the ending. Only God can see the big picture of our lives. Only God can look around all the corners in the road and see what is coming. Only God knows how things will turn out for us. We must rely on God's definition of *good* before we declare something to be good.

GOD'S PERSPECTIVE ON OUR NEEDINESS

A need, from the scriptural standpoint, is *anything that keeps a person from being whole or from fulfilling God's purpose for his life.*

Wholeness is a vital concept for us to understand regarding the work of God in our lives. So often we get bogged down in our grappling with this problem, that symptom, this situation, that difficulty, this obstacle, that concern. God sees the big picture of our need. He sees us in our perfection—who we *can* be, what we *might* do and become, how we *should* live in order to receive the maximum amount of His blessing. God sees us as whole men and women. Therefore, when God compares what we were created to be and what we are destined to become with who we are right now, the difference is our need. It is the sum of all that keeps us from wholeness.

Time and again we find Jesus saying as He healed various people, "Be made whole." Jesus always had a person's wholeness as His goal.

GOD SEES YOUR LIFE AS A WHOLE

God sees your whole life, and He sees your life as a whole. You cannot divide your life into compartments and say, "This is my spiritual life and this is my material life and this is my home life and this is my financial life." Your life functions as a whole. And the whole of you is in Christ when you become a Christian. Christ is involved in every area of your life. He makes you whole; He does not divide you or separate the areas of your life one from another. This means, of course, that Christ Jesus is involved in every aspect of your neediness. He is concerned not only with your spiritual neediness, but also with your financial, material, physical, relational, and emotional needs.

In every circumstance, situation, place, time, or incident you are in union with Christ because you cannot separate yourself from Him once you have accepted Him as your Savior. He is involved with you every moment of your life. You cannot shut Him out or turn Him away. There is not a single moment or situation with which He is unfamiliar or uninvolved.

Does God care that you just bounced a check and are in need of cash?

Does God care that the air-conditioning in your car no longer works?

Does God care about your tendency to oversleep and arrive at work late every day?

Does God care that your feelings were hurt in an argument that you had with your stepmother?

Yes! God is aware of, concerned about, and involved in every area of need you have, great or small.

Too often, however, we want to face and deal with only our external needs. We want God to provide a quick answer for us only in the tangible, material realm of life. To dig deeper into our neediness is something we perceive as painful, unnecessary, or too spiritual. God doesn't agree with that approach. While He is concerned about the needs we face in the practical and natural realm of life, He is even more concerned about the needs that impact our very identity and our potential as human beings. Rarely are the obvious external needs separate from deeper and more pervasive internal needs.

ALL NEEDS ARE INTERRELATED

All of the needs in your life are interrelated. Imagine for a moment a three-legged stool. If you take away or break one leg, the stool is going to collapse. It cannot stand. If one leg is weakened or splintered, the stool is likely to give way if any pressure is exerted upon it. So it is with the basic needs in your life, be they physical, spiritual, or emotional. Soundness in each area of life is required for wholeness, and strength in each area is necessary for you to withstand the pressures, trials, and traumas that come to you at some point.

Furthermore, each area of your life must exist in balance. If a three-legged stool has one leg that is longer or shorter than the others, the stool is out of balance. It is unstable. God's desire for you is that you be emotionally stable, consistent, reliable, and even in your temperament. He desires for your physical needs to be satisfied. He desires for your spiritual life to be balanced and growing. His will is never for one of His children to be on an emotional, physical, or spiritual roller coaster of extreme highs and lows. Rather, He desires that you be in balance and that you be able to confront both positive and negative situations with a consistency of joy, love, and peace.

The person who is filled with God's Spirit is not a person who experiences love one day and no love the next, joy one day and no joy the next, peace one moment and no peace the next. God's Spirit is not a come-and-go presence in someone's life. God's character does not change; He is without "shadow of turning" or variation in His personality. (See James 1:17.) So, too, with the genuinely Spirit-filled person. Such a person has a consistency of character, an even temperament, a reputation for steadiness.

We can seem whole in one or two of these areas, but that is not sufficient for us truly to be whole in God's eyes. Wholeness from God's perspective is to be complete; to know with deep assurance that we are beloved by God with an everlasting, infinite, and unconditional love; to be able to move forward with boldness and confidence that we are God's children; to claim God's promises that we are victors through Christ Jesus over every negative situation and circumstance; and to be able to stand up to the enemy of our souls regardless of what the devil may throw at us.

Wholeness is more than feeling peace and harmony within. It is a prerequisite for being productive and effective in the kingdom of God and a prerequisite for bringing the maximum amount of glory to God. Wholeness is not just a nice idea or a nice goal to have for our lives. It is absolutely essential to experiencing joy, witnessing for Christ, and receiving eternal rewards.

Wholeness is an inner work that God does in our lives. But we are never the sole beneficiaries of our wholeness. God makes us whole so that we might help and bless others. Wholeness is the work that God does in us with a twofold purpose: that we might be sound in spirit, mind, and emotions, and that we might influence others to accept God's love, forgiveness, and help.

OBVIOUS EXTERNAL NEEDS VS. HIDDEN NEEDS

In my work as a pastor, I have discovered that very often what the person thought was the foremost need in his life did not turn out to be the real need or the only need.

The woman who was having disturbing nightmares and an ongoing inability to sleep thought she had a need for sleep and for inner peace. The real need was to confront the incest that had occurred in her childhood and the deep feelings of unworthiness that had developed in her as a result of that abuse.

The young man who had a fight with his father thought his need was for a place of his own. The real need was his need to develop a new relationship with his father and to come to grips with the feelings of incompetence that had developed from years of belittling criticism in his father's home.

Throughout the Gospels we find a number of people who came to Jesus asking for one thing only, to be healed of all that truly kept them from wholeness. Consider these examples:

In healing a woman who had suffered for twelve years with a flow of blood, Jesus not only met her physical need, but in the very act of touching her, He also restored her to the greater community in which she lived. Her friends and neighbors had not associated with her for years because she was "unclean." Jesus said to her, "Daughter, be of good cheer; your faith has made you well. Go in peace" (Luke 8:48). To live in peace meant to be at peace in her body, free of her affliction, and to be at peace with all those around her. Her need had not only been an uncontrolled hemorrhage and a lack of financial resources as she went from physician to physician seeking a cure. Her need had also been to have fellowship with other people and to be part of a community of friends.

When Jesus healed a paralyzed man who had been lowered by his friends through a rooftop, the first thing He said to the man was, "Son, your sins are forgiven you." Jesus was soundly criticized by some of the scribes for blasphemy—for claiming to have the power to forgive sins. Jesus asked them, "Why do you reason about these things in your hearts? Which is easier, to say to the paralytic, 'Your sins are forgiven you,' or to say, 'Arise, take up your bed and walk'? But that you may know that the Son of Man has power on earth to forgive sins." He said to the paralyzed man, "I say to you, arise, take up your bed, and go to your house" (Mark 2:8–11). Jesus apparently recognized that the root cause of the man's paralysis had something to do with sin in his life. The greater issue related to the healing of the man had to do with a forgiveness of sin—he was in need of a spiritual healing as well as a physical healing.

The healing work of Jesus was first and foremost a spiritual or inner work of healing because Jesus knew that first and foremost, we must be well on the inside if we are truly to become whole.

Because all of our needs are connected, every need we face is related to God and in some way, to some degree, is connected to our spiritual relationship with our heavenly Father. All external needs are to some degree a reflection of inner needs.

GOD'S DEFINITION OF *WELL* IS NOT THAT OF THE WORLD

Spiritual health cannot be defined by the world because the world cannot bring about that health. Why not? In the first place, you must understand what it truly means to be healthy in order to create that state. If you do not know all that is required for a person truly to be healthy, how can you create health or engineer the circumstances that will create health?

We see many conflicts in the medical community when it comes to physical health. One scientific report will tell us that a certain product or substance will promote health, and a few months later, another scientific report will tell us that this product or substance is of little or no effect and that a different product or substance is required. Highly knowledgeable people disagree about what substances are needed in which quantities and at what times of life to promote or produce physical health. The bottom line is that the world does not have an absolute, or even a very solid, consistent definition about what it means to be healthy physically, much less healthy emotionally, spiritually, or psychologically.

Only God knows fully what is required for wholeness because only God knows fully what it means to be whole, perfect, and complete. Only God knows what is missing in our lives because only God sees the total picture.

Furthermore, only God knows how to bring into our lives the missing elements, and only God can cause a person to be made whole. Only God can extend our perfection into the realm of eternity. Only God can heal us fully and cause us to live forever in complete perfection.

Are you willing to face up to your neediness today? Are you willing to face the fact that everything in your inner life isn't as whole, complete, and sound as God would desire for it to be? Are you willing to admit your sinfulness to God? Are you willing to humble yourself and admit that you can't do it all or be it all by yourself and in your own strength?

If you are willing to say yes to these questions, then Jesus is waiting for you to turn to Him and allow Him to heal you, restore you, and make you whole. He wants to be your Savior. He wants to forgive you, to cleanse you of the guilt you have been carrying, and to restore you to a full and right relationship with God the Father. Jesus wants to begin a work in you that will result in your wholeness. Jesus wants to send the Holy Spirit to dwell within you so that you might have the divine Helper, Comforter, and Spirit of truth available and working in you at all times.

GOD'S EXTENDED OPPORTUNITY FOR GENUINE WHOLENESS

I have a strong belief that God gives every person an opportunity—indeed, repeated opportunities—to experience genuine wholeness. I believe that God confronts every person with his neediness and that He offers Himself as the solution for the neediness. He extends an opportunity for healing and wholeness to every person.

When do many people seem to hear this message from God?

I have spoken to a number of people in the last decade about the emotional healing process they have experienced in their personal lives, and I have asked many of them, "When did you first feel the restlessness in your soul that drove you to seek wise counsel and help?" In virtually all cases, they have responded, "Oh, somewhere in my forties."

I don't know why this is the case, but it seems to be part of our human experience to feel this need in our lives when we are forty-something. Perhaps it is that we are so driven to get the external factors of our lives in place prior to that time—we choose a career and work in it, we choose a mate and develop a marriage and perhaps have children, and then we spend a couple of decades working hard at building good associations, good patterns, good habits, raising good families, and achieving successful careers. It seems that once all of these external things are in place, the Lord says, "Now, about those internal things . . ."

Or perhaps it is that at forty, some of the external things that we have so diligently tried to create and produce begin to show cracks. The perfect girlfriend didn't turn out to be a perfect wife, and conversely her perfect boyfriend didn't turn out to be a perfect husband. The children who seemed so perfect lying in their infant cribs suddenly seem to have problems. A career that seemed on the rise takes a nosedive or becomes dissatisfying. In our forties, we often are forced to reappraise and reevaluate our priorities, the success of our past efforts, and the validity of our future goals. As part of our reevaluation, we are confronted with our inner state of being.

Regardless of *why* the forties may be a major time for facing emotional wounds, the fact is that every person I know comes to the point—sooner or later—of saying, Is this all there is to life? Is this truly why I was created? Am I truly fulfilling God's intended plan and purpose for my life? And if not, why not?

When these questions are asked and the answers are not immediate, satisfying, and in keeping with God's Word, the person is forced to ask, What's wrong? In all likelihood, some inner healing needs to be done. God has a work that He desires to do that may be revolutionary and that will also be a work of refinement.

The good news is that God does not leave us where we are, no matter how excellent or how whole we may become. He is always in the process of producing in us more and more of the likeness of Jesus Christ. Surely none of us would be so presumptuous to say, "I am 100 percent like Jesus in all ways." Hardly. God still has a work to do in us. And He continually seeks to do that work. He will not let us remain in our current state without challenging us to greater growth.

The good news is also that once we have developed an intimate relationship with the Lord, the process required for the healing of our old wounds becomes less and less painful. The most painful part of the healing process is nearly always the initial breaking of our stubborn pride, the breaking up of the crusty emotional soul of denial, the breakthrough into the territory of past pain, and the first instances of our "breaking down" and weeping as we face old memories that cloud our ability to see things clearly. The more we desire to be in close fellowship with the Lord, the more we rely upon Him to do His healing work within us, and the more we trust Him to produce in us the nature and character of

· 2 ·

What Doesn't Work in the Meeting of Our Needs?

Are you aware that Jesus did not heal every sick person in the land of Palestine when He walked the earth? Jesus healed every sick person who was brought to Him or who came to Him. Jesus taught: "Those who are well have no need of a physician, but those who are sick . . . For I did not come to call the righteous, but sinners, to repentance" (Matt. 9:12–13).

What does this mean? It means that Jesus made Himself available to all those who knew they were in need and who came to Jesus to be their Great Physician. If you don't think you are sick, you probably aren't going to seek out a doctor. If you don't think you are a sinner, you aren't going to ask God for forgiveness.

People who recognize that they are sick seek help. Those who recognize that they need forgiveness confess their sins and repent of their sinful lives.

Even though God confronts every person with his neediness at some point in his life, God never forces anyone to accept the healing and wholeness He offers. He does not move beyond the boundaries of human will.

"But," you may say, "God can do anything."

Yes, He *can* do anything. It is not a matter of God's ability but a matter related to the freedom that God has given to mankind. God willfully

13

has chosen not to deny the freedom He gave us as individuals to accept or reject His presence and power in our lives.

Most of this book will deal with what *does* work in meeting our needs, but I believe it is important at the outset of our discussion to address several things that *don't* work.

SUPPRESSION DOESN'T WORK

The typical initial response to a need is to cry, "Help!" Most people when faced with a need feel a sense of inner urgency that may be coupled with frustration, anxiety, or a general feeling of unrest, uneasiness, or even fear. A person is likely to say to others and to God, "Can't you see my need? Meet my need! I want this need to be met—and the sooner, the better!"

If a need is not met, it may take on even greater urgency with the passage of time, compelling a person to take action lest the pain or distress continue. A person who has an immediate need for air, for example, is going to take quick action because without oxygen, death is imminent. The longer the person goes without air, the greater the sense of urgency to the point of panic! A person who is drowning or who is freezing doesn't hesitate to cry out and to do everything possible to stay afloat or move to safety. All effort is focused on meeting the urgent need.

Inner emotional and spiritual needs, however, sometimes are not voiced. We may feel the urgency of the need, but we don't display urgent actions or responses. A number of reasons may be given for this. A person may be embarrassed to admit he has an inner need or to seek help from others. A person may be in rebellion against God and may choose to blame God for the need and lack of provision. Still others feel the need but don't know how to define it or express it; they have an unlabeled frustration or sense of anxiety that they don't understand and, therefore, can't articulate.

Over time, these unmet needs tend to take on a "state of being" status. The needs may grow stronger, leading to aberrant behavior, deep depression, or sickness. In those cases, the needs erupt from the spirit and soul of man into the physical, natural, or material world where the symptoms are often addressed, even if the underlying need is not addressed.

In other cases, unmet emotional and spiritual needs merely smolder. They continue to exist, to gnaw, nag, and fester within, but they do not disappear.

Some people seem to have become discouraged, thinking that a particular need in their lives will never go away. Therefore, they conclude, "I just have to learn to live with this."

Others perhaps hope that the need will disappear if they ignore it long enough. That is rarely the case, however.

I have talked to people who are in their sixties and seventies and feel a sense of restlessness and anxiety deep within, and they still don't know the reason for their feelings of neediness. Time alone doesn't automatically bring about either an awareness or an understanding of our neediness. Don't err by making the assumption, "All of this will become clear someday," or by concluding, "These feelings will pass eventually." In most cases, our neediness does not dissipate with time, and neither does it disappear unless we truly address the root problem of the neediness and allow God to heal or resolve the problem.

DENYING THE NEED DOESN'T WORK

In some cases, a person hears from others, "You don't really have a need." Without a sympathetic ear, he simply stops talking about the need. It exists nonetheless.

And in other cases, a person may move into self-denial, claiming to himself and others, "I don't have a need," when in reality, the need exists and has only been buried deeper into the person's soul, psyche, or spirit.

For many years, I lived in a state of denial regarding my father, who died when I was nine months old. If a person asked me about my father, I replied, "I never had a dad. He died when I was a baby. I never knew him." If a person asked me what impact my father had on me, I replied, "No impact. I never knew him, so he had no effect on my life."

Then one day when I was in my forties a secretary in our church brought her nine-month-old baby girl into the office for me to meet. As I held that baby and talked to her, telling her how wonderful she was, she responded with big grins and a real sense of understanding in her eyes. After the mother and child left my office, the thought struck me,

That baby knew me! She responded to me. She felt my words and my touch. That's how old I was when my father died. I did know my father!

The following Saturday afternoon as I was praying in the prayer room at church, I had a strong mental picture of my grandfather and my father. They were talking and laughing while they were sitting on a log in some woods. Suddenly I had a deep ache in my heart to be with them. I wanted to be in the middle of their conversation, share their laughter, and feel their close presence.

The more I thought about my grandfather and my father, the angrier I became at God. "Why did You take my dad from me?" I prayed. And that was the beginning of a breakthrough for me. In that moment, nearly twenty years ago, the hard shell of denial was cracked. I had a father. I had a relationship with him. I had feelings about my relationship with my dad. And I could no longer stuff those feelings away and deny their existence. I had to examine them and deal with them.

Denial manifests itself in numerous ways.

A person may say, for example, "I certainly don't have an emotional or spiritual problem. What I have is a financial need! I need more money."

On closer examination, however, one might ask the person:

- Why do you need more money?
- How did you come to the place in your life where you have a financial need?
- What is your understanding of money and its purpose in your life?

These questions eventually compel an emotional and spiritual response. A person may say that he needs more money because he is in debt and has unpaid bills. On closer examination, a pattern of indebtedness and overspending is uncovered. What causes that person to overextend his resources? Is it presumption that God will provide? Is it a feeling of inferiority that the person hopes will be met through the accumulation and display of material possessions? Is it a lack of discipline? The underlying issue is not truly a financial one, although the external surface symptom of the problem is financial. The underlying need is in the emotions and in the spirit. It is related to the person's understanding about God and His commands and desires related to stewardship of resources.

Let me give you another example of denial at work.

A woman whom I will call Sarah recently told me this story. A friend of Sarah's was experiencing serious marital difficulties, and as she confided them to Sarah, Sarah asked, "What do *you* think you might have done to contribute to these problems in your marriage?" Sarah's friend said, "Not a thing. Even my counselor said that this problem is all his fault." Sarah related this incident to me, then asked, "Will a counselor ever place total blame on one person in a relationship?" My answer: "It's not likely."

What was at work? A denial about the root need underlying the external surface problem. If this woman remains unwilling to face her emotional and spiritual needs, she will never come to an understanding about how the needs drive and define behavior, including her behavior toward her spouse.

When another person doesn't treat us the way we desire, we must ask, Why is this person responding to *me* in this way? What is it about my behavior that brings out this response? An honest look at ourselves is likely to reveal an unmet emotional or spiritual need.

AVOIDING CONFRONTATION DOESN'T WORK

At times we adopt a number of behaviors to avoid confrontation and thus avoid the rejection that is a possible consequence of confrontation. These behaviors become "structures" that we build—they serve as walls or barriers in our relationships. We may think we are protecting ourselves with these structures, but in the greater reality of God's purposes, these structures close us off from other people and from God's presence.

DISTANCE
We may not want to get too close to another person, even someone we love dearly, out of fear that he may "see through us" or discover something in us that he will not like.

PROJECTION
Perhaps we say to another person, "You have a problem." In truth, the very problem we identify in that person is *our* problem. A person may

say, for example, "You are always so selfish." The truth is that the person saying this is the self-centered one. A truly selfless, other-focused person rarely sees others as selfish!

Why do we project our faults onto others? In hopes of deflecting blame or fault away from ourselves. We want to appear faultless so that others will love us.

LYING

At times, people cover their bad behavior with a self-justifying lie, such as, "If you were in my position, you'd do the same thing." Or we say, "Everybody does this. Everybody feels this way." We think that if we can hide our guilt under a cover of excuse, we'll be more acceptable and lovable.

ACQUIESCENCE

Do you know a person who always gives in to what others desire in order to avoid conflict? Many a spouse has said, "Whatever you want, dear," to avoid an argument. Many a person has said, "Whatever you say," to avoid facing the truth of an attitude, feeling, or behavior that may be painful to face.

CONFORMITY

Often, we try to blend in with others with a hope that if we are *like* others, others will accept and love us. We become like putty in a mold so that we won't risk rejection for standing out in some way. We lay down our unique identity and our strength in a desire for acceptance.

When you find yourself engaging in these behaviors, you need to stop what you are doing and ask, Why am I so afraid to be myself? Why am I afraid to have an opinion, to face the truth, to get close to someone, to open up and reveal who I am? Why am I lying or projecting my faults onto others? What do I think I will gain, or lose, by this?

When we build these structures into our relationships with others—and with God—we cut off the flow of God's power in our lives. We damage our communication, we stifle our creativity, and we fail to reach the full potential of any relationship. These structures are walls that keep us from the very intimacy we desire so intensely.

RELYING ON ANOTHER PERSON DOESN'T WORK

When I learned a little bit more about this situation, I could see clearly some of the needs that existed. The woman was what we used to call a clinging vine. She relied heavily upon her husband to make her happy; she expected him to meet her every need, including every emotional need. No man is capable of doing that, of course. Only God can meet all of our needs with His infinite power, love, and wisdom. The more the woman clung to her husband, demanding that he meet all of her emotional needs, the more he withdrew. He couldn't stand the pressure. He spent more time alone and away from their home. He was less likely to engage in conversation and to express himself to his wife. He had moved into a self-preservation mode that the woman couldn't begin to understand because she didn't see her neediness as influencing his behavior.

In a number of cases a person will turn to another person or to an institution for the total provision of need in his life. That person may be a spouse, a parent, a child, or an employer. It may be the welfare office, the government agency, the law, the system.

Let me assure you of two things: no one person, and no one agency or system, can meet all of the needs in your life, and certainly not the deep inner needs that are vital to wholeness. A knight in shining armor who rides in to rescue the needy person and save the day so that everybody lives happily ever after is a character in a fairy tale. People can help people, but no one person can completely resolve all of the needs in another person's life.

Husbands and wives get along so much better when both realize they cannot fully meet all needs of the other person.

Parents and children get along better when both realize that all of their needs cannot be met through a parent-child relationship, no matter how good that relationship might be.

Friendships are improved when both friends realize that they cannot provide all the emotional support they require as individuals.

Employers and employees get along better when each realizes that the other side is not the end-all and be-all for meeting needs.

Yes, even pastors and churches get along better when neither looks solely to the other to supply all of the inner needs.

Furthermore, if you are looking to people to resolve all of your needs—and factoring out God—you are going to be sorely disappointed. If you had all of the people in the world working in a concerted manner on your particular need, you still would not experience a full provision for your need. People, individually and collectively, will eventually let you down, especially when it comes to what you need for inner emotional and spiritual health.

As quickly as you hear the praises of other people, just as quickly you are likely to hear their cutting remarks and criticism.

One moment the world may clamor for you and call you great, fabulous, the best, a star, the most desirable of all people. The next moment the world, in its fickleness, is likely to drag your name through the mud and despise all that you do, say, and stand for.

You cannot count on other people to be your source of self-worth and value. If you do, you eventually will be disappointed.

STRIVING TO MEET THE NEED ON YOUR OWN DOESN'T WORK

In a number of cases, when a person discovers that another person or a group of people has let him down, he will conclude, "I'm just going to have to do this for myself." Each of us seems to have a strong drive for self, self, self. We all try at some time in our lives to meet our inner needs through our own efforts. And ultimately we fail in our efforts because no amount of self-effort or self-supply can satisfy a deep emotional or spiritual need. In fact, attempting to do it on our own will make matters worse. Anytime we try to meet our needs in our own way, bypassing God and acting on our own will and impulses, we dig an even deeper hole in our emotional structure. We simply cannot make ourselves whole.

Self-striving—the seeking to accomplish things totally on your own strength, effort, and creativity—produces two very negative results in you. First, it nearly always generates anxiety, which may manifest itself as worry, frustration, or an inner agitation. These feelings come because deep down inside, you know that your striving is in vain and that you cannot be and do all that you desire in your own strength. Even so, you refuse to turn over the reins of your life to God; you keep pushing forward, trying to do what you know you cannot do. You push and strain and groan against needs, all the while with a churning in your stomach or a headache born of stress and worry.

In Matthew 6, we find Jesus speaking to people who were in need. Many of the people who heard Jesus give what we now call the Sermon on the Mount were simple people who had very basic needs for food, clothing, shelter. They lived from day to day in the material meeting of their needs. They also had the same emotional and spiritual needs that all human beings have had in every generation. Many of these people apparently were guilty of striving to meet their needs without seeking God's help, and they were frustrated, anxious, and filled with worry in the process. Jesus said to them,

> *Do not worry about your life, what you will eat or what you will drink; nor about your body, what you will put on. Is not life more than food and the body more than clothing? Look at the birds of the air, for they neither sow nor reap nor gather into barns; yet your heavenly Father feeds them. Are you not of more value than they? Which of you by worrying can add one cubit to his stature? So why do you worry about clothing? Consider the lilies of the field, how they grow: they neither toil nor spin; and yet I say to you that even Solomon in all his glory was not arrayed like one of these. Now if God so clothes the grass of the field, which today is, and tomorrow is thrown into the oven, will He not much more clothe you, O you of little faith? Therefore do not worry, saying, "What shall we eat?" or "What shall we drink?" or "What shall we wear?" For after all these things the Gentiles seek. For your heavenly Father knows that you need all these things. But seek first the kingdom of God and His righteousness, and all these things shall be added to you. Therefore do not worry about tomorrow, for tomorrow will worry about its own things. Sufficient for the day is its own trouble. (Matt. 6:25–34)*

How do you get beyond a spirit of striving and instead have a spirit of total trust in and dependency upon God? Jesus gave the answer in this passage. He said that you must turn your mind away from a preoccupation with acquiring things and focus upon God and His kingdom. You must shift your priorities when it comes to the things you think about, dream about, and desire.

What do you think about the most today? Is it that new red sports car in the car dealer's showroom? Is it remodeling your kitchen? Is it about what you will fix for tomorrow's dinner? Is it where you will get your next drink or your next fix of drugs? Is it how you can manipulate that troublesome or weak person at work to do your bidding?

Most of us don't like to admit to such thoughts as being our predominant thoughts, but so often they are! Stop to consider your last thought before you go to sleep at night. To what does your mind turn when you find yourself in heavy stop-and-go traffic? What do you think about when you engage in routine chores that require little concentration? What do you dream about doing, being, or having?

The anxiety that comes from self-striving is nearly always related to the fact that you are spending way too much time thinking about the wrong things. You are so concerned about self and self-defined priorities and needs that you fail to focus your heart and mind on the very things that will bring you peace and a solution for your needs.

The second great negative result of self-striving is this: depression and frustration that arise from a sense of failure. When you focus on the things that you want, you will always reach a point at which you realize— perhaps not consciously but certainly in your deep subconscious being— that you cannot have all that you desire to have, and neither can you control or manipulate other people in the ways that you desire.

Stop to consider the truth of these statements:

You cannot make another person love you.

You cannot always have your way in every situation.

You cannot own everything you want to own right now.

You cannot achieve anything totally in your own strength and ability.

You cannot do anything to absolute perfection.

You cannot persuade everybody to think the way you think.

If we are truly honest with ourselves, we will admit that we don't like the fact that we can't control these things. Yet no one is capable of doing anything that exists as an absolute. In other words, you cannot control anything *all* the time, *every* time, *totally,* for *all* people. Only God is absolute. He alone is omniscient, omnipresent, and omnipotent. He alone governs and rules the universe according to His laws, which are unchanging. He alone is the Father who is without "variation or shadow of turning" (James 1:17).

When we come face-to-face with our inadequacies, failures, and limitations, we are prone to frustration, worry, and anxiety. We don't like recognizing that we cannot control all that we desire to control or that the world does not spin around us.

Jesus said, in effect, "Rather than focus on what *you* desire, which will always lead to the realization of what you cannot do and be in your own strength, turn your attention to what *God* desires! Focus instead on what He can enable you to do and be. Concentrate on what He has prepared for you and desires for you. He will provide!"

No method and no relationship we can ever devise is going to work when it comes to our emotional and spiritual healing. Why? Because God did not make us to go through life on our own. He made us for Himself. He created us to be in fellowship with Him, first and foremost. Certainly God wants us to have good relationships with other people, but the number one relationship for each of us is a relationship with Him.

When we try to get our needs met apart from God, our efforts lead only to disappointment, discouragement, disillusionment, and despair. Only God can fill the emptiness of the human heart. Only God is sufficient to meet our deepest needs for acceptance, love, and worthiness. And only as these needs are met can we truly experience wholeness.

Are You Willing to Take the First Step?

Are you willing to admit that you have inner emotional needs?

Are you willing to stop suppressing or denying your needs in hopes they will go away or resolve themselves without action on your part?

Are you willing to turn to Jesus and trust Him to be your Great Physician?

The way to move beyond neediness is to be active. If you truly want to experience wholeness in your life, God requires something of you. And even as He requires something of you, He offers you *all* of Himself to help you do what He has required.

I invite you to go to your heavenly Father today and say,

Here is my need, Father. I admit that I've been suppressing my neediness. I have been living in denial. I admit that I have tried to meet this need in my own way or by my own method, and what I have done hasn't worked. I turn to You fully and ask You to meet my need in Your way and in Your timing. If there is a need in my life that I haven't faced, I ask You to help me discover it. I trust You to meet my need, and I thank You in advance for meeting it. I ask this in Jesus' name. Amen.

Make a decision today to become a whole person and to live in wholeness, trusting God to meet *all* of your needs.

· 3 ·

The Most Basic Need of Your Life

Have you dealt with the bottom-line need of your life?
Have you resolved the number one need that you share in common with every other person?

Have you resolved the one need that you must resolve during your lifetime on this earth?

Every human being ever born and every human being alive today has had one need in common. This need is the most basic one of life, and ultimately it is the only essential need. It is the need to be forgiven of one's sin nature and come into right relationship with God so that one might experience an abundant life now and in eternity hereafter.

One of the great truths is this: all other needs are secondary to this need to be born again spiritually. It is equally true that once this need is met in a person's life, all other needs *can* be met, and until this need is met, most other needs *cannot* be met.

Try as you might . . .

- you can love a person, but you'll never fully know what love is until you begin to receive God's love.
- you can communicate well with a person, but you'll never fully know what it means to communicate completely until you can communicate freely with God.
- you can establish a relationship with a person and be committed to

it, but you'll never know the full power and comfort of what it means to be in a relationship until you establish a relationship with God.

All of the things that we so much desire as human beings flow from and are enriched greatly by the establishment of an intimate, loving relationship with our Creator, almighty God, our heavenly Father. Emotional and spiritual health does not arise and cannot arise from anything that a person does in his own strength or in relationship with other people. Genuine emotional and spiritual health must flow from the relationship with God.

WHAT IS YOUR PERSONAL RELATIONSHIP WITH GOD?

Ask yourself today, Do I have an intimate relationship with God?

Some people must admit, "I don't have *any* relationship with Him." Others nearly always must admit, "I don't have as intimate a relationship with God as I would like to have."

Begin at that point. Deal first with your relationship with God. Move toward God. He most certainly is moving toward you already. Tell the Lord how you feel, what you desire, where you hurt, why you think you are hurting. Read God's Word with your eyes wide open to the many possible ways that the Lord wants to speak to you personally, through His Word. You are likely to discover valuable nuggets of wise counsel that you had no idea were buried in God's Word. Spend more time with the Lord, talking to Him and listening to Him. Spend more time in His Word, reading with your heart open to the work that God desires to do in you. Build a relationship with God.

As the Lord reveals areas of hurt and pain to you, ask Him to heal you of that pain. Be willing to weep in the Lord's presence. Allow Him to use your tears to cleanse from your inner soul the impurities and bitter memories that keep you from being emotionally whole.

Ask the Lord to reveal whether you need the wise counsel of a pastor or Christian psychologist. Avail yourself of the help that the Lord makes available to you. Be willing to talk to Christ-following, godly men and women and to seek their insights into God's Word and God's healing process.

Don't begin at the symptom level. Begin at the root level—your need for an intimate, loving, and healing relationship with God.

Every Person Needs a Spiritual Rebirth

Nicodemus came to Jesus at night. He didn't want anybody to see him consulting the man named Jesus, who was considered by many of Nicodemus's peers to be nothing more than a low-class, itinerant carpenter who claimed to be a prophet. Nicodemus said, "Rabbi, we know that You are a teacher come from God; for no one can do these signs that You do unless God is with him" (John 3:2).

Nicodemus came to Jesus with what he thought was an intellectual need—a question that he hoped Jesus might be able to answer, a problem that he hoped Jesus might be able to resolve for him so that he would know what and how to think. Nicodemus had seen and heard many things, but he hadn't been able to put it all together. He sought clarification, enlightenment, and a rational, understandable, definitive answer from Jesus.

Jesus, however, perceived more than an intellectual need. He answered Nicodemus's question by addressing the underlying spiritual root: "Most assuredly, I say to you, unless one is born again, he cannot see the kingdom of God" (John 3:3). Jesus further said, "Unless one is born of water and the Spirit, he cannot enter the kingdom of God . . . You must be born again" (John 3:5, 7). Jesus didn't try to prove His divine nature; rather, He went to the core of Nicodemus's need, which was to have a spiritual rebirth.

Every person needs to be cleansed from sin. Every person needs to be released from the burden of guilt, filled with the Holy Spirit, and made whole spiritually.

So many falsehoods are circulating today about how a person comes to be a Christian. Let me state it very plainly for you:

Salvation isn't gained by being good.

Salvation isn't gained by doing good.

Salvation isn't gained by thinking good thoughts and having good attitudes.

Salvation isn't gained by joining a good church or by being baptized in a good baptismal service.

Salvation isn't gained by having someone else state that you are good.

Salvation isn't gained by thinking good things about Jesus.

Salvation is gained by your receiving Christ into your life and dwelling in Him even as He dwells in you.

Some time ago I was at an In Touch (the name of our ministry) dinner in Chicago, and I happened to sit at a table with people who were from a denomination other than mine. I asked them how they happened to start listening to the In Touch programs. One of the women told me that she had always believed in Jesus. She had seen statues and paintings of Him all her life.

She said, "When I heard you say, 'Receive Jesus into your life with your faith,' suddenly it was as if a light was turned on inside me. I thought, *Now I know what to* do *with Jesus.*" Up to that point she had known about Jesus, but she hadn't known what kind of relationship with Jesus she might have. He had been "out there" on the walls and in the stained glass windows and in the words of her church ritual, but He had never been "in there" in her heart.

She said, "I am nearly seventy years old, and for more than sixty years Jesus was someone I called *the* Savior. But now I know Him as *my* Savior."

Salvation is a union with Jesus Christ that is initiated and implemented by God the Father when you believe that Jesus Christ is God's provision for your eternal salvation from sin's death consequences. As the apostle Paul wrote so clearly: "For by grace you have been saved through faith, and that not of yourselves; it is the gift of God, not of works, lest anyone should boast" (Eph. 2:8–9).

What is our position when we are in Christ? We are fully adopted into God's immediate family! We are joint heirs with Christ Jesus. We are God's sons and daughters. We have an eternal relationship with God. You are in union with Christ Jesus. The Holy Spirit of almighty God is living His life in you and through you.

A Spiritual Relationship with Christ Jesus Is Forever

Once this relationship is established, it can never be taken away from you or even destroyed by you. Why? Because of the way you entered the relationship.

Who initiated the relationship? God the Father.

Who made the relationship possible? Jesus Christ on the cross, and in an ongoing daily way, the Holy Spirit who brings us to a full knowledge of what Jesus Christ did on the cross.

God Himself, in His fullness, brought about the union we have with Him by Christ Jesus, and nothing that any human being does can undo what God has done. You don't have that power, and neither do I. God's work in saving us is just as definitive as Christ's death on the cross.

We can cause ourselves not to feel the union we have with Christ. We can lose some of our joy about being in union with God. We can sin and become estranged from our heavenly Father. But we can never break or destroy the union that is forged with God when we are genuinely saved. Those who have been spiritually birthed cannot be "unbirthed." Just as after a baby is born, he can never be returned to his mother's womb, so the person who has been born again spiritually cannot be returned to his previous state.

"But what about when I sin?" you may ask.

God sees your sin, grieves your sin, and moves immediately to convict you of your sin so that you will confess it to Him, receive His forgiveness for it, and then not sin again.

"But what about when I sin repeatedly?" you may say. "Eventually God is going to get tired of my sinning since I have experienced His grace and know better. Eventually He is going to turn away from me."

No, He is not. He is there to stay. He will continue to work in your life with a great motivation of love so that you might return to Him and renew your commitment to walking in right paths. He will be with you in every storm of your life. You have never even been in a drizzle or a gentle mist without Jesus' knowing it and being at your side. He is always with you.

You may ask, "Well, where was I before I was in union with Christ? In what state of being was I living before I was born again?" The Bible answers that question clearly in 1 Corinthians 15. Paul stated that before we were in Christ, each of us was "in Adam." We had Adam's propensity to sin. We had his nature to seek after our own will and to attempt to do things our own way. We had Adam's death sentence on our lives because we had Adam's built-in estrangement from God. Adam's sin has tainted the souls of all who were born after him. In Adam, each of us was in a state of spiritual death, a state of spiritual sinfulness.

Once we were born again, we began to live in Christ, and we were sealed forever into an eternal newness of life. As Paul wrote, "For since by man came death, by Man also came the resurrection of the dead. For as in Adam all die, even so in Christ all shall be made alive" (1 Cor. 15:21–22).

When you come to God to claim a promise of God in His Word, you come to Him on the basis that you are His child. You have a position in Christ Jesus. Because you are in Christ, you have access to everything you need.

Take another look at Romans 8:32, which says, "He who did not spare His own Son, but delivered Him up for us all, how shall He not with Him also freely give us all things?"

At the cross, God demonstrated His goodness to us in the most unforgettable, meaningful, and eternally beneficial way possible. It was through the death of God's beloved Son, Jesus Christ, that God perfectly and intensely demonstrated to us His awesome, indescribable love. There is nothing more dramatic or absolute that God could have done or could ever do to show us how much He loves us.

In giving us Jesus as our Savior, God gave us His absolute best gift for all eternity. And, Paul reasoned, if God gave us such a supreme and wonderful gift, why wouldn't God give us every other and lesser good thing? If God has already given us the Gift of gifts, how much more likely is it that God will give us all of the lesser gifts that we desire?

There isn't anything greater than Jesus that God could give us. And in giving us Jesus, He hasn't closed the door to our receiving other things from His hand. To the contrary, He has shown us that all good things are ours to receive, in His timing, according to His methods and purposes, and for our benefit.

Let's assume for the moment that you are a great lover of fine art. You are invited one evening to have dinner with some friends who are also art lovers and who hold your friendship in high regard. At the close of the evening, one of your friends says, "My wife and I have been praying about this, and we have decided that we would like to give you a painting as a gift." Let's further assume that this painting is one that you have admired often in their home. You know that at last appraisal, this painting was valued at more than $10,000. You know about the artist and his work. How would you respond?

Well, if you are really honest with yourself, you'd be thrilled! You might hem and haw a little and say, "Oh, you really shouldn't," but deep inside, you would be leaping for joy.

Now do you suppose for a moment that if these friends had offered such a generous and astonishing gift, and you graciously received it, they would hesitate for even one second if you asked them, "May I have a piece of paper to use in wrapping this painting so I can take it home without damaging it?"

Of course not! They would be quick to respond to your request for materials to ensure that the painting was protected and valued. They would be delighted that you wanted to safeguard the painting.

In like manner, your heavenly Father has offered you the most amazing gift that you can ever receive—the gift of His Son and full forgiveness of your sin nature through believing in His Son. He is not going to withhold from you anything that will enable or assist you in taking Jesus into the world in which you live and work. God desires for you to display your relationship with Jesus in every facet of your life, and He will grant every request you make that furthers the witness of Christ Jesus in you and through you.

EVERYTHING IS PROVIDED FOR GOOD AND GODLY LIVING

Once you are in union with Christ Jesus, everything you need for good and godly living is made available to you. In 2 Peter 1:3–4 we read these encouraging words:

> *His divine power has given to us all things that pertain to life and godliness, through the knowledge of Him who called us by glory and virtue, by which have been given to us exceedingly great and precious promises, that through these you may be partakers of the divine nature, having escaped the corruption that is in the world through lust.*

Peter said three things in this brief passage: First, Peter said that God intends for us to be full partakers of the divine nature of Jesus Christ. God intends for us to escape the consequences associated with sinful living.

We have been freed from the grip of sin, and we have been freed from the sentence of eternal death. God intends for us to live in as much provision and victory as Jesus lived when He was on this earth.

Second, Peter said that we not only have Jesus Christ as our example of a perfect life, but we have Him inside us to enable us to live in a way that is pleasing to God and totally in line with God's commandments.

Third, Peter said that all things that pertain to life and godliness have been given to us. God has provided the things that pertain to life, or in our terminology today, "making a living." He has given us all things in the natural and material realm that we need in order not only to survive but also to live a sufficient life on this earth. And God has provided all the things in the spiritual and inner realm of life so that we might live in godliness, which is to be in right relationship with God, in right relationship with others, and whole in our emotions and spirits. Nothing that you need for good living and godly living is kept from you.

In Romans 8:15–17, Paul wrote,

> *You did not receive the spirit of bondage again to fear, but you received the Spirit of adoption by whom we cry out, "Abba, Father." The Spirit Himself bears witness with our spirit that we are children of God, and if children, then heirs—heirs of God and joint heirs with Christ.*

God intends for you to live without the guilt and fear that come from the bondage of sin. God desires for you to live in the full freedom of knowing that you are a child of God. Furthermore, He intends for you to have access to everything that Jesus has access to—you are an equal heir with Jesus Christ to all of God's supply.

What does Jesus have access to? Everything that is good and beneficial and leads to wholeness!

CHRIST'S POWER IS RESIDENT IN YOU

Are you aware of the power that is available to you if you are one with Christ Jesus? This power is not your power, but Christ's power. His authority, His ability, His wisdom, His effectiveness.

In John 17, Jesus said of His disciples, "They are not of the world, just as I am not of the world." And then Jesus prayed for them and for us,

"I do not pray for these alone, but also for those who will believe in Me through their word; that they all may be one, as You, Father, are in Me, and I in You; that they also may be one in Us, that the world may believe that You sent Me" (John 17:16, 20–21). What a glorious and awesome thing it is to be one with Christ Jesus, who is one with God the Father! What a privilege we have!

At times I hear people talking about demons, and I am amazed at the great power they ascribe to the devil and his cohorts. While I certainly believe in demonic power, I don't quake at the thought of it. I am in union with One who is so far greater than all the demons of hell put together that there truly is no comparison. The devil is a creature, made by God and always under God's dominion. He exists only because God allows him to exist. He has no authority over God, no ability to win a victory over God, and no power equal to that of God.

As believers, we should give very little credit to the devil and demons. They exist, they exert influence, but they are totally within the confines of God's authority. The Bible states very clearly that the Holy Spirit resident in us is far superior to any power manifested by evil. John wrote, "You are of God, little children, and have overcome them [the spirits that do not confess Christ], because He who is in you is greater than he who is in the world" (1 John 4:4).

NOT FEELINGS BUT POSITION

When we approach and claim the promises of God in the Bible, we do so on the basis that our position is in Christ. We do not claim the promises of God because we feel at one time that the promises are true for us or we feel positive in a particular situation that God is going to act on our behalf. We claim the promises of God as true for us because of what Jesus has done for us, what God has said He would do for us, and what the Holy Spirit is available to do in us, through us, and for us. Our access to the reality of God's promises is not based on anything that we are or have done; it is based on who God is, what Jesus Christ has done, and what the Holy Spirit desires to do.

We are to live out our lives on the basis of our position in Christ Jesus. We are to come to the Father in prayer with boldness and confidence, fully aware of our position in Christ and fully aware of what Christ Jesus is both capable and desirous of doing on our behalf.

As long as we refuse God's love and His offer of forgiveness through Jesus Christ, we cannot be made whole within. We cannot make ourselves whole. Only the Holy Spirit can do that work within us. And the Holy Spirit will not act to perform this work within us until we actively receive Jesus Christ.

Our part is to receive and to accept God's forgiveness. Our part is to believe that Jesus died on our behalf and for our sins.

God's part is to assure us of His love and forgiveness by giving us the gift of the Holy Spirit to reside within us and to heal us from the inside out.

Plain and simple—until we accept the shed blood of Jesus as having been shed on our behalf, we cannot be whole. Jesus is the only One who can meet all of the needs in our lives in a definitive and lasting way.

CHRIST GUARANTEES GOD'S PROMISE TO MEET OUR NEEDS

What is a guarantee? It is a pledge or formal vow that a person will do what he has promised to do. God makes us a promise in Philippians 4:19, a promise that He will supply all of our needs according to His riches in glory by Christ Jesus. What is the foundation for this guarantee? The foundation is to be found in the phrase "by Christ Jesus." We see this much more clearly if we switch the structure of the verse around: "According to His riches in glory by Christ Jesus, all your needs shall be supplied by my God."

Our position in Christ Jesus is the foundation for our having all of our needs met. The supply of our needs is guaranteed by our position in Christ.

Our position in Christ is our relationship with Christ. If we do not have a relationship with Christ, we are not in a position for Christ to meet our needs. If we have a weak relationship with Christ, we are in a weak position for having Christ meet our needs.

The phrase "in Christ" is found more than 130 times in the New Testament. It is the very heart of what it means to be a Christian. It is the foundation for all that the apostle Paul taught.

John recorded this teaching of Jesus:

Abide in Me, and I in you . . . I am the vine, you are the branches. He who abides in Me, and I in him, bears much fruit; for without Me you can do nothing . . . If you abide in Me, and My words abide in you, you will ask what you desire, and it shall be done for you. (John 15:4, 5, 7)

To abide in Christ is to be in union with Christ. It is to dwell in Him completely, without any part of our being kept outside Him. We are entirely submissive to Christ and subject to His command over our lives. We do not choose to do anything without Him. In fact, we *can't* succeed at doing anything without Him. Christ lives in us and we live in Him. And as we abide in Him and in His teaching, we make our requests and receive God's provision.

Paul wrote to the Colossians, "As you therefore have received Christ Jesus the Lord, so walk in Him, rooted and built up in Him and established in the faith, as you have been taught, abounding in it with thanksgiving" (Col. 2:6–7). Paul did not say to walk "after" Christ or "in the footsteps of Christ," he said to walk "in" Christ, rooted or abiding in Him. And, Paul added, be grateful for the life you have in Him. Be thankful for this abundant life you have been given in Christ.

When you receive Jesus Christ, the Holy Spirit comes to indwell your spirit, and the very life that you begin to live is His life, manifested through your talents, your gifts, your personality, and in your circumstances and the context of your life.

People who have never accepted Christ do not have the life of Jesus Christ flowing in them and through them. They cannot experience the fullness of God's promises because these promises are only manifested fully by Christ Jesus.

ARE YOU IN THE RIGHT POSITION FOR CHRIST TO MEET YOUR NEEDS?

Let me repeat again the truths with which I began this chapter. They are vital for your life now, your eternal life, and your ability to grasp and claim the material in the remaining chapters of this book:

All of our needs are secondary to our need to accept Jesus Christ as our Savior, to be born again spiritually, and to live in right relationship with God our Father.

All of our needs *cannot* be met apart from Christ Jesus.

All of our needs *can* be met in Christ Jesus.

If you have never accepted Jesus Christ as your personal Savior and been born again spiritually, I invite you to take that step today and pray with me:

Father, I admit to You that I am a sinful person. I have thought, said, and done things that are not pleasing to You. I know I am not in right standing with You. I believe that Jesus died on the cross in my place, and I accept what He has done on my behalf. I ask You to change my sin nature and to fill me with Your Holy Spirit. Help me to live the new good and godly life that You desire for me to live so that I might become all that You created me to be. I ask this in the name of Jesus. Amen.

· 4 ·

All Manner of Need

Many people I know believe that God will meet some of their needs, solve some of their problems, grant them some of their desires. That is not what Paul wrote to the Philippians: "My God shall supply all your need" (Phil. 4:19).

"All, Dr. Stanley?" you may be saying. "You don't know my needs!"

All. Regardless of your needs.

When Paul wrote that all of our needs are met in Christ Jesus, he knew that Christ Jesus was more than capable of meeting our needs. We see that manifested in numerous examples throughout the earthly life and ministry of Jesus.

The Very Purpose of Jesus Was to Meet Need

One of the reasons that God came in the form of human flesh, in the life of His Son, Jesus Christ, was to show us that God is concerned about human need. Jesus Christ identified with human need. He confronted, dealt with, and fought against human need of all types. Jesus did not sit afar off, passing judgment on those in need or ignoring the needs of the people. To the contrary! He rolled up His sleeves and marched straight forward into the greatest needs known to man.

Furthermore, Jesus knew from the outset of His ministry that His purpose on this earth was to confront and meet human need. In Luke

4:18–19, we find Jesus taking the scroll in the synagogue in Nazareth on the Sabbath and reading from Isaiah 61:

The Spirit of the LORD is upon Me,
Because He has anointed Me
To preach the gospel to the poor;
He has sent Me to heal the brokenhearted,
To proclaim liberty to the captives
And recovery of sight to the blind,
To set at liberty those who are oppressed;
To proclaim the acceptable year of the LORD.

As soon as Jesus had closed the scroll and handed it back to the attendant, He said, "Today this Scripture is fulfilled in your hearing" (Luke 4:21).

Jesus was declaring to the people that He knew that His very purpose on this earth was to meet the needs of people—to preach good news to those who were poor in spirit, to heal the brokenhearted, to set free those who were in the bondage of sin, and to reveal the Father in a way the people hadn't been able to see Him before.

If one statement could sum up the earthly ministry of Jesus, it would probably be this: He met people's needs. Repeatedly the writers of the New Testament told how Jesus met people *where they were* and met *whatever need they had*. No need was off-limits to Jesus; no need was too great or too small. He confronted physical needs as well as spiritual and emotional needs. In Matthew 4:23, we read about the beginning days of Jesus' ministry: "Jesus went about all Galilee, teaching in their synagogues, preaching the gospel of the kingdom, and healing all kinds of sickness and all kinds of disease among the people."

In Acts 10:38, Peter—an eyewitness of Jesus' ministry—characterized the work of Jesus this way: "God anointed Jesus of Nazareth with the Holy Spirit and with power, who went about doing good and healing all who were oppressed by the devil, for God was with Him."

Throughout the New Testament, we find a wide assortment of needs that the apostles and others met in the name of Jesus. Today, we know that Jesus acts as our Mediator, sitting at the Father's right hand and bringing our needs to the Father. Some of them are the needs that we expressly bring to Jesus and lay at His feet, saying, "I can't handle this. I can't resolve this. I can't meet this need in my life. Please help me."

However, Jesus brings other needs to the Father that we do not bring to Him of our own volition. Why don't we bring these needs? Sometimes we are rebellious or stubborn. Sometimes we don't know our deepest needs.

Yet Jesus knows these unrecognized needs in our lives. One of the attributes of Jesus is that He knows the hearts of men and perceives what goes on in our spirits. (See Mark 2:6 and Luke 9:47.) In knowing our hearts, Jesus knows our motivations, desires, and yearnings as well as our inadequacies, ineptitudes, and deficiencies. He sees what we need. And out of His deep love for us, Jesus brings our needs to the Father.

The Father always responds to what Jesus brings to Him. There is no prayer that Jesus prays on our behalf that goes unheeded or unanswered by the Father. So even though we have not brought our need to Jesus, Jesus brings our need to the Father, and the Father takes action on our behalf, for our good, in order to meet our need.

JESUS CONFRONTED ALL MANNER OF NEED

In the next few pages, I invite you to take another look at several examples of need meeting in the Scriptures. Notice not only what type of need Jesus confronted, but also the underlying factors related to the need. These are stories you likely know well. Take a fresh look at them from the standpoint of your need.

THE NEED FOR PHYSICAL SAFETY

On one occasion, Jesus traveled with His disciples in a boat across the Sea of Galilee, and a great storm arose. The Bible tells us that the "waves beat into the boat, so that it was already filling." In other words, the wind and waves were so fierce that the boat in which they were traveling began to capsize. The disciples awoke Jesus, who was asleep in the stern, and they said to Him, "Teacher, do You not care that we are perishing?" Jesus immediately arose, rebuked the wind, and said to the sea, "Peace, be still!" The wind ceased and there was a great calm. Jesus then said to the disciples, "Why are you so fearful? How is it that you have no faith?" The disciples were in awe of what Jesus had done, and they said to themselves, "Who can this be, that even the wind and the sea obey Him!" (See Mark 4:36–41.)

The disciples asked, "Don't You care?" Jesus answered by His actions, "Yes, I care!"

Our need for physical safety is always a primary concern to us. Preservation of life is a basic human instinct. God made us with a will to live and to be safe, and God is not in the least callous toward our fears or our need for physical safety. Far from it. Time and again throughout Scripture we have examples of God protecting His people in sovereign ways. We see God calming the fears of those who were frightened by evil as well as those frightened by His angels and miracles on their behalf. God understands our need for physical safety, and He is present always to reassure us that our ultimate safety rests in Him. Regardless of what may happen to us on this earth, He is Life. The Lord is our Protector and our Champion.

THE NEED FOR REASSURANCE

After Jesus had multiplied the five loaves and two fish of a boy to feed some five thousand men and their families, Jesus "made His disciples get into the boat and go before Him to the other side." In the meantime, Jesus sent the multitudes away, and then He went up on the mountain by Himself to pray. Again, a storm arose on the sea, and the boat in which the disciples traveled began to be tossed about by the waves. The disciples rowed for hours, but still didn't reach the opposite shore.

Then the Bible tells us, "In the fourth watch of the night Jesus went to them, walking on the sea. And when the disciples saw Him walking on the sea, they were troubled, saying, 'It is a ghost!' And they cried out for fear. But immediately Jesus spoke to them, saying, 'Be of good cheer! It is I; do not be afraid'" (Matt. 14:25–27).

What were the needs of the disciples in this scene from the New Testament? Certainly they had a need for physical safety—a need to arrive at the opposite shore. By that time, they also had a need for rest. They had rowed for hours, and their energy was no doubt sorely depleted. No doubt they had a need for encouragement. They had no understanding of how close or how far they were from the land, only that the wind was contrary and they were fighting to stay afloat and make progress toward their destination.

Jesus came to them to meet all of those needs. In the course of His coming to them, however, the disciples experienced yet another need—fear. That was the first need that Jesus addressed. He said to them, "Be of good cheer! It is I; do not be afraid" (v. 27).

Once Jesus got into the boat with them, the Scriptures tell us that "the wind ceased" (Matt. 14:32). Their fear also ceased. Jesus' presence provided total reassurance and a total meeting of the need.

An old and familiar story is told of a young child who was troubled by a thunderstorm. She sought refuge in her parents' bedroom as the lightning flashed and the thunder rolled in the night sky. Her parents hugged her and cuddled her and attempted to comfort her by saying, "You are going to be all right. God is with you. He will take care of you." The little girl replied, "Yes, but I still want to be with someone who has arms."

In many cases, I have seen God provide someone "with arms" to comfort those who are grieving, those who are troubled, or those who are sick or suffering. God sends His ministering servants to those in need as an expression of His reassurance and comfort.

THE NEED FOR DELIVERANCE FROM EVIL

When Jesus entered the country of the Gadarenes, He encountered a man with an unclean spirit who dwelled among the tombs. Others greatly feared the wild man, who could not be controlled. He had often been bound with shackles and chains, but he always managed to break his shackles and pull apart the chains. The Bible says, "Neither could anyone tame him" (Mark 5:4). Day and night, he could be heard crying out as he cut himself with stones.

When the man saw Jesus from afar, he ran and worshiped Him, crying out with a loud voice, "What have I to do with You, Jesus, Son of the Most High God? I implore You by God that You do not torment me" (Mark 5:7). The man, filled with demons, still worshiped Jesus. Even the demons are smart enough to recognize that Jesus is the Son of God and to give Him homage.

Jesus said, "Come out of the man, unclean spirit!" And then He asked, "What is your name?" The man replied, "My name is Legion; for we are many" (Mark 5:8–9). Then the demons within the man begged Jesus earnestly that He would not send them out of the country. Jesus gave the demons permission to enter a herd of about two thousand swine, and no sooner had they done so than the herd ran violently down the slope of the mountain and into the sea, where they drowned.

The man was gloriously delivered. The Bible tells us that he was found "sitting and clothed and in his right mind" (Mark 5:15). The possession by demons had been the root cause of need in the man's life, but look at the three related needs that were met when Jesus delivered the man.

1. *The man was found sitting.* The man had been continually moving about, tearing apart any form of chain or ropes put upon him. The demons at work in him had created a great restlessness in the man's soul—an irrational agitation, a fomenting turmoil. Jesus changed all of that. The man who had roamed the tombs day and night, crying out and cutting himself, was sitting quietly and peacefully at Jesus' feet. He had a settledness about him. He had a quiet spirit.

I once counseled a woman who was extremely distraught. Her face was puffy from countless hours of crying. Agony was written all over her face. She had numerous questions about her future in the wake of her husband's death. She certainly wasn't under the influence of demons as the man in the tombs had been, but she was nonetheless very troubled in her spirit. Several times during our session together, she dissolved into tears and could hardly be consoled.

I prayed for her, and she was calmer when she left my office. I was grateful for the help I was able to offer her, but I knew in my spirit as she left the church that she needed an inner and ongoing healing that only Jesus could provide day by day.

Several months later I saw the woman again in a public gathering, but I didn't recognize her at first. She was the picture of serenity; she seemed to radiate peacefulness. I told her how peaceful she looked, and she replied very simply, "Pastor, I've been sitting at the feet of Jesus."

She told me how much the story of Mary and Martha had ministered to her in the months since I saw her. She recalled how Mary had sat at the feet of Jesus, hearing His words, while Martha was concerned about serving Jesus and the disciples. She specifically recalled the words of Jesus in Luke 10:42: "Mary has chosen that good part, which will not be taken away from her."

She said, "Pastor, I realized that Jim had been taken away. But if I would only sit at the feet of Jesus, listening to His words, I would not only receive help and encouragement from the Lord, but something would be given to me that could never be taken away.

"I started spending as much time as possible every day sitting in my big easy chair, reading the Scriptures aloud to myself, listening to the Bible being read on tape, and listening to good Bible teaching on the radio. I still did my daily chores and exercised daily and talked to friends every day, but several hours each day were devoted to sitting at the feet of Jesus. I can't tell you how much that has meant to me."

She didn't have to tell me. I could see it in her expression and in her demeanor. She had gone to the best place she could ever have gone for help that was both priceless and eternal. Her spirit was at peace.

2. *The man was found clothed.* The man was described in Luke 8:27 as wearing no clothes. He was without restraint, including the restraints of culture and custom. His nakedness, as much as his violence, estranged him from other people. He bled openly from his self-inflicted wounds; his raw flesh was no doubt infected, and thus, the man's wounds made him unclean to others. And then Jesus delivered him. He sat clothed, which included being bandaged. He was restored to other people.

For so many people, the very thought of sharing their inner hurt, painful memories, and ongoing struggles with a group of people is not only frightening but painful in its own right. And yet very often as we share our pain with others, we no longer feel shame, exposed, or frightened that others might discover our inner secrets. Loving believers in Christ Jesus, and especially those who love the Lord and may have undergone similar experiences to ours, can be of great comfort and help.

The Bible teaches, "Confess your trespasses to one another, and pray for one another, that you may be healed" (James 5:16). In some translations, the word *trespasses* is stated as *sins* or *faults.* These are the sins we have committed and the ones that may have been committed against us. We are to confess the times in which we have ignored the NO TRESPASSING posted by others and trampled on their hearts, as well as the times in which others have trampled on our hearts. In the process of confessing these painful and hurtful times, the Bible teaches, we are healed.

The nakedness we feel in our guilt—the exposure, the shame, the feeling as if everybody knows how terrible we are and how much we deserve the consequences of our sin—is clothed when we allow others to bandage our hurts and to restore us to a community of loving fellowship.

I certainly am not recommending that you confess your faults to strangers or the first sympathetic ear you seem to find. Doing that can result in more harm than good. Find a group of people that you trust and that operates according to strict rules of confidentiality, or work with a Christian counselor who has a reputation for being a person of high integrity, trustworthiness, and good results in those with whom he has worked.

In addition to trust and confidentiality, any setting in which you confess your faults must include a time in which you receive the forgiveness of God and embark on a new path in your life. The very purpose of confession is forgiveness and repentance, which means to turn from the way you were going to the direction that is pleasing to God. Find a counselor or a group that will pray with you to receive God's forgiveness in your life and then support you as you begin to lead a new life.

3. *The man was found in his right mind.* The man had been incapable of rational thought or decision making. He had lived totally on the impulses of the demons that raged within him. He had lost all awareness of conscience. He no longer had an understanding of right and wrong on which to base his life's choices. But then Jesus healed him. He sat "in his right mind." He was able to speak intelligently and to make sound choices. In fact, he begged Jesus that he might go with Him. Jesus, however, said to him, "Go home to your friends, and tell them what great things the Lord has done for you, and how He has had compassion on you" (Mark 5:19).

The man was both willing and able to do what Jesus commanded him to do. The Scriptures tell us that "he departed and began to proclaim in Decapolis all that Jesus had done for him; and all marveled" (Mark 5:20). Jesus sent the man, now in his right mind, to proclaim the need-meeting gospel of Jesus to perhaps the toughest audience in all that region—the ten cities known as the Decapolis that were entrenched in pagan Roman customs and had virtually no regard for the Jewish laws, customs, or people.

I once heard about a woman who was released from a mental hospital. On the way home, the friend who had picked her up from the hospital suggested that they stop by a Bible study fellowship group in their neighborhood. The woman did not resist the idea, although she had little understanding about the nature of the group meeting they were going to attend, and so the two of them showed up at the meeting. The woman who had been suffering from anxiety attacks heard the Bible teacher say, "God wants to renew your mind and your heart so you won't be troubled by thoughts that seem to take control of your mind and return to haunt you day after day after day. One of the ways He renews our minds is through His Word. Take your Bible and read the Gospels aloud to yourself. Fill your ears, your mind, and your mouth with the words and stories of Jesus. Then go on to the rest of the books of the New Testament. Read and read and read. God will retrain your thoughts and reprogram your mind as you do this."

The woman decided to give the advice a try. And over the next few months, God did precisely what the Bible teacher had said. The thoughts and fears that had plagued her day and night disappeared, and in their place were the words of the Lord. The New Testament literally became the "way she thought." It became the way she perceived herself—as God's beloved child for whom Jesus Christ had died and rose again. It became her understanding of God—as a loving Father who longed to spend all of eternity with her. It became the way she viewed others—as fellow believers in Christ Jesus. It became her daily guide for loving and giving to others, and trusting and seeking God in every decision she made. She truly was restored to her right mind, and with such quickness and completeness of healing that her psychologist and family physician asked her, "What kind of therapy have you been undergoing?" Her answer was very direct: "Bible therapy!"

What God did for this woman I believe He can and will do for you as you read His Word on a daily basis and at sufficient length for God truly to speak to your spirit and begin to renew your mind and heart. The psalmist knew what it meant to be "led and fed" by the Lord. He said,

> *The LORD is my shepherd;*
> *I shall not want.*
> *He makes me to lie down in green pastures;*
> *He leads me beside the still waters.*
> *He restores my soul;*
> *He leads me in the paths of righteousness*
> *For His name's sake. (Ps. 23:1–3)*

As we trust the Lord to lead us daily and to feed us daily by His Word, we, too, can know what it means to have our souls restored and to know how to walk in the ways pleasing to Him. We can know what decisions to make and when to act. We can know that we are in right standing with the Lord every moment of our lives. We can be restored to the "right mind" that the Lord intended for us at our creation.

THE NEED FOR PHYSICAL HEALING

In Mark 6:54–56, we read a brief summary of Jesus' remarkable ministry of healing among the people:

> *When they came out of the boat, immediately the people recognized Him, ran through that whole surrounding region, and began to carry about on beds those who were sick to wherever they heard He was. Wherever He entered, into villages, cities, or the country, they laid the sick in the marketplaces, and begged Him that they might just touch the hem of His garment. And as many as touched Him were made well.*

Let me expand on just two examples of Jesus' healing ministry. In Matthew 8, we read that a man with leprosy came to Jesus, worshiped Him, and said, "Lord, if You are willing, You can make me clean." This is the statement many of us make, isn't it? "Lord, if You are willing." We believe Jesus can heal today, but we wonder if He is willing to heal, and specifically if He is willing to heal *us*.

Jesus responded, "I am willing; be cleansed." Immediately the man's leprosy was cleansed. Then Jesus said to him, "See that you tell no one; but go your way, show yourself to the priest, and offer the gift that Moses commanded, as a testimony to them" (Matt. 8:1–4).

Why would Jesus tell the man to go to the priest and make an appropriate offering? Everybody in the entire community would then know that the man had been healed by Jesus and that he was healed completely. A verification by the priest was necessary for the man to be restored to his family, friends, and neighbors. Jesus healed the man physically, and He made it possible for the man to be healed in his broken relationship with others. More was involved than physical healing.

Another healing in Matthew 8 involved Peter's mother-in-law. Jesus entered Peter's house and found the woman lying sick with a fever. Jesus touched her hand and the fever left her. The Bible says that she then arose and served them. The woman was restored to a functioning relationship with other people. More was made right in that moment than the departure of a fever.

The healing that Jesus brings to us may be manifested by a physical healing, but in every case in which I have witnessed a miraculous physical healing, more was healed than just the body. In virtually all cases, the person was restored to greater service, fellowship, or loving relationship with others.

GOD'S PURPOSE IN MEETING OUR NEEDS

We will take a more in-depth look at this point in a later chapter, but at the outset of this book, I want you to see that the meeting of our needs is

- essential for our well-being and wholeness.
- essential to an ongoing, developing, and deepening relationship with God, our loving heavenly Father.
- essential to a positive and enriching relationship with other human beings—both those who are close to us and those who are acquaintances or strangers.
- essential to a greater understanding of ourselves and to a growing sense of our worth and value.

God does not place needs within our lives so that we will be imperfect, incomplete human beings. These needs exist within us to compel us to seek God and to rely upon Him to make us whole and completely productive and effective within the greater plan and purpose He has for us on this earth. Our needs, in other words, become our potential. In the resolving and the overcoming of needs through the power of the Holy Spirit, we truly come into the fullness of all that we were created to accomplish, achieve, and fulfill in our lives. Our needs are the launching platform for us to accomplish the purpose for our lives. They are the starting point for us to learn, grow, develop, and eventually come into the fullness of the stature of Christ Jesus.

Praise God for the needs He has built into you. They are the evidence

· 5 ·

Symptom or Root Problem?

Recently I was on my way to the church to perform a wedding, and while I was stopped at the red light of a certain intersection, I saw a man who was standing on the street corner holding a sign: NEED FOOD. WILL WORK. That was not a particularly unusual sight to me. I pass that intersection often, and I have seen countless people standing there with similar signs.

That night I found myself staring at the man. He was about my height. He had a wrinkled and weathered face, disheveled hair and clothing, and he was dirty and ragged in his overall appearance and very sad-looking. I put myself in his shoes for a moment. I imagined what it must be like to stand there hour after hour, without sufficient supply in one's life, looking at people in cars who were staring back blankly. How would I feel if I were standing on that corner hungry, without work or money, without someone to care enough for me to take me in or help me? How would I feel if I were as lonely as that man appeared to be? How would it feel to be empty inside, without accomplishments or purpose, without any direction or future, perhaps with an addiction to alcohol or drugs? And how would it feel to be standing on a corner early in the evening, gazing at a man in a tuxedo on his way to someplace where he was wanted and needed? How would it feel to be ignored by that man and the person behind him and the person behind him until the light changed and yet another group of people stopped, but failed to offer assistance?

49

My attitude toward people in his situation changed dramatically in that moment.

"But," you may say, "he was probably looking for a handout so he could buy a bottle of liquor."

Perhaps.

"He might have been a con artist, looking for a handout so he didn't *have* to work."

Perhaps.

In either case, he was a person with a need. He was a person who at some point in his past had strayed away from God's intended plan and purpose for his life. Regardless of the true motivation of that person, standing on a street corner with a sign that indicated he was begging for work and food was *not* what God had in mind for that person when He created him and placed him on this earth. That person was standing on that corner because he had an unmet need deep inside his heart, an inner need that was far deeper than the outer need scrawled on his handmade sign. That person had at some point in his life been given wrong direction or had listened to the wrong voices. He had made wrong choices. And the result was that he was not doing what God had destined for him to do and he was not in the process of becoming what God desired for him to become in the Lord Jesus Christ.

So often we look at people's appearance and their outer behavior, and we draw conclusions about them and their motivations that may not be at all the true state of their lives. So often we fail to see the deep inner needs and drives that compel a person to say and do things that are contrary to God's purposes. And yet it is at the deep inner level of our lives that the most profound changes are needed. It is at the deep inner level that all outer, surface needs must first be addressed if the solutions we seek are to be definite, productive, positive, and lasting.

THREE COMMONLY MISUNDERSTOOD NEEDS

As a pastor, I have had countless people come to me with a need. Three needs often seem to loom very large in people's minds and emotions, but as great as these needs may be, they are not the real needs. Rather, they are needs that are symptoms of much deeper and more basic needs. I believe there is value in exploring these three symptomatic needs.

1. THE NEED FOR A SEXUAL RELATIONSHIP

Within marriage, nothing can be more comforting and satisfying. Outside marriage, nothing can be more disastrous.

Many people have a sense of need in the area of their sexual desire. This is often expressed to me by single people, those who have gone through divorce, or those whose spouses have died. The automatic assumption seems to be: I need a sexual relationship, and the only solution for this inner frustration and desire that I feel is a sexual relationship.

I certainly do not deny the reality of sexual desire that God has built into us as human beings, yet I have also come to recognize that in the majority of cases where this need is felt intensely and is expressed repeatedly, the real need is for intimacy. Ultimately the need is for a more intimate relationship with God.

The person who has a need for intimacy feels estranged, cut off, separated, unfulfilled. These feelings are defined as sexual desire, but they are really symptoms of a need to be loved in a way that is comforting, consistent, and unconditional. Only God can provide this kind of love in its purest and richest form. People often use phrases such as "if I could only be held by someone" or "if I only had someone who really knew me and really loved me completely" to express the root need, "I need to be embraced by someone who will never let go of me and never stop loving me." That Someone is God.

A number of years ago I counseled a young couple who were having problems in their marriage. The man's complaint was that his wife always seemed to be too tired for sex. The woman's complaint was that her husband never took time to kiss her and hold her, but was too eager for the culmination of the sex act. The longer we met together, the more it became obvious that the root problem was not related to sexual behavior; the root problem involved issues of intimacy and unconditional love.

The husband was truly longing for affirmation. After a long day at work, he came home desiring to be appreciated, valued, and made to feel worthy. Sexual activity was the only way he had been taught to receive appreciation and value. His wife had no idea that was truly what her husband desired, so it never occurred to her to praise him for his efforts or to tell him how much she valued him as a man.

The wife was also seeking affirmation. Alone all day at home with the children, she wanted her husband to notice that her contribution to their family was valuable and appreciated. She wanted her husband to see her as a desirable woman, not merely as a housekeeper, childcare provider, and sexual partner. She wanted him to tell her in words and by deeds that he liked spending time with her, thought she was beautiful, and enjoyed being close to her. She was seeking intimacy and unconditional love.

When the two young people learned how to express value to each other in ways apart from the act of sexual intercourse, their entire marriage blossomed, and before long, the issues that had first brought them to me disappeared. They were addressing the root needs and problems inherent in a marriage, not merely the surface issue of too little/too much sexual activity.

Our culture sends numerous messages through all forms of media to each of us every day that say, "If you feel general uneasiness or tension, it must be the result of sexual desire." There is almost an automatic response in some people to conclude, "I feel restless, so I must need sexual intercourse." The root, however, is not a need for sexual release but a need for emotional intimacy.

Transparency. Sharing. Being together. These things build intimacy. When intimacy is established in marriage, sexual behavior becomes a beautiful expression and a fulfilling activity. When intimacy is missing, sexual activity can be frustrating, and the ever-present concern about sexual behavior can be exhausting. God never intended for sexual intercourse to become a substitute for intimacy. Rather, He desires for it to be an outgrowth and an expression of intimacy. In that context, sexual activity provides joy.

Ultimately only God can truly fill the vacuum in each of us for intimacy. No person can completely satisfy that need. Two people may love each other the best they know how to love, but genuine unconditional love—love that gives and gives and gives without recrimination or any tinge of retribution—is divine.

When a person turns to God and seeks to build a relationship with God, when a person receives God's forgiveness and love, when a person spends time with God, shares his heart fully and honestly with God, and engages in frequent and in-depth conversations with God, such a person knows truly what it means to be in an intimate relationship. Once a person knows that, it is so much more meaningful, and so much easier, to develop an intimate relationship with another person. And when both partners in a marriage understand and experience intimacy with God, and are seeking to develop intimacy with each other, richness in marriage is sure to result.

2. THE NEED TO BE MARRIED

So many people have said to me down through the years, "Pastor, I just need to get married." In most cases, marriage is not a need—it is a perceived solution to one or more needs. The root needs are much more likely to be loneliness, financial insecurity, emotional insecurity, or unfulfilled sexual desire. In other cases, the person is looking to a spouse to do what only the Lord can do—in other words, be the source of emotional, spiritual, financial, material, physical, and psychological support.

Let me ask you, "Who wants to get married for the sole purpose of being used by the other person to get all of his or her needs met? Who on this earth could remotely feel that it was either possible or equitable to spend one's life solely for the purpose of meeting another person's needs?" And yet many people who say with a tone of desperation in their voices, "I *need* to get married," are looking for precisely that—somebody to meet all of their needs for them.

To this point, I have never had a person say to me, "I need to get married because I have a very strong desire to meet all the needs in that other person's life." The need to be married is a me-centered need in most cases.

The reality for most people is that in marriage, some of their needs are met, and they are able to meet some of the needs of the spouse. No person, however noble, great, fantastic, or talented he may be, is fully capable of meeting all the needs of another person, and no person should expect another person to meet all of his needs.

Too many marriages are in trouble today precisely on this point. People are looking to their spouses to meet the needs that only God can meet.

This is also likely to be the root cause for many teen pregnancies and sexual encounters. Young people are looking for someone to meet their emotional needs for acceptance, love, and value. The young person believes that if someone has sexual relations with her, he automatically will accept her, love her unconditionally, and place high value on her and the relationship. That is never the case—at least not in a lasting way. Words of acceptance, love, and value may be spoken. But over time, the very act of immorality erodes the underlying foundation that is required for true acceptance, genuine love, and lasting value.

If you are under the impression that you can meet all of the needs of another person, I suggest you reexamine your position. Jesus Christ is the only person who could meet all of another person's needs, and even He could fulfill the needs only after His death, resurrection, and ascension to the Father in heaven. Paul taught, "My God shall supply all your need" (Phil. 4:19). God alone is capable of fully meeting your needs. Look to Him!

A woman told me that she felt a great need to be married. She longed for a husband to value her, love her, and build a relationship with her. I encouraged her to trust God to bring this person across her path and, until He did, to rely upon God to meet her inner needs for validation, self-worth, and love.

She did that for a while, but then a friend convinced her that she needed to get out and play the field. The young woman began to attend parties every night of the week, and many of the parties were ungodly in all sorts of ways. The men she met wanted her all right, but not as a godly wife. They wanted her sexually as a plaything for the night. Within a matter of weeks, she found herself pregnant, and in the process of her undergoing pregnancy-related medical exams, she also discovered she had a sexually transmitted disease.

Her situation discouraged her further. She reasoned, *What man will want me with a child and with a sexually transmitted disease?* She got an abortion. That compounded the guilt she felt in her heart. She lowered her standards even more when it came to the men she dated. Eventually she hit bottom emotionally and cried out to God, "Oh, God, I have so many needs! Help me!"

God heard her heart's cry, and He responded to her with all the love and forgiveness He had always had for her. Over months and years as she trusted God with her life, she slowly regained her sense of self-worth. God eventually did bring a man her way who accepted her as she was and loved her for who she was in the Lord, regardless of her past.

But oh, the years she wasted and the pain she experienced. She could never undo the facts of the pregnancy and abortion in her past. She could not undo completely the disease she had acquired, although she could control its effects to an extent through medication. She could not get back the years she lost or fully restore the relationships she had damaged in her rebellious choices that were against God's plan for her.

And when did that sad decade of her life begin? In the instant she determined that she had to take the matter of meeting her perceived need for marriage into her own hands and do something to find and marry a man of her choosing.

Her friend had convinced her that trusting God wasn't enough. She had convinced her that "God helps those who help themselves"—which is true to an extent, but which is true only if the person is helping herself in a way that is right and good in God's eyes. The young woman could have limited herself to dinner invitations and parties hosted by Christian friends. She could have chosen to go on Christian cruises and retreats, or to get more involved in church-related social activities and ministries. Her friend, however, had convinced her that it was actually good for her to go to non-Christian places because the men there were more plentiful, interesting, and exciting, and that it would all be okay in the end because she could convince any man she met at an ungodly party to accept Jesus Christ and be born again before a wedding took place.

Was it the friend's fault that the woman chose the path she followed? No. The woman allowed herself to be deceived. She knew enough to say no to her friend's arguments at every turn of the road. She knew enough to choose good and refrain from evil. Her error was the age-old error— I can do this on my own, independent of God.

If you are single today, trust God to bring you the spouse who is right for you. Don't compromise your standards or flirt with evil. Keep yourself pure.

3. THE NEED FOR LOVE

Too many people in our world today have grown up without unconditional love from their parents. One parent or both parents may have abandoned them when they were children, either physically or emotionally. They may have felt intense loneliness as children. They may have felt that they were continually shunned, sent to be with others, put in the care of baby-sitters, or ignored while parents worked or partied. They may have felt misunderstood, underappreciated, or not valued. They may have heard all kinds of critical assessments of their worth and their worthiness: "You'll never amount to anything," "We never wanted you anyway—you were an accident," "You never do anything right," "You are a real *problem* child."

When children are mistreated in these ways, they grow up with an intense desire to be counted worthy. They have a strong inner need that they generally conclude is a desire to be loved.

The problem is, many of these people enter relationships that fail to satisfy. In some cases, they enter marriages with a person who is just as needy as they are, and in their intense desire to receive love, they fail to give unconditional love—and vice versa—and the result is two people grasping at each other to receive the very thing that they feel they need most but that they have virtually no capacity to give. In other cases, they enter relationships seeking love, and they genuinely are given such love but they do not know how to receive it. Thus, their feelings of neediness remain.

What is the root problem? They need to be healed of the emotional wounds of the past. The real need is not to be in a loving relationship, but to be brought to a place of inner wholeness where they can truly be a partner in a loving relationship.

A woman once came to me with eyes nearly swollen shut from many hours of crying. "My husband just doesn't love me," she sobbed.

"Why do you believe that he doesn't love you?"

"He is staying at work later and later every night. I know he's doing that so he doesn't have to be around me."

"Have you talked to him about this behavior?"

"Yes," she sobbed. "He said he was working longer hours to win a promotion so he could provide more for me and the children, but I know the real reason is that he just wants to be away from us and especially away from me."

"Has he expressed dissatisfaction with you?" I asked.

"No," she admitted.

"Then why are you concluding that his long hours at work are a direct response to his feelings for you?"

She cried quietly for a moment and then blurted out, "He's just like my dad."

"Tell me about your father," I said.

"He was at work all the time I was growing up. I hardly ever saw him. When he came home he was too tired to play with me or to hug me. He never asked me how I was. He never kissed me good night or tucked me into bed."

The issue became very clear. The woman had deep inner needs related to the way her father had treated her as a child, and she was transferring those needs to her husband. Her father had been a cold, aloof man. As it turns out, he was an alcoholic and was not at work nearly as much as the woman had thought; he had spent much of his after-hours time at bars and clubs. Her father's inability to express love was the real issue that was acting as an undercurrent of uneasiness and tension in her marriage. Her husband—a warm, loving, ambitious, and caring man—was not at all like her father, but she perceived that he was like her father because of surface behaviors. She was looking at symptoms, not root needs and problems.

When the woman began to realize that the real issue before her was not a problem in her marriage but a problem in her past, and when she recognized that she needed to be healed of the emotional wounds she had suffered as a child before she would be in a good position to assess and then address the current issues in her marriage, she was on her way toward healing and wholeness.

As the months passed and the woman worked with a good Christian counselor to gain a new perspective and to receive Christ's love and healing regarding her past, she saw the behavior of her husband in an entirely new light. Rather than be resentful of the time he spent at the office, she became thankful for his concern for her and their children. Rather than be frightened that her husband was moving away from her emotionally, she recognized that he was acting out of love for her. Rather than confront or withdraw from her husband, she had the strength to express herself directly and honestly. Together, she and her husband struck a new balance between hours spent at work and hours spent at home.

The underlying root problem had not at all been an issue of love, but issues of old, lingering, and festering emotional wounds that needed to be healed.

The best time to deal with emotional wounds related to one's past is prior to marriage, of course. The problem is that too often we fail to recognize these emotional wounds before we marry. We transfer the set of feelings we have had in one relationship to a new relationship where they are often unwarranted.

A woman said to me in the wake of a very painful separation from her husband, "I always knew he would leave me."

"Why did you believe that?" I asked.

"I just knew he would."

As much as I probed, she would not admit to a reason why she held that opinion. Over time as we discussed various issues in her childhood and younger years, I realized that she had very likely drawn this conclusion about her husband and her marriage because her father had never been faithful to her mother, or to any of the other three women he had married. She automatically assumed that her husband would treat her the same way her father had treated her mother and her various stepmothers. In the end, she had been the one to separate from her husband, thinking that she would be better off to initiate what she perceived to be the inevitable outcome of their marriage rather than wait for him to leave her as she was certain he would.

The real need in the woman's life was not counseling for the present marital situation, but counseling for the inner emotional wounds that she had carried in silence for more than forty years.

Not all emotional wounds are experienced in childhood. Some people are scarred by the behavior of adults who have mistreated them or rejected them. Many people bring the wounds of past relationships— dating relationships, engagements, marriages—into new relationships. Some bring the wounds experienced in previous places of employment to their new jobs. Some bring spiritual wounds they experienced in previous church settings to their new church homes.

Every emotionally wounded person I know is seeking love to heal his wounds. He believes that the number one need in his life is love. "If I can just find someone to love me, I'll get over that previous relationship." "If I can just find an employer who will appreciate me, I'll recover from being fired." "If I can just find a pastor who loves me enough regardless of my sins, I'll rebound from that bad church experience."

The truth is, the wounded person needs to be healed of the old wounds so that he can receive love and be a full partner in an unconditional love relationship. The jilted or abused person needs to be healed emotionally before he enters a new relationship. The person who has been mistreated in the workplace needs to recover from the wounds and learn from them so that he can experience happiness in a new position. The person who has been spiritually wounded needs to address the wounds and be healed so that he can find satisfaction and fulfillment in a new church setting.

If healing of the past does not occur, the problems will carry over into the new setting. Words of love and appreciation will help, but they will not truly heal. Time will pass, but it will not heal. Only the presence and power of Jesus Christ in a person's life truly heal and make whole.

Only God can heal deep, inner emotional wounds, especially ones that stem from early childhood. Some incidents occur at such an early age that the victim of abusive, neglectful, or hurtful behavior cannot even remember what happened or the context in which it happened. Only God sees the beginning from the ending in a person's life. Only God knows *why* some feelings exist in us. Only God knows *how* to unravel the tangled web of emotions that trap us into despair and despondency at the very core of our beings.

The enemy within us is the need that demands attention, that results in nightmares, that causes us to cry out in fear or feel anxious to the point of tears in the middle of a crowd on a bright, sunny day. And the only true victor over that enemy is the power of the Holy Spirit, resident within us to heal, comfort, and give counsel. Human counselors can help, especially if they truly know the Lord Jesus Christ and attempt to live in full accord with His commandments. Ultimately the Holy Spirit will heal us of our emotional wounds.

If you go into a new relationship—personal, career-related, church-related—with the thought, *I'll find love here and everything will be all right,* you are likely to be disappointed. Looking to the love or appreciation of another person to solve your problem should be a giant clue to you that the problem is not one that the other's love or appreciation can solve. The problem lies within you. Something is festering deep within. And until that "something" is addressed, cleansed, healed, or restored, you will not be in a healthy position either to receive love fully or to give love generously.

Go to God and express your feelings. Ask Him to reveal the real nature of your problem and to heal you of its root cause. Ask for His guidance in finding the right Christian counselor who can help you uncover the old wound festering within. Ask God by the power of His Holy Spirit to bring the light of truth to bear on old issues and old feelings that you have tried to bury. Put yourself into a position to be healed of the past so that you can embrace fully and successfully the future that God has for you.

THE NEEDS WE KNOW AS ADDICTIONS

Do you crave a cigarette?

Do you need a drink?

Do you think only about the next fix?

Do you count the hours until you can take the next pill?

In raw form, addictions are perhaps the ultimate symptomatic needs.

What is an addiction? Why does a certain thing or behavior become what we think we must have in order to live or at least to live a desirable life?

An addiction is a repeated form of behavior that brings some form of result that keeps a person repeating the behavior. The result may be highly destructive in the long run, but seem appealing or pleasurable in the short run. The actual result of the behavior may not be physical but emotional. Just about all the people I know who have become addicted to alcohol or nicotine have told me that they disliked their first taste of an alcoholic beverage or their first puff on a cigarette. They kept drinking and kept smoking, however, because they did like the result of having their peers think they were acceptable, cool, neat, or hip.

Even knowing the long-term damage that drinking alcohol and smoking cigarettes might cause to their bodies, they continued in the behavior because they liked the short-term benefits that were psychological and emotional. They also came to like the physical benefit of relaxation they felt with alcohol or nicotine, far more than they ever liked the taste of the alcohol or tobacco, the smell of tobacco on their clothes and in their homes and cars, the shortness of breath, the nausea from over-drinking, or other aspects of the habit.

Positive behaviors can also become addictive because of the rewards associated with them. People who run regularly like the good feeling they get while running or after they have completed a run. People who spend quality time in prayer and meditating on God's Word have a sense of spiritual withdrawal if they go for a period without praying or reading the Scriptures.

The results keep a person returning again and again to any particular behavior. That is the way habits are built—good or bad. That is the way addictions start.

ADDICTIONS DIFFER FROM HABITS

The difference between a habit and an addiction is that a person still exerts control over a habit. Not engaging in the behavior brings no sense of irretrievable or grievous loss. In an addiction, the behavior begins to exert control over the person. A real sense of loss, a deep craving, or a sense of being deprived, is felt in an addiction. An addiction is always associated with an insatiable drive or desire, a hunger for the activity or substance, and a dependency upon the chemical or the mental hormones that are released during a particular activity.

Persons often engage in habitual behaviors without thinking much about them. In addictions, persons can think of little else than the addictive behavior. The person addicted to alcohol is always anticipating to some degree the next drink. The person addicted to gambling is always looking for the next betting opportunity. The person addicted to a prescription painkiller is always counting the minutes until the next pill can be taken.

People can be addicted to numerous things other than chemical substances.

I have met a few people who were addicted to keeping an immaculate house, perfect in appearance and clean in every crevice to the point that maintaining cleanliness was not only valued but also felt to pressure them to act. Such addictions are often termed compulsive emotions with obsessive behaviors.

Some people are addicted to sex. Others are addicted to a particular kind of activity, such as exercise or work. Some are addicted to overeating, especially unhealthy foods.

People who are addicted never started out intending to become addicted. Nobody who has become a drug addict said upon taking his first dose of drugs, "My goal is to become addicted to this drug." No person who has become addicted to gambling ever said upon placing his first bet, "My goal in life is to get to the place where I can't live without turning virtually every activity in my life into an opportunity to place a wager."

In the development of habits, however, people often say, "I want to have the habit of . . ." Habits are generally rooted in positive intention. They are outgrowths of one's will, and in most cases, they are aimed at the development of a positive trait or a healthful activity.

In addictions, people tend not to be thinking. Many people who become addicted to various activities or substances later find themselves saying, "Where was my mind? What was I thinking when I started doing this? Was I nuts?"

ADDICTIONS NEVER FULLY SATISFY

An addict never has enough. A person addicted to alcohol never has sufficient alcohol to last him the rest of his life. A person addicted to prescription medications never feels so good that he never needs another pill.

Good habits satisfy. They bring a sense of order, balance, and harmony. Bad habits do not satisfy, but in most cases, when a person recognizes that a bad habit exists—and it is not an addiction—the remedy for the bad habit is the exact opposite behavior. The person who has a bad habit of chewing his fingernails can develop a good habit by not chewing his fingernails and by routinely manicuring his nails. The dissatisfaction that arose from having ugly nails gives way to satisfaction at having healthy, appealing nails.

The person who is genuinely addicted does not feel an immediate sense of satisfaction if the addicted behavior is stopped. Alcoholics still have a desire for alcohol long after they have had their most recent drink. I have met people who quit smoking twenty years ago but still have a desire for smoking. Addictions grip the inner physical and psychological nature of a person. They are more than merely bad habits.

The symptoms associated with addictions are often perceived to be needs, but the addiction itself is not the root need. The symptoms of being out of control, of being "out of it" mentally, of losing the ability to function in vital areas of life, of being forever broke, and of feeling constantly driven are all very real. Such symptoms give a strong feeling to the individual experiencing them and to others who witness them that need is present.

But the real need is not for a drink or the need to be freed from feeling the desire for a drink. The real need is not for a fix of some kind or to be freed from having the compulsion for a fix. The real need is something more basic to the human heart. In most cases, it is a need for acceptance.

The inner drive for acceptance first leads the addicted person to take a drink. In some cases, the acceptance that is being sought is not the acceptance of another living person, be it spouse, friend, colleague, or close relative. Rather, it is the acceptance of a person long since dead or a person from long, long ago. I have met people who are addicted to compulsive behaviors because they are still seeking, at a very deep inner level, the approval of Mom or Dad.

Still others are in need of self-acceptance. They engage in certain behaviors in a desire to prove to themselves that they are valuable, desirable, beautiful, or worthy. Their initial act may be one of rebellion, but in a warped and twisted way it is also an act of seeking self-acceptance. The desire is to say, "I can act on my own. I am independent. I can make this decision myself. I can engage in this adult behavior now."

At the core of it all is ultimately a deep need to be accepted by God. The person who becomes addicted always has, at some point in the cycle of addiction, an unexpressed need to prove himself worthy to God and to be accepted by God. Or the person feels that he is not accepted by God and therefore seeks to deny that such acceptance is important to him. Of course, acceptance is important, and all of his efforts at denying this need in his life drive him to deeper and deeper addiction.

How These Needs Relate to Wholeness

Wholeness cannot be achieved unless one factors in emotional and spiritual need. A person cannot claim to be whole just because he is healthy physically, has his material needs met, and has good relationships with his spouse, children, colleagues, and friends. The person who ignores his emotional and spiritual self is not whole from God's perspective. Rather, he is missing pieces or is sorely deficient in areas of his being.

God created us to be spiritual and emotional beings. In that way we are most like God—in the spiritual, inner dimension we have been created "in His own image" (Gen. 1:27). The spiritual, emotional, psychological nature is the foremost aspect of who we are. It is the part of us that has a capacity for eternity. After having created this essential and vital aspect of man's being, God then put man in a physical body, set him in a natural environment, gave him material substance, and blessed him with human companions. When we neglect or negate the emotional and spiritual part of who God made us to be, we are immediately in a state of need, lack, want, and disharmony.

The symptoms of frustration and a general restlessness of spirit—perhaps even anxiety, a lingering melancholy, a sense of things being not quite right—are symptoms of this lack of wholeness, and only when we are willing to go to the very core of who we are as human beings and invite God to do a work that makes us whole in spirit and soul are we going to experience wholeness and a lasting solution for the symptoms of our restless hearts.

Any attempt to alleviate symptoms without going to the root need will have two negative results:

First, symptoms will recur. The alleviation of symptoms is only temporary and never complete when symptoms alone are addressed and root causes remain. In many cases, the symptoms will multiply and spill over into other situations, circumstances, or relationships in our lives.

Second, wholeness will be postponed. The underlying situation will remain and fester. A preoccupying concern with alleviating symptoms often pushes the real solution for the real problem to a future date and then a more future date and yet a future date.

If you are addicted to something today, if you feel driven to have a sexual relationship, if you can think of little else other than getting married, if you feel you are starving for love, ask God to reveal the deeper inner need that is driving these symptomatic needs. Ask Him to heal you where, indeed, you are hurting the most.

· 6 ·

A Close Look at God's Promise
to Meet Our Needs

Do you truly believe that God is capable of meeting your needs and that He desires to meet all of your needs?

Some people ask, "If God is all-powerful and all-knowing, and if He loves me with an infinite and unconditional love—and therefore, He not only is capable of meeting all my needs but also desires to meet my needs—why doesn't God just meet all my needs right now? Why do I still have needs? When the apostle Paul wrote from a prison cell, 'My God shall supply all your need,' why do I still have a lack of supply?" (See Phil. 4:19.)

Others say, "I know God is capable of meeting my needs, but since I still have needs, God must not want to meet them."

Still others question sincerely, "Why didn't God meet all my needs the moment I accepted Jesus Christ as my Savior?"

These are excellent questions, worthy of close examination.

At the outset of our discussion about these questions, let me assure you again that God is committed to meeting all of your needs according to His riches in glory by Christ Jesus. A commitment is a pledge, a statement of a sure promise. The value of any commitment is based upon two things:

1. The *ability* of the promise maker to fulfill the promise.
2. The *integrity* of the promise maker, which might also be stated as

the character to follow through on what has been said and do what has been promised.

God certainly qualifies as One who will stand behind His commitments on both accounts. He has all of the wisdom, power, and ability necessary to fulfill His promises to us. He also has proven integrity— God has always done what He has said He would do. God is utterly faithful to His Word. He is holy and immutable; He is unchanging. His character is impeccable.

There are those who say, "Well, the Bible's promises are fine for the people back then, but Paul was writing to the Philippians, not to me. Times are different now. Things have changed."

Friend, all of God's Word is for you, right now, right where you are. It all applies to you. Why is this so? Because the Author of the Bible hasn't changed. The Scriptures are true today because the Author still stands by His Word! His commandments, statutes, and promises have not changed; they reflect our unchanging God. He is the same "yesterday, today, and forever" (Heb. 13:8). The only times in God's Word in which God has not done what He said He was going to do are times when God's promises were conditional and man's behavior was an intervening factor.

WHAT IS THE NATURE OF THE PROMISE?

The better we know God—the more intimate our fellowship is with Him—the more we will trust God to do what He has said He will do. And the more we know about a promise in the Bible, the more we understand our role in bringing a promise to fulfillment.

As we study the Bible, we must ask several questions anytime we come to a promise in the Scriptures:

- To whom is the promise given?
- Who is making the promise?
- What is God really saying?
- What does God desire for me to do?
- How does God desire to act on my behalf?
- What is the end goal or the purpose for the promise?
- What is God's motivation in making this promise?

The more we know about the promise, the more we understand whether it is a conditional or unconditional promise.

TWO CATEGORIES OF PROMISES

All of God's promises fall into one of two categories: unconditional or conditional. As we read, memorize, and quote God's Word, we must be very careful to discern clearly the difference between these two categories.

Unconditional promises. In an unconditional promise, God states that He will do something regardless of man's behavior. In other words, God is going to do what He desires to do with or without any input or response from mankind. Nothing will interfere with or keep God from doing what He has said He will do.

An example is the promise of Jesus to His disciples that He is going to return one day. Absolutely nothing that man does or does not do can keep Jesus from fulfilling this promise in the fullness of God's timing and according to God's plans and purposes. Christ *will* come again.

Another unconditional promise is the promise of Jesus that He would never leave or forsake His disciples. Regardless of what people do or don't do, regardless of circumstances or situations that may arise, regardless of any mediating or intervening factors, Jesus will not forsake those who have put their trust in Him. That unconditional promise stands for all disciples at all times in all places and in all situations.

Conditional promises. In a conditional promise, God's actions are based in part on man's responses to God's commands. What man does, therefore, influences God's fulfillment of a promise.

Too often, people take some of God's *conditional* promises as being *unconditional.* That is a very dangerous error to make, and it can lead to frustration, disappointment, disillusionment, and even doubt about the goodness of God. How so? Well, if a person regards a promise of God as being unconditional when it is actually a conditional promise, he may very well fail to meet the conditions associated with the promise because he isn't looking for any conditions. He assumes that God is going to do everything and he is required to do nothing. In his failure to meet the conditions, of course, he negates the promise. Not realizing this, however, he begins to wonder why God is taking so long to meet his need. He begins to doubt whether God really meant what He said. Soon he doubts whether God cares or whether God is truly to be trusted on any matter.

Consider a situation in which a father says to his son, "I will buy you a new car when you finish college." The son is very excited—so excited that he fails to hear the full meaning of his father's statement. The boy goes to college for two years and decides that he has had enough of college. He gets a job and starts wondering when Dad is going to provide the new car he promised. The fact is, the boy did not finish college— in the sense of completing a college degree. He just finished college from the standpoint that he stopped attending classes! The promise was a conditional one, and the error occurred because the son defined the conditions in a way the father had not defined them.

Too many people make this same mistake when it comes to our heavenly Father. They decide when the conditions are met rather than trust God with that determination. The results are failure and disappointment. We must be very careful in reading God's promises to determine precisely what the conditions of a conditional promise may be.

Look again at Philippians 4:19: "My God shall supply all your need according to His riches in glory by Christ Jesus."

Ask yourself, Is this a conditional promise of God, or is this an unconditional promise? This passage happens to be a conditional promise. How is it conditional?

First, Paul said, "My God." If a person cannot say, "My God"—in other words, if a personal relationship has not been established with Jesus as Savior—then this promise is not in effect.

Second, Paul said that needs will be met "by Christ Jesus." If a person looks to any other person or source to meet his needs, the promise is not in effect.

This promise is based upon a relationship between Christ Jesus and those who follow Him. We might call this a family promise. It is in effect only for the family of God. It is not a promise for the unbeliever or the person who does not trust Jesus as Lord of his life.

Note that I did not say that this promise is limited to a particular church, denomination, or group of believers within the body of Christ. God has only one family—people who confess Jesus Christ as Savior and seek to follow Jesus as Lord.

What about the Christian who doesn't have all of his needs met?

The first place you need to look when a need is not being met is not at God or at His Son, Christ Jesus, but at yourself. You err greatly when you ask, Why hasn't God lived up to His promise? You are wise to ask instead, What am I doing that is keeping God from fulfilling this promise in my life?

You may respond, "Well, I'm not doing anything to keep this promise from being fulfilled! If you knew my circumstances or my situation . . ."

Let me assure you that no circumstance or situation is going to keep God from acting on your behalf. Nothing is too great or too powerful to stand in the way if God chooses to act. The real question remains, What are you doing in the midst of your circumstances or situation?

Do you already have a preconceived idea about how God should act to meet your needs or whom God may use to meet your needs?

I have encountered a number of people who have said to me, "Well, if he would just do such and such and she would agree to do so-and-so, then my need would be met." Or they have said, "Well, I did such and such and therefore God must do this and that."

Those who make such statements are not trusting God to be their Need Meeter. Rather, they are asking God to exert His power on behalf of their wishes and commands. We are called by God to trust Him, and Him alone, to meet our needs and to be our total source of supply. Furthermore, God requires that we obey Him as a part of our trusting Him. We have the situation completely backward anytime we start expecting God to trust us to know what is right and to obey our commands so that He might prove His love for us.

Our position is one of standing before God, declaring, "I trust You completely to meet my needs in Your timing and according to Your methods." Anyone who takes the stance before almighty God, "You must do things *my* way," is presumptuous and foolish.

God's Motivations for Meeting Our Needs

What's in it for God?

Why does God give to us?

What are His motivations for meeting our needs?

MOTIVATED BY LOVE

God's foremost motivation for meeting all your needs is this: He loves you. Yes, He loves you, loves you, loves you, loves you. I would repeat it a thousand times and more if I could. There is no bottom to His divine heart.

Why, then, must we do certain things in conditional promises? Why doesn't God just pour out to us all that we need?

Because ultimately God is about building a loving relationship with us.

Obedience to His conditions is part of having a loving relationship with God. Obedience is evidence that we are trusting God to be the source of our lives. He wants to be the One on whom we depend for provision, the One to whom we look for wise counsel, the One on whom we rely for protection.

Obedience in fulfilling God's conditions is also related to our growth and development as Christian believers. We've all heard the old song that says, "I know that you know that I know that you know . . ." That's what happens when we obey. We know we are obeying, and our obedience creates in us a greater strength to ask for what we desire and to act more quickly when God directs us.

CONFORMITY TO CHRIST

Often we come to a promise in the Word of God and we know it is true in our minds, but we have difficulty believing it to be true in our hearts, and especially we have difficulty believing that the promise is true for us. One of the reasons we find it difficult to claim God's promises as true in our personal lives is that we do not fully understand what God is seeking to do in our lives.

We must understand that God's primary purpose in our lives is not to meet our needs but to conform us into the likeness of His Son. Many people make God out to be some kind of sugar daddy, always ready and willing to give them precisely what they crave at any particular moment. They see God as the wish fulfiller, the One who turns all of our dreams into reality, the ultimate fairy godfather, the One who makes all things just the way we desire for them to be. While it is true that God is our Father and our Provider, and while it is equally true that God desires only the best for us for all eternity, God is not present in our lives to do things our way. He is present in our lives so that we might desire and choose to do things His way.

God does not exist for our pleasure. We exist for His pleasure.

God does not exist to make all of our personal human and often short-sighted dreams come true. We exist so that we might have a part in His plan and purpose for the ages.

We do not make God and then tell Him what to do for us. God made us, and He is the One who orders and directs our lives.

When we approach the promises of God, we must always keep in mind that God's ultimate purpose in our lives is to conform us into the image of Jesus Christ. God desires for us the same relationship He had with Jesus—a close intimacy so that we do only what the Father directs us to do and all that we do is for His glory. Jesus was 100 percent obedient to the will of God the Father in all things. He relied exclusively upon God the Father for direction, wisdom, sustenance, provision, and power. Jesus drew His identity solely from God the Father—everything about the character of Jesus was identical to the character of God the Father.

Like Jesus. That is what the Father has in mind for you and for me. He is creating in us the character of Christ. He is molding us to be obedient to His plan for us and in intimate loving relationship with Him.

God meets your needs always in the context of making you more like Jesus.

A FRESH AND DAILY RELATIONSHIP

A prominent Hebrew name for God is El Shaddai—God who Provides. El Shaddai was a living presence to the Israelites, the God who guided them in a pillar of cloud by day and a pillar of fire by night, the God who gave them manna every morning, the God who provided water from solid rock, the God who protected them from Pharaoh's armies, the God who met with Moses face-to-face. El Shaddai was *the* Provider, their only Provider.

The Israelites knew from their experiences in the wilderness that El Shaddai provided their daily needs. Jesus spoke of this also when He taught His disciples to pray, "Give us this day our daily bread" (Matt. 6:11).

The prophet Jeremiah wrote,

This I recall to my mind,
Therefore I have hope.
Through the LORD's *mercies we are not consumed,*
Because His compassions fail not.
They are new every morning;
Great is Your faithfulness.
"The LORD *is my portion," says my soul,*
"Therefore I hope in Him!" (Lam. 3:21–24)

The One who meets our needs is fresh and new in His supply every day. He doesn't give us stale leftovers. His supply is precisely what we need in the moment we need it. Everything He gives us is fresh, new, alive, vibrant, powerful.

We cannot awaken on any given morning and be without God's mercies and His compassions. Regardless of what we have done or said the day before, God is with us in a fresh new relationship every morning.

Every night before we go to sleep, we need to confess our sins to God and receive His forgiveness. We need to do this not so that God will awaken the next morning full of love, forgiveness, and mercy toward us, but so that *we* will awaken the next morning able to receive the fullness of the love, forgiveness, and mercy He extends to us. God never drags around our unconfessed sins, but we do. The burden of guilt is something we carry. It is vital that we set down the burden of those sins so we can take up the blessings that God has prepared for us to have.

You can trust God to meet your needs with a provision that is fresh and good—it will be exciting and life-giving, satisfying and sufficient.

AN EXTENSION OF HIS GLORY

I once overheard a child offer this as an excuse for his behavior: "I just couldn't help myself." To a certain extent, God meets our needs and desires to give us good gifts because it is His very nature to do so. He cannot fail to give. He cannot fail to love.

God's good gifts flow from His goodness. God's very nature of goodness motivates Him to give good gifts and to give them and give them and give them. There is no end to either God's desire to give good gifts to His children or His ability to give good gifts. And therefore, we can never fully exhaust the storehouse of good gifts that are laid up for us.

I once took an informal poll and asked people at random to tell me the first word that came to their minds to describe the nature of God. Many people responded with these words: *holy, righteous, just, absolute, eternal.* A few people said *loving* or *forgiving.* But it was only after asking dozens of people this question that someone responded with *good.*

Most people don't seem to think of God as being good to them. They tend to think of God as being demanding, exacting, and unrelenting. They see Him as prosecutor, judge, and jury. They see Him as distant, remote, and unfeeling—the Creator, the Higher Power, the Almighty. While God certainly bears all of these titles and attributes, He also bears the attributes of faithful, merciful, forgiving, loving, kind, gentle, nurturing, providing, protecting, and good.

We have a lot more ability at times to imagine other people—from close family members to total strangers—doing something good for us than we have the ability to imagine that God might truly pour out an overwhelming blessing on our lives.

A provision always for good. All that God has for us is good. His supply is not only ample, but it is of the highest and finest quality. Jeremiah knew this great truth about God:

> The LORD *is good to those who wait for Him,*
> *To the soul who seeks Him.*
> *It is good that one should hope and wait quietly*
> *For the salvation of the* LORD. *(Lam. 3:25–26)*

God sees the whole of our lives, beginning to ending and on into eternity. He knows what is the best for us not only now but tomorrow and next month and next year and twenty years from now. His gifts to us are always good for us.

A good parent does not give a child a gift that will make the child unhappy. Neither does he give the child everything the child thinks will make him happy. A parent gives what he believes is best for the child, in the right amounts, at the right times.

When I was a boy, there were lots of foods that I didn't particularly like. I ate them anyway. I ate them because my mother cooked them for me and she insisted that I eat them. I ate them because I was hungry and what was put before me was all that was available for me to eat. But that still didn't mean that I enjoyed the taste of all the foods that were put on my plate.

An amazing thing happened somewhere along the way to adulthood. I started liking some of the foods that I didn't like as a child. Some of the things to which I would have liked to have said "no, thank you" as a child are things I find myself ordering from menus.

That same thing happens to us as we grow in our relationship with Christ and become more conformed to His nature. Some things that we didn't like when we were in an unforgiven, sinful state become things that we dearly love. Some things that we weren't all that fond of when we were babes in Christ become things that are pleasurable to us as we mature in our faith and in our love relationship with God.

The opposite situation is also true. There were things that I craved and enjoyed as a child that I no longer like. I look back on some foods that I liked as a child and a teenager, and I think, *Why did I ever think that tasted good?* In like manner, there are things that people do when they are in sin that seem good to them at that state of their lives, but that become things they wouldn't dream of doing once they know Christ or are more mature in Christ.

Our minds are renewed when we come to Christ, and a big part of that renewal is a change in the things that we define as good, desirable, pleasurable, rewarding, and satisfying. Our definition of what is good changes as we come to Christ and grow into His likeness. However, God always sees what is absolutely good for us—things that are good for us now, good for us in every area of our lives, good for those around us, and good for us through all eternity. He gives us only the things that are truly beneficial for our growth as His children and that are beneficial for the advancement of His kingdom on this earth.

The question to ask yourself if you have an unmet need today is this: Is this thing that I need something that God defines as good for my life?

Proactive and creative in His giving. A woman once told me that one of the best Christmas presents she ever received was a stereo record player that her parents bought for her when she was eleven years old. She said, "It had never dawned on me to ask for a stereo. I'm not sure I even knew that stereo units like the one I received had been manufactured. I certainly would not have asked for such an expensive present. But my parents in their generosity gave me a stereo, and it was a gift that gave me countless hours of pleasure during my teen years. My parents continued to monitor the records that I bought. Their gift of a stereo wasn't without certain limitations about how loud or how late at night I could play it. Even so, the gift was an overwhelming one to me. It was a gift they knew I would enjoy even though *I* didn't know how much I would enjoy it until months had passed."

This is the way God gives to us. He gives us what He knows will bring us great pleasure and joy, even though we in our finite wisdom and understanding may not know fully what we need or desire.

God does not wait for others to initiate the provision for our innermost needs. He assumes a proactive position in meeting our needs. God may use other people in the process, but He creates, orchestrates, and engineers the solution that satisfies.

Do you believe even for a second that God is surprised by the need you are experiencing? Do you believe that your sudden lack in a certain area of your life is either a mystery or a surprise to God? To the contrary—God knows you far better than you will ever know yourself. He knew about this need in your life today long before you were ever conceived in your mother's womb. Not only did God know about that need, but He knew His provision for meeting that need. Just as your need is no surprise and no mystery to Him, neither is the provision for solving your problem or meeting your need hidden from His understanding or ability.

God will not keep anything from you that you need to know.

God will not withhold anything from you that is rightfully yours as His child.

God will not hide any aspect of His character from you.

God will not deny you any promise that He makes in His Word.

God will not shut you away from any blessing that is for your eternal benefit or that is required for the fulfillment of your purpose on this earth.

And best of all, God has already prepared for you all that you will need for every day of the rest of your life.

· 7 ·

The Provision of Unlimited Supply

Do you believe there is a need that might be outside God's ability to meet it?

In your heart of hearts, do you believe God is going to supply only 80 percent of your needs, or perhaps 90 percent, or even 99 percent?

Not so! When Paul wrote, "My God shall supply *all* your need," he meant precisely that. All. Not a percentage of. Not a fraction of. All.

I have heard people say on a number of occasions, "Oh, yes, I have a need in my life. But God has been so good to me . . ." What is such a person saying? In essence he is saying that he believes he has used up all of his allotted portion of blessings. His current need lies just beyond God's storeroom of supply. His current need pushes him into the category of being selfish or greedy, and therefore, he expects God to turn down his desire for yet another blessing.

Friend, God has more for you. He still has blessings that you have not received. Malachi painted a wonderful word picture about this:

"Bring all the tithes into the storehouse,
That there may be food in My house,
And try Me now in this,"
Says the LORD of hosts,
"If I will not open for you the windows of heaven
And pour out for you such blessing
That there will not be room enough to receive it." (Mal. 3:10)

We are not to think we are asking for too much from God. Malachi pointed us toward the knowledge that God has more for us than we are capable of receiving. An abundance of God's provision for us lies beyond what we have even thought to request.

Not long ago I heard about a man who said, "I cannot contain it all." This man as a child had dreamed of owning a house with a big yard so that he could buy a riding lawn mower to mow it. He loved to be outside as a boy, and he thought the idea of mowing a lawn with a riding lawn mower would be about the best thing a person could do on a Saturday afternoon.

He had been a churchgoer all of his life, and even as a child, he gave his tithes and offerings to God. Over the years, he never wavered from that obedience to the Lord. He was wise in his spending and wise in all of his business practices. Decade by decade, his fortune grew, and along with it, the amount of his tithes and offerings. He thanked God for all things. And by the time he was sixty years old, he lived on an estate in which he had more than an acre of lawn. Sure enough he had a riding lawn mower. And not only did he have this estate, but he also owned houses in two other areas of the country. In each place he had two automobiles, one for himself and one for his wife. And in each place, he had a riding lawn mower. Finally at age seventy-five, he said to God, "There's too much for me to contain. I don't need three riding lawn mowers, six cars, three houses, and a boat to maintain. This blessing You have poured out for me from heaven—well, Lord, I just don't have room to receive it all!"

Most of us don't have the problem that man had. But then again, most of us don't have the simple trust in God that he had all of his life. He had no doubt that God would meet his needs, and that God would meet them with an overflowing abundance. He believed that God had the ability to do or accomplish anything. And in believing that he was a beloved son of God, he had no trouble receiving the blessings that God showered upon him from above.

The man ardently sought out every bit of wisdom that God might send his way as he conducted his various business affairs. He asked God to help him in every relationship he had—not only in his relationships with his wife and children, but in his relationships with employees and even those who serviced his riding lawn mower. He asked God to help him grow in his spiritual life and in his ability to be an effective minister to others. God had given him numerous opportunities to share his business expertise with others in one-to-one counseling and in providing business wisdom to his church and various community groups. The man truly believed that God would meet *all* of his needs—not some, but *all*—and that God would meet his needs in a way that was overflowing in generosity and abundance.

Do you believe about God what this man believed about God? Do you know God and trust Him as this man did? Are you truly trusting God to meet all of your needs—not some, not just a high percentage, but all—even to the point that you no longer can contain all of the blessing that God pours out on you?

God's Storehouse of Supply

God does not meet our needs according to our resources—the talents we have, the gifts we offer, the numbers we have associated with our bank accounts or investment portfolios. No. God meets our needs according to His resources.

And what are God's resources?

My! You cannot begin to count all of God's resources. The oceans and seas are His. The continents are His. The atmosphere and all of outer space are His. All that is under the continents and all that is locked away as potential for life-giving blessing in plants and animals—*His!* We cannot begin to calculate all of God's resources that are available for His use on this earth, and we haven't even begun to count the unseen resources of heaven. His resources are immeasurable, indestructible, and inexhaustible.

God's bank account has no limitations. His storehouse of supply is beyond our imaginations in size, scope, and magnificence.

How rich is God? What does God possess? The psalmist recorded this about God's wealth:

I am God, your God! . . .
Every beast of the forest is Mine,
And the cattle on a thousand hills.
I know all the birds of the mountains,
And the wild beasts of the field are Mine. (Ps. 50:7, 10–11)

In Haggai 2:8, the Lord declared, "The silver is Mine, and the gold is Mine."

ALL THINGS ARE GOVERNED BY GOD

Everything that is in existence is owned by God, governed by God, and available to God at any given moment. He is in absolute control over anything that we might call a resource, be it animal, mineral, plant, or atmospheric in nature. He has created all and sustains all. At any given second, God could wipe out everything we know as being real, including our lives, because His power over His creation is all-encompassing.

As Christians, you and I are living in union with the Sovereign Power of the universe.

Not only is God in total and absolute authority over all *things* in the universe, but also over every *process* of the universe. The laws by which nature operates are God's laws. He made them, He can alter them, and He can change them if He so desires. All of the scientific laws that we associate with healing, growth, development, and fruitfulness are His laws.

Furthermore, all things that exist but are unseen—in other words, the spiritual realm—are governed by God and are subject to His command. All of the rules or laws that pertain to good relationships, good marriages, good psychological and emotional health, a sense of well-being, effective communication, leadership, a righteous community of people, a godly attitude, development of a good character, and many other laws related to our inner being and our relationships with others are God's laws. He established them, and He continues to rule over them.

We often think of the natural world as being subject to the laws of nature, but when it comes to human nature, many people factor out God's sovereignty. God is the Author of the laws that govern human nature just as He is the Author of the laws that govern the natural environment in which we live.

Friend, there isn't a resource or a process, seen or unseen, known or unknown, that is outside God's domain and God's governance. You are in union with Christ Jesus, God the Father, and the Holy Spirit simultaneously and continually. You are in union with God in His fullness, and that includes the fullness of His authority and power over all things.

Surely at this point Philippians 4:19 becomes really exciting! "My God shall supply all your need *according to His riches in glory.*" We are privileged by God and given the right by God to tap into His riches in glory—riches that are far beyond anything that we can fully understand or comprehend. As Paul wrote to the Ephesians, God "is able to do exceedingly abundantly above all that we ask or think" (Eph. 3:20). In other words, you can't begin to ask God for all that He desires to give you. You can't imagine all that He has for you. I have a pretty good imagination and a pretty good boldness in asking things of God. What an awesome statement about God's supply house to think that we can't even imagine all that is contained in God's riches and that we don't have enough time on this earth to tap into all that God has made available to us!

One of the words that most toddlers learn quickly and use to great advantage is *more.* Give a young child a sip of a milk shake or a spoonful of good-tasting pudding and that child is likely to respond, "More." Even if the child doesn't say the word, the look in his eyes is one of eager anticipation, *More!* As little children before our heavenly Father, we are like toddlers desiring more of God's goodness and more of God's riches in our lives. And just as a loving parent does not give a child just one taste of an ice-cream cone and then deny the child a second taste, neither does our loving heavenly Father give us just a taste of His goodness and then deny all future requests for His blessings.

GOD IS OUR NEED MEETER

We must recognize three significant truths about God's provision and His storehouse of unlimited supply. The first of these is that God, and God alone, is the One who provides. He is the One who holds the keys to the storehouse of unlimited supply. He is both the originator and the giver of the supply.

Paul wrote very specifically that God will supply all our need "according to *His* riches in glory" (Phil. 4:19). *His* supply, *His* storehouse, *His* riches, *His* possessions.

How many people in the world today believe that all of their needs can be met by a government agency or by a special program of some kind? Let me assure you, no government or special program can ever meet all of a person's needs, and certainly not the most fundamental and basic of all needs: spiritual and emotional needs. No amount of government aid can ever instill self-worth. In fact, government aid too often becomes a detriment to self-worth.

The quicker we come to the understanding that only God in Christ is the Need Meeter, the sooner we will release other people from the tremendous burden we try to place upon them to meet our needs to provide for us all of the emotional support and love that ultimately God alone can provide. I cannot convey to you how important this is to our developing healthy and joyful relationships with other people. As long as we look to others to satisfy the deep inner longings that we sometimes cannot even fully define or describe, we will remain in a needy state. God alone is capable of meeting our deepest inner needs.

God may use certain people to meet your needs, but you must never look to those people or require them to meet your needs. To do so is to set yourself up to be devastated when those people fail you either through a willful act or through a lack of ability. No person, or persons, can be or should ever be counted upon to be your source of hope, joy, peace, contentment, creativity, or emotional security. God alone is your source for the meeting of these needs!

God Meets Our Needs by Christ Jesus

God has a method for making available to us the riches of His unlimited storehouse. That means of availability is Christ Jesus. This is the second truth we must learn.

Many people, including a good percentage of those who sit in churches every Sunday, do not know the position they have in Christ; therefore, they do not understand the privileges that are theirs in Christ. Many people live their entire lives without knowing the fullness of the provision that God has for them.

Many companies today issue identification passes to their employees. These passes give them entrance into the company and, in some cases, restrict or give access to various departments or physical locations within the company. Our "pass" into all areas of God's storehouse is Christ Jesus. Paul wrote to the Philippians that God supplies our needs "by Christ Jesus."

Jesus brought us to the Father and mediates for us before His throne, saying, "This one believes in Me." Because of what Jesus has done for us and what Jesus declares about us, we are forgiven and cleansed of all our sin. Jesus gives us access to God the Father.

Jesus brings us again and again to the Father and says, "This is the need in Our beloved one's life. This is what We must meet."

"By Christ Jesus" we are in relationship with the Father. And thus, by Christ Jesus we are in a position to receive all that the Father has for us in the way of our inheritance as His children.

Jesus knows my name and my address. He knows precisely where to deliver God's "riches in glory."

We have the position in Christ to receive God's ample supply. Christ has an ample supply to give. And we have the privilege of receiving His supply.

THE PRIVILEGE OF INSTANT ACCESS

Furthermore, we have instant access to God's provision. There is no time in our lives when we are cut off from God, and therefore, there is no time when we are cut off from His supply.

You can be on a gurney being rolled into a surgical suite.

You can be standing at your kitchen sink washing dishes.

You can be sitting at your desk shuffling papers.

You can be out on the golf course just about to make a putt.

You can be driving in your car on a freeway.

One of the greatest privileges of your life is that you have instant access to God. You do not need to complete a certain protocol, accomplish a list of prerequisites, or be in a certain place, holding your hands in a specific way or reciting a particular statement. You can get in touch with God instantly, directly, and personally at any time of day or night, in any situation or circumstance, either verbally or silently.

Let me paint a picture for you. Suppose that a person sees the brochure we publish about our In Touch cruise to Alaska, and he decides he wants to go on a trip like that. He makes his reservation, saves his money, and buys his tickets. He packs his bags, and finally the day comes when he boards the ship. He goes to the first sitting of the first dinner meal and takes a look at the long, sumptuous buffet table. Then he sits down, opens a little sack, and pulls out a few crackers and a jar of peanut butter.

Someone asks him at that point what he's doing, and he replies, "I'm having dinner." This person obviously doesn't know that all of his meals on the ship are covered by the price of his ticket.

When you came to Christ, *all* of the provisions and abundance of Christ Jesus were made available to you. You don't have to remain in a needy state. Christ has what you need in sufficient supply, and it is available for you to access right now.

A Full Provision for Every Need

The good news for us is that these are not only needs in our lives, but because they are needs that God has created within us from birth, they are also needs for which God has created a full provision. God never sets up a situation or creates a circumstance without also building in the full provision, expression, or potential for success in that situation or circumstance. This is the third significant truth about God's provision.

God creates needs so that we might trust Him to provide for the needs, and in the process, we might grow in our relationship with Him and strengthen our ability to be and do what He has created us to be and do. Stated another way, any lack in our lives is an opportunity for us to grow in our relationship with God, and an opportunity for us to grow in our abilities and in our faith so that we can be even more effective servants of God and witnesses to God's love and grace.

For God to give His people needs and then fail to provide for the needs would be punitive and hateful. God certainly is neither! It is out of God's great love and mercy that He has built a God-shaped vacuum into our lives and then offered to freely, generously, and abundantly fill that void with His love, presence, and power. Friend, there isn't a single verse in all the Bible that describes God as uncaring, unfeeling, stingy, or tight.

Your Supply Box Is Full

In Ephesians 1:3 Paul declared, "Blessed be the God and Father of our Lord Jesus Christ, who has blessed us with every spiritual blessing in the heavenly places in Christ." I want you to notice that this statement is in the past tense. Paul did not say that God is *going* to bless us with spiritual blessings once we are in heaven, or even once we fulfill certain duties, roles, or commands. Paul wrote that Jesus Christ already *has* made all of these blessings available to us. They are blessings that are already laid up in God's storehouse for us to claim.

God does not have to go out and work to refill your supply box. Your supply box is already full to overflowing. Everything you are ever going to need to fulfill God's plan and purpose for your life has already been placed in your supply box, and it has been there since the moment of your conception. God has already deposited to your account all that you will ever need to withdraw.

In other words, you cannot have a need that is too great for God to meet. You cannot have a need that takes God by surprise. You cannot have a need that is beyond the supply that has already been provided by your heavenly Father and made available to you by Christ Jesus!

· 8 ·

The Provision of a Way Out

Have you ever confronted a problem and said, "Where's the exit sign? I want out of this situation"? It might have been a financial problem, a career-related problem, a family-related problem, or a personal problem. When anyone is in need, the first thought is usually, *How can I escape this?*

If that is the way you are feeling and thinking about a need in your life, you should be encouraged today. God *does* have a way to resolve your need!

Three questions are related to virtually all types of needs:

1. Who or what is responsible for causing the need?
2. What is necessary for the need to be met?
3. Who is responsible for meeting the need?

I believe a powerful principle related to needs ties together the answers to these questions: *Whatever created the need in your life will determine how God supplies the need and who is responsible for meeting the need.* In other words, the one responsible for causing the need is ultimately the one responsible for meeting the need, and the condition caused by the need is directly related to the solution for the need.

Financial needs require financial solutions.

Physical needs require physical solutions.

87

Relational needs require relational solutions.

Spiritual needs require spiritual solutions.

Needs that arise from hatred require solutions rooted in love.

In nearly all cases, the way out of a need is the same way you got into the need—only in reverse. The person primarily responsible for meeting the need is the person involved in creating the need.

NEEDS THAT GOD CREATES

God created some needs. Many Christians have not stopped to thoroughly consider that truth. They automatically assume that God solves needs, and therefore, the devil or the evil nature of man must create them. Just because God is the supreme Need Meeter does not mean that needs are not sometimes created by God in our lives so that His plan and purpose can be realized in us and through us.

Have you ever stopped to consider that God created a need in the life of Moses? Moses had been tending sheep for forty years on the back side of the desert. He was married, had children, and had a good relationship with his father-in-law, who was the priest of the people with whom Moses had settled. He had a career, a family, and a degree of status and wealth. And then God showed up.

The Lord revealed Himself to Moses in a bush that was ablaze with fire but was not consumed. God spoke to Moses and created a major problem for him: "Go back to Pharaoh. Lead My people out of Egypt and to the promised land." Moses was wanted on murder charges in Pharaoh's court. He had no status with the Hebrew people or authority to lead them anywhere. And furthermore, he had no public-speaking ability. Problems? Yes, huge problems.

As is true for all problems that God creates, we have only one choice: obey or disobey God's demand on our lives. To obey is to put ourselves into a position for God to provide for our need. To disobey is to put ourselves outside the boundaries of God's provision. Moses obeyed.

Consider the situation of a thirty-six-year-old man who is married, has a family, has a good job, and has bought a house in a nice neighborhood. And then, consider what happens if God calls that man to preach the gospel. God creates a whole host of needs for that man—where to go to seminary, how to pay for seminary, where to live, how to help his children and wife make the move, and on and on. To obey is to see God's provision. To disobey is to be miserable.

Many people respond to God's demand on their lives by blaming God, blaming others, or sulking in their pain. The better approach is to ask, "God, what is Your goal for me? What do You want me to do? Help me to trust You to fulfill what You are calling me to do and be."

When God creates a need, He determines what is necessary for meeting the need, and He is responsible for meeting the need.

Needs That We Create for Ourselves

We create other needs for ourselves. Needs in this area are very often material, physical, financial, or relational.

Many of our self-created needs arise because of unwise decisions. The need will be met, in part, by our making wise decisions and having the courage, skill, and determination to follow through on them. Let me give you an example. Suppose you have engaged in a bad health habit, which over time has caused an unhealthy situation in your body. Perhaps you have eaten foods that are too high in cholesterol and fat content, and you are now facing a higher risk for heart attack and stroke. What will solve this need? Well, the solution in part will involve your making a wise decision to cut down your fat and cholesterol intake, to engage in more active exercise, and to have periodic physical checks on this condition.

What is the way out of a need created by an unwise decision? A wise decision. And who is primarily responsible for meeting the need? The person who has made the unwise decision.

What is God's role in this? I believe that God will give any person wisdom if he asks for it. James 1:5–6 tells us, "If any of you lacks wisdom, let him ask of God, who gives to all liberally and without reproach, and it will be given to him. But let him ask in faith." I believe that God will give daily guidance to any person who requests it, and that He will give courage, fortitude, and willpower to any person who requests these qualities.

In some cases, people create needs in their relationships, perhaps through ignorance and carelessness, but often through rebellion and self-centeredness. Hurtful words may be spoken; estrangement may arise; divisiveness may take root. The relationship is in need.

What is the way out of this type of need? Generally speaking, it will be the opposite of what created the need. Consider the man who is neglectful of his wife. Perhaps he spends fifteen hours a day at the office and gives his wife no priority when it comes to scheduling his weekend hours. What is the solution for the need? A big part of it is likely to be a reprioritizing of plans and schedules so that the man can spend more time with his wife. Who is responsible for meeting the need? The man. What is God's role? I believe God will give the man wisdom about *how* to reprioritize his time and efforts, and will help heal the heart of the wife and make her more open to a full reconciliation with her husband.

If unkind words have been spoken, kind words need to be spoken.

If dishonesty has become a pattern, honesty needs to prevail.

If lies have been told, the truth needs to be told.

If hateful actions have been taken, loving actions need to be pursued.

Jesus told a parable about a man who created needs for himself. We know it as the parable of the prodigal son. (See Luke 15:11–24.) Through a series of wrong conclusions and bad decisions, the young man created needs in his life. He learned what we all learn: bad decisions produce bad consequences.

Some of the needs in the young man's life were no doubt legitimate. He had a need to prove himself and fulfill his personal destiny, as well as a need to establish his own identity. Other needs might *not* have been of his own choosing. He might have experienced feelings of rejection. The problem, however, arose because the young man did not know *how* to resolve his needs. He *left* home rather than confront his neediness *at* home. We can never outrun or escape our neediness.

The prodigal son ended up homeless, hopeless, rejected, criticized, left out, and with a deep longing for love. The good news of this story is that no matter how needy we become—and regardless of the fact that we might have brought some needs on ourselves—God loves us, accepts us, forgives us, and *helps us to resolve our needs.* He will not do our part, but He will assist us so that our efforts will succeed and we will have both the courage and the endurance necessary to see a problem resolved fully or a need met fully.

NEEDS THAT ARE CREATED BY OTHERS

There are some needs that we don't ask for and we don't create, but that others create for us. Joseph was certainly a person who experienced this type of need. He was sold into slavery by his brothers through no fault of his own, other than telling his brothers two of his dreams. While in Egypt and in slavery, Joseph was falsely accused by Potiphar's wife, and as a result of the false charge, he found himself in prison even though he had acted righteously before God. Yes, Joseph had problems created by others!

One time after an In Touch rally, a woman greeted me. She put a note in my hand and said with great insistence, "Please read this." When I opened her note later, I found that it said:

> I feel hopeless. I have no purpose in life. I am angry with God. But I believe what you said tonight and I am accepting Jesus Christ as my Savior. Suicide and hell would be worse.

At the bottom of the note she had written: "Adult 24. Child of alcoholic father. Mother in mental hospitals most of my life. Sexually and physically abused as a child."

This young woman, like Joseph, had not asked for the troubles of her life. But also like Joseph, she had made a decision to trust God with her life.

In cases where others create problems for us, God's role is one of deliverance from evil. Total and abiding trust in God is our only hope.

NEEDS THAT WE INHERIT FROM OTHERS

Some people have had some needs so long that they can't remember how they acquired the needs or from whom. Needs in this category are very often emotional in nature, and a good number of them relate to needs that begin early in life.

Some of these emotional needs are rooted in parental rejection, abuse, separation, hateful criticism, cutting remarks, or neglect. Others arise out of repeated failures. What can be done in these cases?

Well, first we must recognize that these needs are usually deep-seated and that they will take time to reverse. There are no quick cures for the feelings, hurts, and emotional needs that arise from bad parenting early in a child's life. Long-term and loving commitments are required. What brings about the healing, however, is often the opposite of what caused the pain—being accepted, loved, nurtured, praised, valued, included, honored, treated with dignity and respect. In cases of repeated failures, the need may be best met through information, wise counsel, acquired skills, and opportunities for incremental and consistent successes.

The person primarily responsible for meeting needs arising from repeated failure is the "bad teacher" or the "inattentive student." The failures may be self-created through rebellion that caused the person to reject sound teaching or through lack of discipline that resulted in a failure to practice or maintain good skills and habits. The failure may result from bad information or bad role modeling. The need will be met through good teaching, good role modeling, diligent practice, a submissive attitude, and an eagerness to be instructed and to learn. The errant student is responsible for finding a good teacher since in all likelihood, the bad teacher will be incapable of providing good teaching.

In both the case of an emotional need arising from bad parenting and the case of a failure-related need arising from bad past performance, the person must be able to recognize his own need if he is going to be able to participate in meeting his need. One difficulty in solving these types of needs is that the needy person often admits only to having rather nebulous, undefined, foggy or fuzzy types of inner feelings. There is restlessness, but there is little understanding of what originally caused such vague, yet persistent feelings. The person tends to know that something is wrong or missing, but he is unsure about what.

In my experience, a critical step is taken when the person will ultimately admit to having one or more of these needs:

- I need acceptance.
- I need successes in what I attempt to do.
- I need approval.
- I need to be loved genuinely and unconditionally.
- I need attention.
- I need friendship or companionship.
- I need to feel that my life is worthwhile and valued.
- I need to be needed by someone.
- I need a vacation (or a break).

- I need a rest.
- I need a challenge.

Identifying the type of need is the first step toward recognizing what the solution for the need might be. If a vacation or a prolonged break is needed, the need will be met through planning and then taking a vacation or prolonged break. If the need is friendship or companionship, the need will be met through engaging in activities that give an opportunity for friendships to develop.

And ultimately when it comes to meeting the emotional or deep inner needs of another person—the needs that may have no known source or specific cause—the responsibility for need meeting is going to fall upon three sources, each of which may have a different level of responsibility: (1) the person with the emotional need; (2) loving Christian friends; and (3) God Himself.

It is very difficult to help a person with a deep-seated or long-standing emotional need unless he is willing to receive help and in some way engage actively in meeting the need. The person who turns his back on all help, wise counsel, or prayer will probably continue to experience need regardless of what others do.

In some cases, people will say to themselves and others, "Well, if this is a problem, God will fix it." In saying this, they expect God to completely override their will, emotions, and thought processes—something God does not do except in the most extreme cases where His eternal plan and purpose are involved. A do-nothing attitude toward a need results in a nothing-done state. We are never to expect God to do everything while we sit back and do nothing. In the Gospel of John, Jesus described the Holy Spirit as our Helper, our Counselor, our Advocate. He is not described as the One who will do everything for us and require nothing of us.

An older farmer gave this advice to a younger farmer: "Ask God to show you what to plant and when to plant. Then plant the best seed you can buy. Ask God to grow the seeds. Then cultivate the ground, pull the weeds, and fertilize the plants as they grow. Ask God to produce a great harvest. Then go out and gather the harvest when it is ripe. Ask God to show you how to market your produce. Then take your produce to market. Don't try to do God's part. And don't expect God to do yours."

INVOLVEMENT BY OTHERS

No one person's needs can be met fully by just one other person. The reason lies in the question, How much is enough? You can ask that question of virtually anything in life. In human terms, there is never enough that any human being can do, have, or be in order to meet a need completely, especially an emotional or spiritual inner need.

A human being who is starving for affection can never get enough affection from one other human being. A person who is frightened and lonely deep down inside can never get a feeling of security or companionship. He or she can never get close enough to another human being.

I have watched with sadness as marriages have become estranged over this very issue. One person in the relationship is needy and so desperate to have a deep inner need met that he or she will cling to the spouse until the spouse is drained dry and is left feeling bewildered, exhausted, sad, angry, and frustrated—often all at the same time. A person with deep inner needs seems to draw upon others with a relentless, insatiable emotional hunger, and virtually nothing that any other person does is enough to satisfy the inner need.

Friends, contributors, employers, employees, volunteers, family members, skilled consultants and experts, hired specialists, and numerous other categories of people are required in some way for nearly all types of material, physical, financial, and relational needs to be met.

In the realm of emotional healing, the person with a need will need a body of believers to bring about a total meeting of the need. If the person needs approval for the talents and gifts that God has given him, he will need approval from several people, not just one, for him to feel that the approval is valid. The body of Christ should provide such approval.

If the person needs friendship, he will need the friendship of several people, not just one person. The body of Christ should provide such friendship.

If the person needs sound teaching or new skills, the person will need several teachers to provide that instruction, not just one teacher. The body of Christ should provide such instruction in the form of pastors and teachers who are good role models and who provide consistently wise instruction from the pulpit, in Sunday school classes, in small group meetings, at retreats and seminars, over the airwaves, in the form of books and tapes, and through one-on-one conversations and counseling sessions.

Again, an inner need cannot be met by an external solution, including the external solutions manifested in another human being. No one person can totally satisfy all of the inner need in another person. We are called to be part of and to participate fully in the body of Christ.

FALSE SOLUTIONS TO NEED MEETING

In many cases, the behavior of a person is rooted in his perception that what he is doing *externally* will bring about the solution to his deep needs *internally*. But external solutions don't work for deep emotional or spiritual needs.

Let me give you a couple of examples.

Let's consider a man who works sixty hours a week at his job. All of his energies, seven days a week, are aimed at getting ahead in his career. Outwardly this man claims that he must work long hours either to keep his job or to advance in his job. Or he may claim that he is expending all of the time and effort for the good of his family. At the core of his being, however, is a deep need to be accepted, recognized, and rewarded for who he is as a person. He has a deep need to achieve in order to have a place in the social world that he doesn't have. All of his energies are channeled into the workplace in hopes that somebody will value him enough, recognize him enough, reward him enough, or accept him as being worthy. He is trying to meet internal needs through external needs.

If you were to ask such a person whether he had needs, he would likely say, "No, I don't have any needs. I'm just a hard worker." The reality is, such a man often does not know within himself the true nature of his inner needs, and he has been deceived into thinking that he can increase his value to others, and ultimately to God, through hard work. Such a person is driven by inner needs, but he will not solve the needs through the work he does.

Let's consider a woman who gets involved in every volunteer effort and every church committee available. From dawn to dusk she does good works for her church and her community. She says she is just trying to be a good Christian. In reality, however, she is struggling with a sense of failure before God. She feels unworthy of God's love and acceptance. She is haunted by incidents long in her past in which she felt rejection, pain, and sorrow. She might have been involved in some type of sin, either her own or that of another person, and she feels unclean and of little value before God. Her efforts are an external attempt to compensate for an internal need.

Such a woman likely does not know that she is attempting to meet inner needs through her relentless work on behalf of others. In truth, she feels driven to give of herself to make herself worthy of God's love and forgiveness. She is striving to earn what Jesus has already offered to her freely.

I have talked to a number of men and women who fit the profiles I have given here, and in every case, if I am able to talk to the persons long enough and they are willing to be honest with themselves and with me, we get to the point where we come face-to-face with a deep emotional or spiritual need in their lives, one that often goes all the way back to their early years.

The same emotional need that drives a person to work himself to the point of exhaustion or illness or perhaps even stroke, heart attack, or death, is the same need that often drives a person to promiscuity, alcoholism, or substance abuse. It is the deep inner need for acceptance, love, value, worthiness, and forgiveness from God.

Until that inner need is faced, and then met through receiving the love and forgiveness of God made possible through the cross of Jesus Christ, the person is likely to continue to pursue external solutions, which are ultimately false solutions.

When Are External Solutions Valid?

Things can never take the place of relationships. Neither things nor relationships resolve inner needs. This is not to say, however, that all external solutions are invalid. External solutions work for meeting external needs.

Consider the situation in which a person has a home literally washed off its foundation by a hundred-year flood. That is an external need. It is not at all rooted in the inner lives of the family members who lived in the home.

What is likely to meet the need that this flood-ravaged family has experienced? Hard work to earn enough money to rebuild the home, wise decisions about where to rebuild, continued love and encouragement to one another in the face of such a challenge. External solutions will work because the need is external.

Consider the situation in which a child falls ill to a fever that was transmitted by a tick while he was out hiking with a group of Scouts. What will bring about a solution to that problem? Good medicine, good support of prayer and love and encouragement from family members and friends, and ongoing precautions. External solutions will work because the need is external.

External solutions work for external needs.

Internal solutions are required to meet internal needs.

WHAT IS GOD'S ROLE?

God's role varies according to the nature of the need. Sometimes God's role is to instruct us in the way we should go. It is then our responsibility to do what He has told us to do.

At other times God's role in meeting our needs is to supply Himself. God the Holy Spirit has been given to those who believe in Jesus Christ to be our Comforter, Counselor, Spirit of truth, and Helper. Jesus used these words to describe the work of the Holy Spirit in us. Guidance, comfort, courage, insight, truth, discernment, wisdom, understanding, peacefulness, strength—all of these are imparted to us by the Holy Spirit to help us see clearly and then walk boldly in the path God puts before us.

What is vital for us to recognize is this: at all times God has a role. Furthermore, we must always acknowledge His role as the most important role.

When we talk about having our needs met, we human beings often look to everyone except to God. We seek answers from relatives, friends, and a host of other sources—some helpful, others harmful to our spirits—rather than look to God.

The ultimate source for meeting all need is God. He uses a variety of methods and instruments to meet our needs, but He is the Author and Originator of all that we need, both in the outer material, natural, and physical realm, and in the inner emotional, mental, and spiritual realm.

Many of the ways in which He helps us can be found in His Word. The Bible not only defines human need but also presents God's methods for resolving human need.

Furthermore, God's Word presents both a right and a wrong way for meeting our needs. Example after example is provided to show how God works and to show the futility of man's methods.

And finally the good news about God's methods for meeting needs is this: there is no negative side effect. When we follow God's method for meeting needs, we are not left with a residual feeling of anxiety, guilt, frustration, or embarrassment. When God meets our needs, He does so in a way that leaves us feeling a deep inner peace, satisfaction, and sense of fulfillment.

Many times God will reveal a plan for meeting your need, and that plan very often includes something specific that you must do.

A young man was discussing his love life—or rather, his lack of a love life—with his grandfather. He admitted to his grandfather that he hadn't been out on a date in several months. He finally gave a big sigh and said to his grandfather, "Gramps, I guess I'm just going to have to trust God to send me a wife."

His grandfather replied with a twinkle in his eye, "I suspect that God would be a lot more eager to help you if He knew you had the nerve to ask the girl He sends you out on a date."

The point is, we usually have to do something to bring God's answer to bear on our need. Certainly we can trust God to help us, lead us, guide us, bring relationships our way, and give us the courage to act. We also must be willing to do our part: ask, seek, knock, work, plan, prepare, initiate contacts, be open to opportunities.

Are you willing to do things God's way?

Are you willing to read God's Word and communicate with God until you have certainty about His plan and His timing?

Are you willing to do what God reveals to you to do?

These are key questions you must ask yourself.

GOD'S PLAN INCLUDES GOD'S PERFECT TIMING

Jesus has a method and a procedure to bring you through the storm you are experiencing, and He also has a specific timetable for His method and procedure. God's timing is perfect, even though His timing may not be your timing.

Notice what happened when Jesus sent the disciples away after He miraculously had fed five thousand families from a few loaves and fish. The Bible says that Jesus "made His disciples get into the boat and go before Him to the other side" (Matt. 14:22). The implication is that they didn't want to go. Jesus insisted. He wanted personally to send the multitudes away, and He also wanted time alone with the Father. His reasons were *His* reasons.

God never has to explain Himself to us or give us a reason for what He does. He never needs to reveal to us the reason for a storm in our lives unless He desires to do so and chooses to do so. There are some reasons that we simply never need to know.

What we do need to know is that Jesus is with us in the storm, regardless of its nature or origin, and that God has a divine plan and purpose in place for our lives.

The storm on the sea, the passage of the disciples from one point to the next, and Jesus' prayer time were all in a perfect concert of time from the Father's perspective.

There is no sense of hurry about this scene, from the divine perspective. Jesus knew the storm was raging, but there is no indication whatsoever that Jesus hurried His prayer time. Jesus knew that the disciples were going to end up exactly where He intended for them to be. He had no fear whatsoever that the storm was going to blow the disciples off course. They might have thought they were going to be off course or late in their arrival, but Jesus knew they were going to arrive exactly where they were supposed to be, when they were supposed to be there.

There is no indication that Jesus was running to them across the sea, as if He had to get there in the nick of time. No! Jesus was walking to them as if everything was happening and unfolding precisely as God had ordained—and indeed, it was.

Jesus was not only the Sovereign of the sea, but also the sovereign Lord of the disciples' lives. That being the case, Jesus was totally in charge of every aspect of the experience.

What a wonderful assurance we should draw from this story for our lives. Is Jesus the Lord of all things or only some things? Is He Lord over time, situations, all the material universe, and all circumstances? Indeed,

He is! Is He Lord over your life? That is a question only you can answer. The truth, however, is that *if* you have made Jesus the Lord of your life, and He is the rightful King of all kings and Lord of all lords, then there isn't a situation, circumstance, or period of time over which Jesus does not have absolute control and sovereignty. He will make certain that all things come together for your good, in His timing and according to His chosen methods, if you will only trust Him completely to be the Lord of your life.

Have you ever thought about the fact that the Lord can cause any storm in your life to blow you to the place where He intends for you to arrive? Many of us think that it is up to us to decide where we are going to be five years from now, or even that it is up to us to decide exactly what we are going to do tomorrow, next week, or next year. If we claim Jesus as our Lord, then those decisions are up to Him, not us. We can make plans, and we are wise to do so, but our plans must always be the result of prayer and made with total flexibility that if this is not what God desires for us to do, we will be quick to alter our course.

James addressed this very issue:

Come now, you who say, "Today or tomorrow we will go to such and such a city, spend a year there, buy and sell, and make a profit"; whereas you do not know what will happen tomorrow. For what is your life? It is even a vapor that appears for a little time and then vanishes away. Instead you ought to say, "If the Lord wills, we shall live and do this or that." But now you boast in your arrogance. All such boasting is evil. (James 4:13–16)

The disciples should never have experienced a single moment of doubt that they were precisely where God wanted them to be and that He was in control of their lives and would bring them through the storm. Why is that so? Because Jesus had insisted that they get into the boat and go before Him to the other side. Jesus will not tell you to do something and then change His mind about it and not tell you. Jesus will not tell you to get into a boat and go before Him to the other side if He does not intend to meet you on the other shore. Jesus had made it very plain to His disciples where they were to go, how they were to get there, and that He would meet them there.

Note what Jesus did *not* tell His disciples. He did not tell them their time of arrival. Neither did He tell them how He was getting to the other side of the sea. He said, "Get in the boat, row to the other side, and I'll meet you over there."

The Lord may not tell you every detail of His plan. Your position is not to require every detail or to know all things, but to obey what the Lord tells you to do. How the Lord does His part, and what the Lord's timing may be, is the Lord's business, not yours.

This is critically important to the way you face needs and storms. The Lord knows precisely how He is going to meet your need or calm your storm. He knows all of the methods He is going to use, and for which purposes He will use them. He knows exactly when He is going to exact His purposes to meet your need or calm your storm. Your position is to trust God and, in your obedience and trust, to do what you know to do and leave all other matters to God's sovereignty.

GOD'S METHODS ARE NOT WITHOUT PAIN

We can and must trust God explicitly when it comes to both method and timing for our needs to be met. That does not ensure, however, that the process will be painless. What we can count on is that God's method will always be effective and eternally beneficial.

As I mentioned earlier, it was not until I was into my forties that I began to deal with some of the inner wounds from my past. I became increasingly restless in my spirit and found myself asking God more frequently, "What's going on here? Something isn't right." I couldn't recognize the cause of my frustration and uneasiness. I asked the Lord to reveal to me the cause of the inner tension I felt. And He began to do His surgery in my life.

The process was not quick and it was not without pain. I had layers and layers of emotional wounds that needed to be revealed and healed: feelings of loneliness, rejection, abusive criticism, unworthiness, and guilt that began early in my childhood. My healing of emotional wounds was not a matter of saying a quick prayer, "Jesus, please heal me. Amen." No, it was a process that required years of introspection, yielding to the healing power of God, and wise counsel from godly men who knew how to listen with an open mind and how to listen to the Holy Spirit and follow His leading in the advice they gave me.

Did I enjoy the process? No, not really. I'm not sure that divine surgery is something that any person enjoys, or even that it is a process that God intends for us to enjoy.

Did I benefit from the process? More than words can convey. I am not the same person I once was in the innermost parts of my being. Through this process of subjecting myself to God's healing power, I learned a great deal more about myself and vastly more about God and His love. I came to experience the feeling of God's love for me in a way that I had never known God's love before. I developed a more intimate relationship with God than I had ever had in the past. My trust in God became complete; my faith grew stronger; my spiritual sensitivity increased; my awareness of God at work became sharper. I developed spiritually in ways I can't even describe other than to say my relationship with God became richer, more intense, more satisfying, and more all-encompassing, and it continues to become increasingly richer, more intense, more satisfying, and more all-encompassing as time passes.

Am I certain without a shadow of a doubt that God heals emotional wounds? Absolutely. Am I certain that He will do in you what He has done in me if you will yield yourself to His healing presence and power as I yielded myself to Him? Absolutely.

PATIENCE IN THE MIDST OF GOD'S PROCESS

Financial problems often develop over months and years. Paying off one's debts can take equally long.

Family and marital problems usually build slowly over years and sometimes decades. Solutions can be slow in coming and may take years of family and personal counseling.

Emotional wounds can occur quickly. It may take only a few minutes for a person to be hurt deeply. But emotional bitterness, resentment, and hatred often seethe for years before a person seeks healing. Emotional healing takes time.

God can heal or resolve both external and internal needs instantly, but in the vast majority of cases, individuals who are truly going to be healed are going to have to walk through a process that takes time.

A woman recently asked a friend of mine, "How long is it going to take for God to heal me of the pain I feel over the incest in my childhood?" The woman had been in therapy for years and was still receiving counseling for problems rooted in that terrible abuse of thirty years ago. My friend replied, "I don't know. Only God has the timetable."

That answer may not be satisfying to the person experiencing pain, but it is an honest answer. An accident can do serious damage to the physical body in a matter of seconds. Healing from those injuries can take months, even years. A disease can be quite advanced before its symptoms drive a person to seek help. Healing from such a disease can require months or years of treatment. So, too, our emotional wounds. A single act of sexual abuse, a particularly embarrassing situation, or one act of rejection can cause emotional pain that may take years to undo or overcome. Only God knows all the pieces to the puzzle and what it will take for a person to regain full health and wholeness.

If you or someone you love is in the process of being healed, have patience. God calls us to be steadfast and to be faithful in our obedience to Him as He renews us, regenerates us, and creates in us the likeness of Jesus Christ.

Even the person who experiences a miraculous physical cure often requires weeks or months of therapy to regain full strength and function. So, too, with emotional healing. The healing process is one of healing and then strengthening for the future. A major part of the process is not only dealing with the past, but also acquiring skills, strategies, and a new perspective for facing the future successfully. Emotional healing requires that we develop new ways of thinking, responding, feeling, and relating. It requires that we approach life with a new outlook and a new level of trust in God.

Don't allow yourself to become discouraged by the pain that you may experience at the outset of an emotional healing process or by the fact that your emotional healing is not instantaneous. Be encouraged that God is at work and He is remaking you into the person He truly created you to be.

Consider again the experience of Jeremiah the prophet, who heard the Lord say to him,

"Arise and go down to the potter's house, and there I will cause you to hear My words." Then I went down to the potter's house, and there he was, making something at the wheel. And the vessel that he made of clay was

marred in the hand of the potter; so he made it again into another ves-
sel, as it seemed good to the potter to make. Then the word of the LORD
came to me, saying: . . . "Look, as the clay is in the potter's hand, so are you
in My hand." (Jer. 18:2–6)

When we undergo an experience of emotional healing, it is often as
if we are broken so that the Lord can completely remake us. Emotional
healing is a refashioning process. The clay is still the same, the end design
is still the same, but the process requires a breaking and a rebuilding so
that the flaws can be removed.

Not only are we to remain steadfast, but we are to be joyful that God
is at work in our lives. We are to thank Him daily that He is healing us,
restoring us, and making us whole. We are who we are, each one of us,
because the Lord is making us who we are. We are His workmanship.
Praise God that He is providing you with a way out, He is with you every
step of the way as you follow His leading, and He will bring you to a
complete resolution of your need.

Paul encouraged the Philippians by writing at the beginning of his letter to them, "He who has begun a good work in you will complete it
until the day of Jesus Christ" (Phil. 1:6).

Paul wrote to the Thessalonians a similar word of encouragement:
"He who calls you is faithful, who also will do it" (1 Thess. 5:24).

Rejoice over the fact that God provides the way out, and His presence
will enable you to pursue that way out until *all* your need has been met!

· 9 ·

The Provision of His Presence

Are you aware that God is with you always?

Many Christians readily proclaim, "God is always there," but if they are pressed for an honest response, they will also admit, "I don't always feel God. I'm not always aware of His presence with me." Too often this is true when we experience periods of intense neediness or when we truly confront our inner state of neediness for the first time.

In the previous chapter we discussed primarily *how* God provides a way out for us when we have need, and we briefly touched upon the nature of God as He walks with us through our need all the way to His full provision and blessing. In this chapter, I want to focus on the nature of God's relationship with us and how we can fully experience the provision of His presence.

DELIGHTING IN THE LORD

Psalm 37:4 gives us one of the most precious and sweet promises of God related to our desires:

Delight yourself also in the LORD,
And He shall give you the desires of your heart.

How many people do you know who have that verse underlined or highlighted in their Bibles?

But look at the first line of that psalm: "Delight yourself also in the LORD." When you delight yourself in another person, you spend as much time as possible with that person, and you get to know that person as well as possible. When you are delighted in your relationship with another person, you are fulfilled, complete, satisfied, content, and joyful in your relationship. If you experience such a relationship, many material and physical things usually become very unimportant.

Think back to a time when you were very much in love with another person. You could spend hours and hours with that person doing virtually nothing, with nothing, and at very little expense. Just taking a long walk with that person or sitting on a porch swing by the hour with that person was sheer delight. Driving to get an ice-cream cone and sitting in the car watching the people go by—those were satisfying and enjoyable moments. You weren't concerned about the designer label on the clothes you were wearing, the make of the watch on your wrist, or even the model of the car you were sitting in. You weren't concerned about having a lot of other people around you. You were fully content just to be in the presence of the one you loved. The most important thing to you in the moments you spent together was the relationship you were building.

And so it is when we come to delight in our relationship with the Lord. Nothing else really matters when we experience an intimate time with the Lord. Everything else pales in comparison to Him. As the old Gospel song "Turn Your Eyes Upon Jesus" says, in the light of Jesus' glory and grace, "the things of earth will grow strangely dim."

Are you content when you are with the Lord? Do you truly delight in Him? Are you spending enough time with the Lord to become delighted in Him?

I have discovered over the years that most people I meet haven't taken the time or made the effort to get to know the Lord. Not really. Not deeply. Not in an intimate way that allows them to feel the heartbeat of God and to know God's vast and eternal love.

The reasons for their failure to know the Lord in a deep and satisfying way are many—fear of God's judgment, fear of what others might say, lack of information, poor teaching in the past, a failure of perception or understanding, a lack of making the Lord a priority.

Once a person truly gets to know the Lord, however, that person is going to discover that it is a delight to know the Lord. No times are sweeter than the times spent with Him. No times are more fulfilling, satisfying, or joyful than the times spent basking in His presence.

When our relationship is one of delight in the Lord, we are not going to want to do things, possess or use things, or enter into any relationship that will damage in any way our relationship with the Lord. Again, think back to the way you felt when you were deeply in love. To the best of your ability, you didn't let anything come between you and your loved one. Nothing mattered as much as keeping your relationship as wonderful as it was on the first day you fell in love.

So it is with the person who delights himself in the Lord. Such a person will not want anything that might inhibit, hinder, stall, or interfere with his relationship with the Lord. In terms we have discussed previously, the person will want only what is good for the relationship.

When we seek the Lord and delight ourselves in Him we want only what is pleasing to Him and only what He wants us to have. Furthermore, we will be satisfied completely with what the Lord gives us.

As 1 John 1:3 tells us, "Truly our fellowship is with the Father and with His Son Jesus Christ." That's the ultimate fellowship! Knowing God. Communicating with Him—pouring out our hearts to Him and hearing His desires, His plan for us, His purposes. Loving Him with all our hearts and receiving an awareness of His vast love. Being at peace with God and knowing God's peace in our hearts. Praising God and being filled with God's joy. Being in a position to say, "*My* God." That is truly what it means to have fellowship with God.

GOD'S PROMISE TO MEET OUR NEEDS

When God meets our inner needs with the provision of His presence, we can be assured always that part of His provision will be to give us these things:

- Contentment—deep and abiding inner peace and calm
- Strength—great courage and fortitude to endure all things
- Fulfillment—a full and satisfying feeling of supply related to our purpose on this earth

Throughout this book, we have been focusing on God's need-meeting promise in Philippians 4:19: "My God shall supply all your need according to His riches in glory by Christ Jesus." To fully understand this verse, we must understand its context.

Paul's entire letter to the Philippians is related to needs and need-meeting. The Philippians were tremendously helpful in meeting Paul's material and financial needs. Paul began his letter to them by saying, "I thank my God upon every remembrance of you, always in every prayer of mine making request for you all with joy, for your fellowship in the gospel from the first day until now" (Phil. 1:3–5). Their *fellowship* in the gospel is translated in one version as their *participation* in the gospel— in other words, the things that the Philippians did to help Paul spread the gospel and teach the new believers.

In the fourth chapter of Philippians, Paul again thanked them for their support:

> *But I rejoiced in the Lord greatly that now at last your care for me has flourished again; though you surely did care, but you lacked opportunity. Not that I speak in regard to need, for I have learned in whatever state I am, to be content: I know how to be abased, and I know how to abound. Everywhere and in all things I have learned both to be full and to be hungry, both to abound and to suffer need. I can do all things through Christ who strengthens me. Nevertheless you have done well that you shared in my distress. Now you Philippians know also that in the beginning of the gospel, when I departed from Macedonia, no church shared with me concerning giving and receiving but you only. For even in Thessalonica you sent aid once and again for my necessities. Not that I seek the gift, but I seek the fruit that abounds to your account. Indeed I have all and abound. I am full, having received from Epaphroditus the things sent from you, a sweet-smelling aroma, an acceptable sacrifice, well pleasing to God. And my God shall supply all your need according to His riches in glory by Christ Jesus. (Phil. 4:10–19)*

I want you to notice two things in this passage. First, Paul was a man who knew about need. He was writing the letter to the Philippians from a prison cell in Rome, so he certainly had a keen awareness of his external needs even as he wrote. Paul never made a claim that the Christian life is a need-free life, or that as Christians, we can mature to the point that we never face need. Paul knew that needs exist for us every day of our lives. We never outgrow our neediness or mature to the point that we don't have needs.

Second, Paul was willing to admit his neediness and to share what he learned about needs and how to deal with them. Paul encouraged the Philippians in the truths he learned from having experienced needs. Never be ashamed of your past needs or your current neediness. Be quick to encourage others by telling them how God has met your needs in the past and how you believe He will meet their needs.

CONTENT IN ALL STATES

Paul said that he learned to be content regardless of his circumstances—in whatever state he was in. Paul was not content *with* troubles, trials, suffering, pain, or need. He felt pain and need just as much as any other person. But he learned to be content *in* times of difficulty. His internal state was one of contentment even when his outward state was one of turmoil, trial, or trouble.

No stranger to outer pain and suffering, Paul was stoned and left for dead in Lystra, beaten and imprisoned in Philippi, and persecuted and defamed publicly nearly everywhere he went. To those in the Corinthian church who compared him to other preachers, Paul wrote that he was "in labors more abundant, in stripes above measure, in prisons more frequently, in deaths often" (2 Cor. 11:23). He then went on to detail for the Corinthians some of the needs and troubles he had experienced in his ministry:

> *From the Jews five times I received forty stripes minus one. Three times I was beaten with rods; once I was stoned; three times I was shipwrecked; a night and a day I have been in the deep; in journeys often, in perils of waters, in perils of robbers, in perils of my own countrymen, in perils of the Gentiles, in perils in the city, in perils in the wilderness, in perils in the sea, in perils among false brethren; in weariness and toil, in sleeplessness often, in hunger and thirst, in fastings often, in cold and nakedness—besides the other things, what comes upon me daily: my deep concern for all the churches. (2 Cor. 11:24–28)*

Few people can match Paul in severity and frequency of need and suffering externally. Yet Paul wrote that in the midst of such outer troubles, he learned to be content internally.

How many truly contented people do you know?

I suspect that the number is very few. And yet if you look closely at the lives of those who truly and genuinely are contented, you are going to find that their contentment has nothing whatsoever to do with material things, relationships, or achievements. I've met truly contented people who were single, and I've met some who were married. I have met genuinely contented people who were poor, and a few who had been given great wealth. I have met contented people who were totally without fame and recognition, and in many ways, without fantastic jobs or great successes, and I've met a few who were content regardless of their fame and success.

In many cases, the very thing that people think will bring them contentment turns out to be the very thing that creates more problems and turmoil for them. In the end, only the Lord Jesus Christ Himself can bring about contentment in a person's life. Paul was able to say, "I have learned in whatever state I am, to be content: I know how to be abased, and I know how to abound. Everywhere and in all things I have learned both to be full and to be hungry, both to abound and to suffer need. I can do all things through Christ who strengthens me" (Phil. 4:11–13).

Be careful that you don't misread these verses. Paul did not say that Christ strengthened him only when he was struggling, suffering, hungry, or abased. Christ strengthened Paul in all states in which he found himself. He strengthened Paul when he was full, abounding, safe, and without pain or struggle. We often don't think about this. Paul had no less need for Christ's strength when things were good. In times of abounding, Paul needed Christ's strength to keep him humble, keenly aware of others and generous toward them, thankful, energized, and an active witness of God's power. When things are going well for us, we need Christ's strength to keep us from pride, laziness, and self-sufficiency.

Paul said that he learned to be content "in whatever state I am." His contentment was in Christ—not in things or in circumstances. His contentment lay in his relationship with the Need Meeter, not in the fact that his needs were met momentarily.

I heard about a man who experienced great contentment and love in the presence of his wife just by holding her hand. The man's wife suffered with a terminal disease for three years before she died, and as she became weaker and weaker in the final months, the man pulled his chair close to hers, and they held hands and stared into each other's eyes. No words needed to be spoken. No physical embrace needed to be shared. The love was just as rich and freely flowing between them through the looks in their eyes and the touch of their fingertips. No grasping. No desperate clinging. No clamoring for attention. No pleas for acts of affection.

True contentment is always marked by a lack of striving—a lack of grasping, a lack of demanding, a lack of insistence.

True contentment lies not in having, but in knowing—of knowing that you are accepted, loved, forgiven, valued in spite of what you may or may not have in your hands or surrounding you.

True contentment is not rooted in environment or in any aspect of the natural and spiritual world. Ultimate contentment is rooted in relationship with Jesus Christ and in Him alone.

STRENGTH TO FACE ALL CIRCUMSTANCES

Paul also taught that he had learned to experience strength in all things. Paul might have had times when he felt weak in his flesh, but he knew that even in those times of natural and physical weakness, he could experience the strength of Christ internally. Paul wrote to the Corinthians about his ability to feel strong spiritually in the face of physical weakness:

> *A thorn in the flesh was given to me, a messenger of Satan to buffet me, lest I be exalted above measure. Concerning this thing I pleaded with the Lord three times that it might depart from me. And He said to me, "My grace is sufficient for you, for My strength is made perfect in weakness." Therefore most gladly I will rather boast in my infirmities, that the power of Christ may rest upon me. Therefore I take pleasure in infirmities, in reproaches, in needs, in persecutions, in distresses, for Christ's sake. For when I am weak, then I am strong. (2 Cor. 12:7–10)*

Paul's thorn-in-the-flesh experience brought him to the position where he could fully allow the strength of Christ to be his strength. Paul was not saying that he delighted in the pain and suffering; rather, he had learned those were opportunities when he could and would feel an even greater flow of Christ's strength in his inner being. Paul's reliance upon

Christ's strength became a vivid witness to others who saw his physical suffering, and for that, Paul was grateful.

Some people today will claim, "Troubles make you strong." They are wrong. Troubles destroy some people. Troubles weaken others. There is nothing inherent about troubles that results in making us strong emotionally and spiritually. The truth, as Paul stated it so well, is that when we rely upon Christ Jesus in our times of trouble, *He* makes us strong. He imparts His strength to us and as we receive His strength, we are made strong.

A FULL SUPPLY FOR ALL THAT IS LACKING

Paul said that he learned to experience "supply" for all his needs. We do not know what gifts Epaphroditus brought from the Philippians to Paul. We do know that Paul regarded their gift as pleasing to God and more than sufficient. To be supplied to the point that you can say, "I have all and abound," is to be fully satisfied. (See Phil. 4:17.) Paul saw all of his needs as being met, and out of that inner feeling of satisfaction, Paul boldly declared to the Philippians his assurance that they, too, would have all of their need supplied by God according to His riches in glory by Christ Jesus (v. 19).

Most people tend to think that the gifts Epaphroditus brought to Paul were only material. The gift no doubt was at least partly material since the family and friends of Roman prisoners were expected to provide material provision for those detained by Roman officials, especially those under house arrest as Paul appeared to be. But prisoners' needs then and now are not merely material. They are also social, emotional, and spiritual.

Paul was undoubtedly encouraged by the friendship of Epaphroditus. Paul could communicate fully with him about matters pertaining to his faith and to the work of the Lord. Paul no doubt could both laugh and cry with him. Such Christ-centered friendship is priceless!

Furthermore, Epaphroditus no doubt brought a good word about Paul's friends in Philippi and elsewhere in the regions where Paul had traveled and ministered. How encouraging that must have been to Paul—to know that his work had not been in vain, that his efforts were bearing fruit, that the work of the Lord was going forward, that the church in Philippi was strong. We all need others to affirm that our efforts have been valuable and beneficial to them. We need their gifts, their friendship, and their encouragement that our lives have had purpose and meaning. Through such affirmation, we experience a full feeling in our hearts that we call fulfillment. A deep satisfaction comes when we know we truly have helped others in an eternally beneficial way.

Paul received a full blessing from Epaphroditus—material provision for his external needs but also emotional and spiritual encouragement that was a provision for Paul's inner needs.

Wouldn't we all like to be able to say with Paul that regardless of what happens to us, we are content, strong, and fully satisfied? In truth, we can have that inner state of being.

A LEARNING PROCESS

We should also note that it was a learning process for Paul. He said very plainly, "I have learned . . ." (vv. 11–12). Paul didn't instantly reach a state of inner contentment, strength, and satisfaction. He grew into that state of being as he "learned Christ."

What Paul had learned, we can learn. Paul made that very clear. Even if you have never felt much peace in your life, you can learn to be content. If you have always thought of yourself as weak and needy, you can learn to be strong, and if you have thought of yourself as strong, you can learn to be stronger. If you have felt uncertain about your purpose in life and whether you are fulfilling it before God, you can learn to experience inner fulfillment as well as learn what it means to receive an abundance of external blessing.

This learning process is part of a growing relationship with the Lord. It ultimately is "learning God." It is knowing the Lord and delighting in Him with increasing delight.

EXPERIENCING GOD'S PROVISION IN CRISIS TIMES

God desires that we experience Him always and that we draw contentment, strength, and total satisfaction from our relationship with Him at all times. It is especially important, however, that we experience the provision of God's presence in the stormy times of our lives, the times when we are keenly aware of our needs or neediness. Such times come for us all.

Every person's life is marked by storms of one kind or another. The reality for each of us is that we are in a storm, have just emerged from a storm, or are about to enter a storm. No geographic area of the earth is immune from natural atmospheric storms, and no person or relationship is immune from inner storms. Since we cannot avoid storms, we must learn to deal with them.

All kinds of atmospheric storms impact us on this earth—windstorms, sandstorms, rainstorms, thunderstorms, snowstorms. At times these storms are driving, blinding, destructive, and costly, even to the costing of life itself. Such storms often make the headlines—they evoke a ripple effect of devastation in the general public and, in many cases, bring about a response of public compassion and concern.

We also face a number of emotional storms in our lives, no less blinding, destructive, and devastating. If these storms are known by the public, even a small group of friends, they also have a ripple effect. No emotional storm impacts only one person.

The response to emotional storms is somewhat different from the response to atmospheric storms. Some respond to the victims of emotional storms with compassion and concern, others shun the persons at the center of the storms, and still others tend to be critical of those who experience emotional storms, usually blaming them in some way for what has happened. In dealing with a storm, we are called to examine the way in which we confront a storm and the manner in which we respond to both the instigators and the victims of that storm.

What happens if the emotional storm a person experiences is not readily known by others? Does the storm impact others any less? Not really. An emotional storm within a person or family will spill over to impact others in ways that may not be readily understood or even identified as relating to the storm. For example, anger that brews within a person is likely to erupt suddenly and sometimes violently, and often it is aimed at someone who was not the initial reason for the anger. The innocent victims of such anger are left wondering, *Where did that come from? What brought that on?* They have no understanding of the inner emotional storm that had been raging and very likely is continuing to rage in silence within the person.

The conclusion we must draw is this: storms occur, and storms cause damage—sooner or later, to greater or lesser degrees—unless they are dealt with by the only One capable of truly calming a natural or emotional storm, Jesus Christ.

In learning to deal with life's storms, we must turn to Jesus and discover the provision that He makes for us when storms strike us.

OUR RESPONSE TO THE STORM

Let us keep in mind as we study Christ's provision that the *nature* of the storm is not at issue. The storm may be in a marriage, in health, in finances, in work, in a relationship with children. What we do in the aftermath of a storm, and especially to keep another storm from arising, is very important, and it relates to the nature of the storm. But while we are in a storm, its nature is not an important issue.

A storm hits the whole of one's life. If you are having financial difficulties, such a storm will have a profound effect on your marriage and family life, your performance at work and in other areas, and ultimately, if the financial difficulty is not resolved, it may even impact your health. A storm in your marriage will impact your children, your finances, your work, and your health.

Neither is the *cause* of the storm at issue. When you are in the midst of a storm, your primary concern is with survival. Pointing a finger at the person or circumstance that caused the storm is not a productive response. After the storm has passed, you may be wise to take a good, long, objective look at what caused the storm so that if at all possible, you can avoid or avert such a storm in the future. You may be wise to alter your relationship with a storm-causing person in some way, preferably to seek loving reconciliation and greater communication and understanding with that person. But during the storm itself, your concern is not going to be primarily with the cause of the storm.

What is your concern in the midst of a storm? How can you survive the storm? How can you live through the situation or circumstance? How can you emerge from the storm?

God's Word assures us that Jesus provides answers to these critical questions. One example of the way Jesus deals with those who are experiencing a storm is found in Matthew 14:22–34. We referred to this story in an earlier chapter, but in this chapter, I want you to focus on several different aspects of the story.

Jesus had just finished a full day of tremendous ministry—preaching, teaching, and healing a great multitude of people who followed Him out into a desolate area. Before sending the people away, Jesus had multiplied five loaves and two fish to feed the hungry crowd of five thousand men and their families. Then, no doubt in exhaustion, Jesus

> *made His disciples get into the boat and go before Him to the other side, while He sent the multitudes away. And when He had sent the multitudes away, He went up on the mountain by Himself to pray. Now when evening came, He was alone there. But the boat was now in the middle of the sea, tossed by the waves, for the wind was contrary. (Matt. 14:22–24)*

In the fourth watch of the night, sometime between three and six o'clock in the early morning, Jesus went to His disciples who were struggling in the storm; He walked on the sea to them. When the disciples saw Him walking on the sea, they cried out in their fear, "It is a ghost!" Here is how Matthew told the rest of this story:

> *Immediately Jesus spoke to them, saying, "Be of good cheer! It is I; do not be afraid." And Peter answered Him and said, "Lord, if it is You, command me to come to You on the water." So He said, "Come." And when Peter had come down out of the boat, he walked on the water to go to Jesus. But when he saw that the wind was boisterous, he was afraid; and beginning to sink he cried out, saying, "Lord, save me!" And immediately Jesus stretched out His hand and caught him, and said to him, "O you of little faith, why did you doubt?" And when they got into the boat, the wind ceased. Then those who were in the boat came and worshiped Him, saying, "Truly You are the Son of God." When they had crossed over, they came to the land of Gennesaret. (Matt. 14:27–34)*

The first thing that we are wise to recognize when a storm strikes is that Jesus is present with us in the storm, just as He was present for His disciples in this story. Jesus is present. He is with us at all times, in all circumstances. There is never a single moment of your life in which Jesus is not there for you and with you.

AWARENESS OF HIS PRESENCE

Nothing can match the power of an awareness that Jesus is present. The presence of friends, advisers, and colleagues can never match the presence of Jesus.

The disciples had been struggling all night without making any progress. Storms arose suddenly in the Galilee area. The winds came across the land from the Mediterranean Sea and then rushed down the steep valleys into the Sea of Galilee, beating the sea almost as if a giant hand mixer were lowered into the waters. The disciples had struggled against such a wind for at least nine hours and had gone a distance of only about five miles, no doubt fighting for every inch of progress they made to keep the boat from capsizing.

Storms strike us quickly at times and often fiercely. We may feel as if there is no way out—everything becomes an intense struggle that seems overwhelming.

A woman once said to me about the day that her husband told her he was filing for a divorce, "Everything began to spin. I felt as if I was hanging on to the edge of a world that had gone out of control. For the next few weeks, it was all I could do to hang on. It was a tremendous effort just to get up and get my children off to school and go through the basic routines of what needed to be done in my life. Nothing else mattered— just getting through the day took all of my energy and strength." Emotional storms are often that violent and all-consuming.

Jesus knows about storms. You can be assured that He knows every detail about the storm you are experiencing. He knows far more about the storm than you know or will ever know. Furthermore, He knew that His disciples were struggling and battling the storm with all their strength. He knew they were in one of those periods that no doubt seemed to them to be the fight of their lives. He knows how you struggle when you are in a storm. And Jesus' response was this: *He came to them.*

Notice that He did not calm the storm from afar, although He could have done that. He had calmed a natural, physical storm on the Sea of

Galilee at a previous time. This time, Jesus chose *not* to calm the storm as He had done before.

Neither did Jesus ignore the storm, knowing in His sovereignty that the storm would eventually blow over without loss of life or property.

Rather, Jesus knew that in this particular storm, the most important thing that His disciples could experience was *an awareness of His presence.*

Note that I said not Jesus' *presence,* but *an awareness of His presence.* Jesus was just as much present with His disciples while He was up on the mountain in prayer as He was when He walked on the sea to them. They were never out of His sight or His concern.

But the disciples were not aware that Jesus knew or cared about them. Their thoughts were not on Jesus, even though His focus was on them. Their thoughts were so much on things other than Jesus that when Jesus appeared to them walking on the sea, they thought He was a ghost! They were frightened at the sight of Him.

We are so like these disciples! We often fail to look for Jesus in the midst of our storms, and we fail to recognize Him when He comes.

The likelihood is that Jesus may not come to you in precisely the way you expect Him to come. He may not come to you in a form that you quickly recognize. Probably the last thing on the earth that the disciples expected that night was to see Jesus walking on the water to them, yet that is the way Jesus chose to reveal Himself to them. Jesus may come to you in a totally unexpected fashion. And if you are not aware that He is present with you or that He cares enough to come to you in your storm, your response to the Lord may be the same as that of the disciples: fear and lack of recognition.

Let me give you a very practical example. A woman once told me of her reaction when her family physician said to her, "You have cancer." She said, "Dr. Stanley, it was as if my doctor had just thrown a black blanket of fear over me. I could hardly think. My eyes wouldn't focus. My ears seemed to ring. I was so stunned I felt paralyzed, incapable of moving. I didn't even hear the rest of what the doctor had to say, which was to tell me that he thought this cancer could be stopped with radiation treatments since it was in very early stages. If my daughter hadn't been with me during that appointment, I'm not sure I could have made it out of his office and to the car—I was that much in a fog.

"The next week, I made my first visit to the radiologist that my physician had recommended. I walked into his office and then into the radiology room filled with fear. What I hadn't expected at all was that this man might be a Christian, or that he might be aware of how I was feeling inside. I was completely surprised when he asked me, 'Are you afraid?' I admitted to him that I was fearful, not only of the cancer but also of the radiation. Then he said to me, 'I am a Christian, and I believe that prayer can help a person in times like these. Would it be all right with you if I said a prayer for you?' I said, 'Most certainly.' He prayed a sweet but very powerful prayer and as he prayed, I could feel my body relaxing. He took time to talk to me about both the cancer and the radiation treatments. I sensed that he truly cared about me, and I became more confident about what I was facing.

"The next time I went to see him I was less afraid. I told him how much his prayer had meant to me, and he asked if we might pray together again before my second treatment. Of course I agreed! This happened each time I went for treatments—thirty-two in all. I tell people now that I had thirty-two radiation treatments and thirty-two prayer treatments!

"By the time I had my last treatment, I was almost sorry it was my last visit to see him—not that I wanted more radiation, mind you, but I had come to appreciate this man's prayers and his calm and reassuring faith. It was a few weeks later that the thought struck me, *Why, that was Jesus coming to me through the form and skills of that radiologist! The love and power of Jesus in him gave me hope and eased my fears. The presence of Jesus in him had become a part of my healing process!*"

I don't know the way in which Jesus will come to you in your storm, but I can say to you in full confidence: Jesus will come to you in the precise way and form that you need Him the most. Trust Him to reveal Himself to you. He wants you to know that He is with you in the midst of the storm.

FEELINGS OF TOTAL ASSURANCE

Why is an awareness of Jesus' presence so important?

When we become aware of Jesus with us, several things happen to us. Taken together, these things add up to total assurance. When we are aware that Jesus is with us, we immediately become comforted.

Comforted. Each of us knows that when we are alone, it is much easier to feel fearful, but if we have even one friend with us in a time of trouble, we take comfort in his presence. Jesus is the Friend of friends. One of the terms given to the Holy Spirit is that of *Comforter.* When you are aware that Jesus is with you in your storm, you can't help being comforted by His presence.

More courageous. We take courage that we can face what lies before us. Who comes to us in our storm? The King of kings, the Lord of lords, the almighty, all-sufficient, all-powerful, all-wise, all-loving Savior and Deliverer! With Jesus beside us, who can stand against us? We cannot help feeling more courageous when we are aware that Jesus is by our side.

More confident. We become confident that God will see us through. Confidence is directly related to our knowing that a current trial or time of trouble will come to an end. When Jesus appears—throughout the Gospel books of the New Testament and in every instance we can cite in our lives today—He comes as Victor. The devil cannot remain where Jesus dwells. The enemy cannot succeed when Jesus arrives on the scene. Our confidence is no longer in ourselves to be able to survive, to endure, or to conquer; our confidence is in Jesus. Our confidence is based upon who Jesus is and what He will do for us, which always will be for our ultimate and eternal good. (See Rom. 8:28.)

NO STORM CAN DRIVE JESUS AWAY

An awareness of Jesus' presence also reminds us that *no* storm can separate us from the Lord. No matter how fierce the storm rages or how powerful it seems to be against us, the storm cannot separate us from God's love, forgiveness, help, or promises. Paul wrote to the Romans,

Who shall separate us from the love of Christ? Shall tribulation, or distress, or persecution, or famine, or nakedness, or peril, or sword? . . . Yet in all these things we are more than conquerors through Him who loved us. For I am persuaded that neither death nor life, nor angels nor principalities nor powers, nor things present nor things to come, nor height nor depth, nor any other created thing, shall be able to separate us from the love of God which is in Christ Jesus our Lord. (Rom. 8:35, 37–39)

The truth of the Lord's ever-presence (omnipresence) comes to us each time we become aware that He is with us in a storm. Just before His arrest and crucifixion, Jesus spoke to His disciples about His abiding presence with them. He said, "I will not leave you orphans; I will come to you" (John 14:18). He promised them that He would send the Holy Spirit to them as their Helper.

As Jesus spoke to His disciples after His resurrection, preparing them for His ascension to heaven, He said, "Lo, I am with you always, even to the end of the age" (Matt. 28:20). In the form of the Holy Spirit, Jesus is with us at all times. He is *always* present in our lives, every minute of every hour of every day.

How blessed we are to live in the time of the Holy Spirit! When Jesus was alive on the earth, He could not be in two places at one time. But now, Jesus is free of all constraints of time and space. By the power of the Holy Spirit, He is with each of those who believe in Him at all times. We never need to call for Jesus to show up. He is already present. We may have a sudden awareness of His presence, so much so that it feels as if He just showed up, but it is not a sudden coming of Jesus—rather, a sudden awareness on our part.

ASK THE LORD TO REVEAL HIMSELF

How might we become aware of Jesus' presence? By asking Him to reveal Himself to us.

So often, we ask the wrong questions of the Lord. We say, "Where are You, God? Why don't You show up? Can't You see what's happening to me? Can't You see how I am struggling? Can't You see the pain I'm in?" The answer of the Lord, of course, is, "I'm right here with you. I know exactly what's going on!"

Our question of the Lord should be, "What is keeping me from seeing You? Help me to see You and to experience Your presence!"

One of the most intense emotional storms described in the New Testament is that experienced by Mary and Martha in the aftermath of their brother's death. Lazarus became sick, and Mary and Martha sent word to Jesus, saying, "Lord, behold, he whom You love is sick" (John 11:3). Jesus responded by saying, "This sickness is not unto death, but for the glory of God, that the Son of God may be glorified through it" (v. 4).

Jesus stayed where He was for two more days, and then He said to His disciples, "Let us go to Judea again . . . Our friend Lazarus sleeps, but I go that I may wake him up" (vv. 7, 11). The disciples couldn't understand Jesus' reasoning since they knew it was dangerous for them to return to Judea, and they also figured that if Lazarus was sleeping, he was getting better. Jesus finally said to them plainly, "Lazarus is dead. And I am glad for your sakes that I was not there, that you may believe. Nevertheless let us go to him" (vv. 14–15).

Now on the surface it may appear that Jesus was not present or aware of Lazarus in that terrible storm of sickness. In truth, Jesus was very aware of all that was happening to His friend as well as what was happening to Mary and Martha. He knew exactly the full plan and purpose of God in the storm they were experiencing. He knew the moment that Lazarus died.

When Jesus arrived in Bethany, He found that Lazarus had been in the tomb four days. Mourners who had filled the house of Martha and Mary were attempting to comfort them. As soon as Martha heard that Jesus had arrived on the scene, she ran out to meet Him, saying, "Lord, if You had been here, my brother would not have died" (v. 21). Even Martha, who knew Jesus so well, assumed that Jesus had not been present in their lives. She went on to make a great statement of faith, however, saying, "But even now I know that whatever You ask of God, God will give You" (v. 22). She didn't expect that Jesus would be able to ask or receive anything related to Lazarus, but her faith remained in Jesus that He was no less the Healer, Deliverer, and Savior.

Martha and Mary might very well have talked to each other prior to Jesus' arrival and said, "Why hasn't Jesus come? Surely He loves us. He has been in our home. We have shared meals with Him, laughed with Him, heard Him teach. He knows how much we love Him, and we know He loves us. So where is He?" Those are the kinds of questions we ask today when we, as Christian believers, experience storms.

The real question, however, should be, "What is Your purpose in this, Lord? Why am I slow to see Your presence and to catch a glimpse of Your plan?"

Jesus did not respond directly to Martha's statements, but He spoke God's plan to her: "Your brother will rise again" (v. 23). Martha did not understand what He meant. She said, "I know that he will rise again in the resurrection at the last day" (v. 24). Jesus then said to her, "I am the resurrection and the life. He who believes in Me, though he may die, he shall live. And whoever lives and believes in Me shall never die. Do you believe this?" (vv. 25–26).

Jesus went on to Lazarus's tomb and insisted that the stone be rolled away. He then prayed, "Father, I thank You that You have heard Me. And I know that You always hear Me, but because of the people who are standing by I said this, that they may believe that You sent Me" (vv. 41–42). He then cried with a loud voice, "Lazarus, come forth!" (v. 43). And Lazarus came walking out of that tomb, restored to life four days after his death.

What was the message of Jesus to Martha and Mary and to all who experienced the evidence of that miracle? It is the simple message that *Jesus is.* Wherever *Jesus is,* there one finds the full operation of the fullness of Jesus.

We say, "Where *were* You, Jesus?" or we say, "When Jesus comes . . ." The fact is, *Jesus is.* God revealed Himself to Moses in precisely this way, saying, "I AM." (See Ex. 3:14.) *Jesus is.*

He is never going to be more your Savior, your Healer, your Deliverer, or your Lord than He is right now. He is the same yesterday, today, and forever. The fullness of who He is, *is* with you right now. There is no more of Jesus left to show up. All of Him is present with you. All of Him has been with you. And all of Him will continue to be with you.

Jesus declared to Mary and Martha the truth that rings down through the generations to us, "I *am* the resurrection and the life." When we become aware of the presence of Jesus with us in a storm, we must become aware that Jesus is with us in the fullness of His power to be the resurrection and the life. No matter how battered, bruised, or even dead we may feel inside as the result of our struggle, Jesus is with us to raise us up into newness of life. No matter how exhausted, broken, or devastated we may feel, Jesus is present with us to restore us, heal us, and energize us. He always comes to give us life and to give us life more abundantly (John 10:10). His very presence with us infuses life into our being.

WHY NOT AN AWARENESS OF CHRIST JESUS SOONER?

Why doesn't Jesus reveal Himself to us sooner than later? Why wait until the disciples were weary from rowing all night against a contrary wind? Why wait until Lazarus had been in the tomb four days? Because then the disciples were ready to become aware of Jesus. Then Mary and Martha, as well as the disciples, were ready to experience the great miracle that confirmed Jesus as Messiah and gave evidence that Jesus would rise from His own death and be the resurrection for all who believe in Him.

The "late" appearing of Jesus was not a lack of Jesus' presence but an appearance of Jesus in such a way and in the fullness of time so that those in need—the disciples, and Mary and Martha—might truly *become* aware of His presence.

If you are not experiencing the full presence of Jesus in your storm or time of trouble, ask the Lord to show you what is keeping you from experiencing His full and immediate presence. Ask Him to show you what He desires for you to recognize, learn, or experience as part of your having an awareness of His presence.

THE SAMARITAN SENT TO YOU

It is also important that you ask the Lord to help you recognize every person He sends to help you. Just as the Lord sent a Christian radiologist to help the woman whose story is told earlier in this chapter, so Jesus may send you very precise help in the form of a specific person. Don't miss that messenger of God's love and mercy!

Jesus told a story about a person who experienced a severe storm in his life. While on the road that led down to Jericho from Jerusalem, the man was beaten, robbed, and left for dead. Two men passed by without offering assistance to the injured man, and then, Jesus said, a man from Samaria spotted him, stopped, assisted him, and took him to a safe shelter in Jericho where he paid for the injured man's lodging and further medical help. Jesus asked those who heard this story, "Which of these three do you think was neighbor to him who fell among the thieves?" The people quickly replied, "He who showed mercy on him." Jesus then said, "Go and do likewise." (See Luke 10:30–37.)

How many times has Jesus come to you in the form of a good Samaritan—someone who rescued you, ministered to you, cared for you, gave practical assistance to you, and looked out for your best interests? How many times have you been the recipient of someone's unrequested kindness? Have you seen Jesus at work in that experience or incident? Have you been aware that Jesus is the One who was behind the scenes all the time, ministering to you through that person, very much present in your time of need?

One reason you are not aware of Jesus' presence is that you have not asked Jesus just who He is using to bring about God's perfect plan and purpose in your life. It may be a person you never would have suspected.

A DIRECT REVELATION OF HIS PRESENCE

Many times, Jesus may not even use a person to make you aware of His presence. He may speak to you directly through a vision, through a message that someone preaches to you, or through the Word of God as you read it.

I once heard about a minister who was pastoring two small churches, preaching in each church every other Sunday. He was weary from the constant travel and the many needs that he saw in each of his small, rural congregations. He was struggling to do his best and remain encouraged in the Lord. He began to doubt his ability to minister adequately to the people.

He walked into his pastor's study on Monday morning and noticed that a Bible lay open on his desk. Thinking that perhaps he had left it open there on Saturday afternoon, he closed it and shelved it. The following Monday, the Bible was again open on his desk. He stopped to read the two pages that were open. Part of what he read was Luke 9:62. The words just seemed to leap off the page to him: "No one, having put his hand to the plow, and looking back, is fit for the kingdom of God."

He immediately fell to his knees, asking the Lord to forgive him for doubting the Lord's call on his life and for failing to rely completely on the Lord for the ability to minister to the people.

The next Monday morning, the Bible again lay open. The minister had no secretary, and as far as he knew, nobody in the church had a key to his private office. Yet Monday morning after Monday morning, his Bible was open on his desk when he walked into his office. Each Monday, words seemed to leap off the pages to him, encouraging him in his ministry and building him up in his faith.

Finally the preacher asked the Lord to reveal to him who was ministering to him in such a profound way so that he might thank the person. The Lord brought to mind the janitor who cleaned up the church after the Sunday morning service. Sure enough, the man had a key that gave him entrance to all areas of the church, including the pastor's study. The preacher went to call upon the man.

He said, "Thank you for leaving the open Bible for me to read each Monday. You'll never know how much the Lord has used these passages of Scripture to help me and to build me up so that I can do the job He has called me to do."

The man seemed a little puzzled. "Aren't you the one who has been giving me these verses to read?" the pastor asked.

The man replied, "No, sir. Wish I was. But you see, Preacher, I can't read. It seems every time I go into your study, though, there's your Bible lying facedown on the floor. I thought you were dropping it on purpose for me to read. So I picked it up real careful like and laid it on your desk to the open part, thinking maybe you'd make a sermon of what was there so I could get the message from the pulpit, seeing as I couldn't read the pages for myself. And sure enough, it seems like you've been preaching right to me these past couple of months."

The preacher never discovered who or what had caused his study Bible to tumble to the floor each week. The cause didn't really matter. What mattered was that the preacher chose to see Jesus in the pages of the Bible that lay open before him, and then to share the Jesus of the Bible with others. He could have dismissed what was happening as coincidence or something very mysterious—not unlike the disciples thinking they were seeing a ghost. Rather, the preacher chose to see Jesus at work. He saw Jesus using an unusual situation in which to reveal Himself and to make the preacher aware of His presence.

As you read the Bible, look for Jesus to speak to you directly and intimately with a message that you know is just for you in the midst of your storm. What is Jesus doing in the passage that He brings to your mind or seems to highlight on the pages you are reading in your Bible? Jesus desires to do that same work or to teach you that same lesson in your life, even in the midst of the storm. He is there with you. Receive His comforting presence!

Jesus *will* show Himself to you. If you are eager to experience His presence, He will enable you to experience Him. He is already present. Ask Him for spiritual eyes to see Him at work, and spiritual ears to hear His words to you.

· 10 ·

Facing the Error That Created the Need

"I wish I hadn't done that."

"I wish I hadn't made that decision."

"I wish I hadn't gone there."

"I wish I had never agreed to that."

"I wish I had never met that person."

"I wish I had never touched that."

"I wish I had never experienced that."

Do you look back over your life and make any of these statements? If so, you very likely have experienced some type of emotional wound, one that may be marked by ongoing regret, guilt, or feelings of shame.

Adam and Eve were certainly in a position to say as well, "I wish I had never . . ."

Never listened to a lie.

Never bought into a lie.

Never began to imagine the possibility of sin.

Never questioned the goodness of God.

Never sought a substitute for a relationship with God.

Never yielded to temptation.

Never pursued sin.

Adam might very well have expressed the responses that are often heard from victims: "I wish I had never been in association with that person . . . I wish I had never given in to that person . . . I wish I had never allowed that person to treat me that way."

"I wish I never had" is a good indicator that emotional and spiritual wounding has occurred. It is a statement that also admits the person knew in some way, at some level, that an error was being made against God's perfect plan and God's absolute commandments. "I wish I never had" is a statement that admits, "I willfully acted in error," or "I willfully failed to act and that produced an error."

If you can look back over your life and say, "I wish I never had," then I invite you to go to God with that very issue or experience and say to God, "Please forgive me for that mistake. Please heal me of that wound. Please help me never to make that error again. Please give me the courage and boldness to live my life fully trusting You and obeying You."

TEMPTATION LEADS TO ERROR

Temptation by the enemy of your soul always leads to error, which in turn leads to need. If you trace a need to an error that you have made in the past, you can also trace that error all the way back to a temptation to do evil.

What exactly is temptation? It is an enticement to get a legitimate need met apart from God's will or outside God's boundaries.

Satan will always begin his temptations by presenting to us something that is a legitimate need in our lives. For example, a person may have a deep feeling of anxiety, frustration, or unrest. Such a person has a need for peace. Satan will hold up that need before a person night and day. His method, however, for meeting that need is not going to be to say to the person, "Now, you turn to God and trust Him." Hardly. Satan is going to whisper, "If you'll only take these pills, you will relax and feel no pain and you will have peace," or "If you'll only have a couple of drinks, you'll feel a lot more peaceful," or "If you could just purchase this particular item, you'll have greater self-esteem and in that you'll be more at peace with yourself."

We must recognize that the needs associated with Satan's temptations are legitimate and real. We must not deny the existence of these needs or discount them as being unimportant, illegitimate, or unworthy. Where Satan leads us astray is not in calling our attention to our needs—certainly some of us ought to identify our needs in a straightforward way and recognize them as needs we should address—but in offering certain methods for meeting our needs.

Some people feel guilty for having needs. That is false guilt. Needs are needs. Many are natural by-products of our humanity or our human error. Some are placed into our lives by God so that He might bring about in us a particular refinement or greater strength. Some are needs that are foisted upon us by the circumstances of a fallen world. Needs are legitimate, and all of our needs are worthy of bringing to Christ so that He might meet them. Don't feel guilty for having needs.

Guilt arises—and should arise—when we attempt to meet our needs by our manipulation or efforts rather than by trust in God. We err when we turn to Satan's illicit methods to meet legitimate needs.

You must make this distinction. The fault lies not in having needs but in attempting to meet them apart from God's plan and purposes.

All temptation is an enticement to act independently of God. When we do, we get ourselves into trouble every time.

There is never a way that is better than God's way. No way apart from God is a way that leads to satisfaction, fulfillment, or any good benefit. We have not been created so that we can violate the principles of God's plan and still live productive, joyful, and effective lives.

UNDERSTANDING HOW TEMPTATION WORKS

In Genesis 3, we find perhaps the most famous, compelling, and significant illustration of temptation in the entire Bible. God had placed Adam and Eve in the Garden of Eden, and He had given them very explicit and absolute instructions about what they were to do there. Nothing was hazy, fuzzy, or questionable about God's instructions. Adam was to give names to every creature that the Lord brought to him. Giving a name to something meant much more than just calling a creature an elephant or a giraffe. To name something, especially in the Bible understanding of "to name," meant to have a complete understanding of that creature and to exert authority over it.

Adam's job was to understand creation fully. He was to be fully aware of all of the characteristics and attributes of every creature and to understand how the creatures functioned in relationship with one another. The purpose for all of that was management. Adam had been given a job of having "dominion over the fish of the sea, over the birds of the air, and over the cattle, over all the earth and over every creeping thing that creeps on the earth" (Gen. 1:26). To have dominion doesn't just mean to be smarter than or to have more power than. It means also to understand, to manage, to control, to maintain, to use.

What a tremendous job that was—and is. Man was to be the caretaker of all God's creation, and not only to maintain it as it was given to man, but to use the creatures of the world in order to "subdue" the earth and to replenish it.

Eve was created to help Adam fully in that awesome responsibility before God. She was to be one with him in purpose and in flesh.

Together, Adam and Eve had the privilege of a walking-and-talking relationship with almighty God, their Creator. They were to undertake their great responsibility with God. God had created them for fellowship with Himself. He desired to communicate with Adam and Eve, laugh with them, delight with them in their discovery of His creation, and counsel them in their exploration and use of the work of His hands.

Our purpose today on this earth is no different from that of Adam and Eve. God has given each of us something that lies in front of us to do that is part of His divine command to have dominion over this earth, to subdue evil, and to bring about the fulfillment of His plan and purposes. God has called each of us to Himself so that we might talk with Him and walk with Him in daily intimacy. God has prepared others to walk alongside us for human fellowship and assistance.

If anyone ever asks you, "Why am I here? Why did God create me?" I hope you have an answer for that person. Perhaps you have asked these questions yourself. The answer at its most basic level is threefold:

1. You were created for an intimate fellowship with God and to have daily communication with Him.

2. You were created to overcome evil and establish God's goodness on this earth. You were created to be an agent of good.

3. You were created to have close relationships with others so that you might have companionship, friendship, and assistance as you praise and worship God and do the work God has put before you to do.

Apart from these three major purposes on this earth, God may have specific things for you to do that are directly related to your specific talents, abilities, capacities, propensities, capabilities, and dreams. Every person has been given one or more talents to use in the fulfillment of his purpose in life. But we are to use these talents within the confines of our greater purpose. We are to use our talents to praise and worship God, to establish God's dominion on this earth through the subduing of evil, and to help others as they praise and worship God or take dominion over the creatures of this earth.

In addition to talents, Adam and Eve were given resources. God made total provision for the external needs of Adam and Eve. He gave them "every green herb for food" and a continual supply of fresh air and fresh water (Gen. 1:30). God had created literally thousands upon thousands of good food sources for Adam and Eve, and He had given them water in abundance—four rivers flowed from the Garden of Eden (Gen. 2:10–14)! All they needed was provided for them in ample supply so that they might fulfill their God-given purpose on the earth.

Furthermore, God gave Adam and Eve access to Himself.

He was present with them daily. For example, Adam and Eve heard the sound of the Lord walking in the Garden in the cool of the day (Gen. 3:8). It was not an unexpected or unanticipated visit by God to the Garden. It was a part of His routine with Adam and Eve. He had fellowship with them every evening; they talked things over and enjoyed one another in close friendship.

You may recall that throughout the creation story we read, "The evening and the morning were the first day . . . , the evening and the morning were the second day . . . , the evening and the morning were the third day," and so forth. From the Bible's standpoint, a new day begins in the *evening*.

We in the Western world think in terms of a day beginning at sunrise, but in the Bible, a day begins at sunset, with rest and fellowship with God, with planning and anticipating the night and day that lie ahead. When God came to Adam and Eve in the cool of the evening, He was coming to "sit a spell" with them, reflect on the day that was past, and anticipate with them what they would be doing during the coming day. And just as God had noted at the end of each day of creation, "And God saw that it was good," so we can assume that on every day after creation, when God came to walk and talk with Adam and Eve, He came to the conclusion about them and about their efforts, "God saw that it was good."

God was the total inner provision for Adam and Eve. He was the One to whom they looked for wisdom, encouragement, and love. He was the fulfillment for all of their inner needs of satisfaction, peace, harmony, and purpose. His plan was their plan. His presence was their source of solace and courage and energy. He was their total source of supply for all of the needs they might have had spiritually, emotionally, mentally, or psychologically.

And when God sensed in Adam a need for a helpmate, God created Eve expressly for him. God met Adam's need for human relationship fully and completely. (See Gen. 2:21–23.)

What God gave to Adam and Eve, He also gives to us. God has made available in Himself all that we need for our spiritual, emotional, psychological, and mental needs to be met. He has given us human beings to be our friends—and for most of us, a human being to be a spouse—so that our needs for relationship, fellowship, communication, and assistance might be met. God has provided all that we need in terms of sustenance so that we will have the energy and ability to fulfill our purpose on this earth. Food and water refer not only to the physical need that we have for food and water, but also to our total need for energy and ability to live and to engage in productive work according to God's purposes. For some, that work might be raising children or engaging in ministry. For others, it might be sitting at a desk in an office or digging a trench or driving a tractor or working in a factory. In whatever area our talents and desires lie, God has already created ample provision for us to be able to do our work productively and efficiently.

There is absolutely no doubt about either God's plan or God's provision in the first three chapters of Genesis.

GOD'S INSTRUCTIONS ARE VERY CLEAR

In addition to telling Adam and Eve very plainly what they were to do, God told them very plainly what they were not to do: "Of every tree of the garden you may freely eat; but of the tree of the knowledge of good and evil you shall not eat, for in the day that you eat of it you shall surely die" (Gen. 2:16–17).

It's amazing that of all the things that God could have set as limitations, He chose only this one thing—this one tree, this one aspect of life—as being prohibited to Adam and Eve.

Let's take a closer look at this one forbidden tree. It is the tree that produces knowledge of good and evil. God wanted Adam and Eve to have full knowledge of what was good. Everything God had created for them was good, and expressly called good by the Lord. Everything that Adam and Eve did prior to the Fall was counted by God as good. We don't know how long Adam and Eve lived before they disobeyed God, but they very likely enjoyed many, many years of goodness before they sinned. They had a great understanding or knowledge of good.

So what did God not want them to know? Evil! God did not want there to be any means of contrast to good in their lives. He did not want them to know the influence of evil, the impact of evil, or the consequences of evil. God said to them, "In the day that you eat of it you shall surely die."

"But," you may say, "Adam and Eve didn't die on the day they ate of the tree." Not physically, although the physical decay and death of their bodies began on that day. What died when they ate of the tree of the "knowledge of good and evil"? Their innocence. Their perfection. Their harmony with each other. Their deep intimacy with God. Their perfect environment. Oh, what a loss! What a death! In many ways, the death was much more severe than physical death. It was a living death that resulted in a daily awareness that Adam and Eve were suspended between the forces of right and wrong, good and evil. Every day, every decision, and every relationship suddenly had the capacity for evil.

Adam and Eve were separated from God. They had never known a need for God before. Now they knew that need.

Adam and Eve were cast out of the Garden of Eden into a world of thorns and thistles. Adam was told, "You shall eat the herb of the field. In the sweat of your face you shall eat bread" (Gen. 3:18–19). Adam had never needed to work hard in a world of pain and obstacles. Now he had that need to provide, a need that involved struggle and hardship.

And yet God had made it very clear to them from the beginning the consequences of knowing evil.

God makes this very same commandment to refrain from knowing evil to us. As His children, born again through the shed blood of Jesus Christ, we are told repeatedly in God's Word to turn from evil and to pursue what is good in God's eyes:

Do not be overcome by evil, but overcome evil with good. (Rom. 12:21)

For the wages of sin is death, but the gift of God is eternal life in Christ Jesus our Lord. (Rom. 6:23)

Let us search out and examine our ways,
And turn back to the LORD;
Let us lift our hearts and hands
To God in heaven.
We have transgressed and rebelled;
You have not pardoned. (Lam. 3:40–42)

Return to Me . . . Turn now from your evil ways and your evil deeds. (Zech. 1:3–4)

Shun profane and idle babblings, for they will increase to more ungodliness. (2 Tim. 2:16)

The Lord holds out a great reward for those who fulfill His good purposes: "Glory, honor, and peace to everyone who works what is good" (Rom. 2:10). Jesus taught that those who work evil will have no reward:

You will know them by their fruits. Do men gather grapes from thornbushes or figs from thistles? Even so, every good tree bears good fruit, but a bad tree bears bad fruit. A good tree cannot bear bad fruit, nor can a bad tree bear good fruit. Every tree that does not bear good fruit is cut down and thrown into the fire. Therefore by their fruits you will know them. (Matt. 7:16–20)

Let's pause now and regain a perspective of the bigger picture. God gave Adam and Eve His presence, each other, and total material and natural provision with one stipulation: do not engage in what will result in your knowing evil and experiencing its deadly consequences.

God gives us as His children today His presence through the Holy Spirit, one another in the form of the body of Christ (the church as a whole), and a promise of total material and natural provision with one stipulation: do not engage in what will result in your knowing evil and experiencing its deadly consequences.

We are to be aware of evil and to avoid it. We are to be wise to the tactics of Satan to tempt us to engage in evil, and we are to be bold in saying no to him.

THE NATURE OF THE TEMPTER

The Bible tells us, "Now the serpent was more cunning than any beast of the field which the LORD God had made" (Gen. 3:1). I want you to notice four things about the tempter Satan.

First, the tempter is not equal to God. God *made* Satan. He is a creature—a rebellious, fallen creature, but always a creature. Too many people seem to believe that God and Satan are on equal footing and of equal stature—the force of good and God on one side, the force of evil and Satan on the other side in a fierce tug-of-war. This in itself is a lie of Satan, exalting himself to such a position. Satan is finite. God made him. He is subject to God's authority even now. He exists solely because God has a reason for him to exist. He is not equal to God, never has been, and never will be, although he continually aspires to the position that he will never attain.

Second, the tempter is "cunning." Satan is smart. He has knowledge that is born of the ages in which he has existed. He knows what heaven is like, and he knows all about how the earth and its creatures were made. He has knowledge about you that you don't even have about yourself. He is a master of disguise and of clever manipulation. His roar is more fierce than that of a lion. His ability to blend in with his surroundings is better than that of a chameleon. His subtlety in stalking is greater than that of a cat about to pounce on a mouse. His ability to spin a web is greater than that of a spider. His ability to disappear quickly is greater than that of a panther. He is the most cunning of all creatures. He is the master of lies and manipulation.

Third, the tempter is always relentless. He came to Jesus three times in the wilderness. He comes repeatedly to those who are serving God. We do not know how often or how many times Satan came to Eve with his temptations, but we can assume that his temptation was intense and insistent. He never gives up. He comes again and again with the same old lies, attempting to wear us out and wear us down until we do his bidding. He is a stalker.

Neither do we know how much time elapsed between the time Eve first listened to Satan and the time she ate of the fruit. Eve might have pondered the situation for a few minutes or a few years. We also do not know how long it took for Eve to convince Adam to eat of the fruit. There is nothing in the Bible that says Adam took a second bite out of the same piece of fruit. For all we know, Eve might have been eating of the fruit for some time before she finally convinced Adam to join her in eating it.

Why do I stress these points? Because we see similar behavior in our world today. One person will say to another person, "I tried that and nothing bad happened to me. In fact, I've tried that several times and I'm still all right." Or a person might say, "I've been doing this for years, and I've suffered no ill effects."

Adam had no initial desire to eat of the fruit. He might have had his own encounters with Satan and resisted them each time. But in the end, Adam gave in to peer pressure.

The results are just as deadly.

I don't care whether Satan whispered into your ear the idea to sin or whether another human being talked you into sinning; the result is the same. And in the end, God does not accept the excuse, "That person made me do it," or "The devil made me do it." Each of us has will, and each has the ability to say no to what is wrong before God. (See Gen. 3:12–13.)

Fourth, the tempter is a formidable foe. Never take Satan lightly. Although he is a limited creation of God, he still is a formidable foe. You are no match for him in your own strength. Only as you rely on Jesus Christ, who is victor over Satan, can you stand strong and say with boldness, "I can do all things through Christ who strengthens me" (Phil. 4:13).

THE TACTICS OF THE ENEMY

We are always wise to become experts on the tactics that our enemies use, especially the tactics of the devil. Notice the tactics of this cunning deceiver in speaking to Eve:

And he [the serpent] said to the woman, "Has God indeed said, 'You shall not eat of every tree of the garden'?" And the woman said to the serpent,

"We may eat the fruit of the trees of the garden; but of the fruit of the tree which is in the midst of the garden, God has said, 'You shall not eat it, nor shall you touch it, lest you die.'" (Gen. 3:1–3)

INTRODUCING DOUBT

Satan introduced doubt. That is his number one tactic. He comes to each of us, saying, "Has God indeed said . . . ?" If he can snare us with doubt, he has us quickly and immediately. And so many people capitulate at this very point. They cave in to doubt. They don't know enough about the Word of God to stand strong and say, "Listen, Satan, this is what God has indeed said!"

Eve, however, was not ignorant of God's word. She did not give in to Satan at the introduction of doubt. Eve responded with a clear statement of God's instructions. What I want you to notice is that Eve knew and understood *precisely* what she was not to do. She did not act out of ignorance or confusion. She was not mixed up. She knew the rule and its consequence.

Note what Satan said next. Then the serpent said to the woman, "You will not surely die. For God knows that in the day you eat of it your eyes will be opened, and you will be like God, knowing good and evil" (Gen. 3:4–5).

DISCREDITING GOD

Satan turned up the heat a notch. He implied that God withheld something good from Eve. He called something good that God called evil. He said, in effect, "God is holding out on you. He has something good that He hasn't given to you. He knows that if you eat of this tree, you will be just like God—you will have complete knowledge." Satan tempted Eve by saying, "You are going to experience something you have never experienced before, and you are really going to like it. It's going to be great! It's going to make you more powerful, more spiritual, more fulfilled than anything else you've known thus far."

Satan accused God of being unfair, punitive, and unjust. Satan cast doubt about the very nature of God. Satan also discounted or cast doubt upon the consequence God stated about eating from the tree. Even as he held out the allure of a "good" thing, he said to Eve, "You will not surely die."

EXALTING THE INDIVIDUAL

The temptation to Eve was highly personal and filled with flattery. The tempter put her on a plane equal to God. He exalted her position. I want you to note the number of times in Genesis 3:4–5 the word *you* is used. I've highlighted them here:

> *Then the serpent said to the woman, "You will not surely die. For God knows that in the day you eat of it your eyes will be opened, and you will be like God, knowing good and evil."*

The implication of the tempter was this: "Others may not be able to handle this, others may not be ready for it, others may not benefit from it, others may not like it, others may not be mature enough for this, but *you* are. *You* are the exception. *You* are special. *You* don't have to obey this commandment of God. Adam may have to for the time being, but *you* are ready for this. The law of God doesn't apply to *you*."

How many people attempt to convince themselves that they are above both man's law and God's law? They have bought into the notion that for whatever reason—perhaps their social status, their parentage, their wealth, their good looks, their past blessings from God, their position, their rank or role in society—they don't have to play by the same rules as everybody else. They have come to see themselves as stronger, smarter, special, or in some way set apart from the masses to what God has said is good and true for virtually everybody else, but not for them.

RELYING ON THE SAME TACTICS

You would think that after thousands of years of Satan coming to every man and woman with the same lies, the same tactics, we would eventually catch on to him and have the ability to see the lies for what they are. And yet men and women are still experiencing needs, and they are still listening to Satan say, "I have just the answer. You desire a little more wisdom? I have just the thing for you. It won't harm you at all to try it. You feel the need for sex? I have just the partner for you. No harm will come to you. You feel the need for greater status? I have just the means for you to get it—no negative side effects. You feel the need for a little more relaxation, fun, and an ease to the tension you feel? I have just the thing for you to try—the things you've heard about it aren't true for *you*."

The tactics are always the same—not just in Eve's case, but in our lives every day. Satan does several things very consistently:

- Satan always attempts to cast doubt on the truth of God's Word. He twists and warps the truth of God's commandments, God's love, and God's mercy at every possible opportunity.
- Satan always attempts to instill doubt about the goodness of God— His fairness, mercy, love, and righteousness. Satan paints an inaccurate portrait of God. He paints a picture in which God is harsh, judgmental and punitive, without mercy, compassion, or loving forgiveness. If Satan cannot get a person to doubt God's commandments, he will attempt to instill doubt about the nature of God.
- Satan always attempts to downplay significantly any and all consequences associated with sin, rebellion, or disobedience.
- Satan always paints a picture for us of pleasure, success, and well- being. He holds out the promise of something that will make us more than what we presently are—more rich, more beautiful, more acceptable, more fulfilled, more excited, more exhilarated, more fun, more peaceful, more happy, more satisfied, more appreciated, more valued, more loved. Satan's great lie is, "I can show you the way to more than God offers you." The implication is always that God is withholding from you something that you deserve or need, or that is rightfully yours.
- Satan always tries to get us to believe that in some way we are above the law or that we are not prone to the consequences that others will experience.

These are the big lies in Satan's arsenal of lies. And like Eve, many of us fall victim to these lies even though we know the truth of God's Word. Knowing the truth and believing the truth—or believing the truth and applying it appropriately to our lives—are vastly different things.

THE TWO MAIN ERRORS WE MAKE

Notice the twofold error that Eve made. First, she listened to Satan. She engaged in conversation with him. She gave him her attention. The number one way to avoid giving in to temptation is to turn away from Satan the moment he whispers something you know to be a lie. Eve knew that Satan's initial statement was contrary to God's word, but still, she continued to converse with him. The time to withstand temptation is the moment it comes. Recognize the lie and turn away from the liar.

Second, Eve began to take a second look at the tree and its fruit. The Bible says that she "saw that the tree was good for food, that it was pleasant to the eyes, and a tree desirable to make one wise" (Gen. 3:6).

Now what did that mean in the bigger picture? Eve began to reason within herself, *This is possible.* The fruit was there. It was ripe for the plucking. She *could* do it. Many people I know have absolutely no trouble withstanding alcohol or drugs as long as these things are far removed from them. But the minute a drink is placed in front of them or drugs are offered to them and it becomes possible for them to reach out and take hold of what has been made readily available to them, they yield to the idea.

A man confessed to me, "I never gave a second thought to having an affair with my boss's secretary until I found myself alone with her at dinner one night. Suddenly there she was. All of the others in the group that had gone to dinner got up and left. She became a possibility for conversation, affection, and relationship for the first time." That's how most sins begin—in the realm of what becomes possible or what we make possible.

Eve also saw that there was something attractive in the fruit. She saw beauty in it—superficial beauty, but beauty and attraction nonetheless. It was pleasant to her eyes. She looked at the fruit enough to convince herself, *This looks good. This looks fun. This looks interesting. This looks intriguing. This looks like something that might be delightful to experience.* Not only was the fruit possible to attain, but it captured her curiosity. She began to think, *I wonder what this will taste like and feel like? It looks good on the outside. Let me explore further.*

The fruit moved from being possible to being promising.

And then Eve saw potential in the fruit. Not only possible for food and promising in its allure, but with a potential for a good consequence.

Very specifically Eve saw the fruit as being "desirable to make one wise." Wisdom—a good thing. Wrong method, wrong fruit, wrong path, but Eve justified all that by seeing that the end result might be worthy. The end began to justify the means. After all, Eve reasoned, God desired for her to be wise.

Oh, how many people follow this same line of twisted reasoning today. "God desires for me to have my needs met and I need money, so it doesn't really matter if I cheat a little here and there, borrow a little I shouldn't borrow from this source and that, shortchange my employer or my customer just a little, all in the name of a bigger profit margin. It doesn't matter if the employees suffer as long as the stockholders are happy and the company shows financial growth. In the end, my needs will be met."

Or a person might say, "I know God desires for me to be with someone who truly loves me. My spouse doesn't seem to understand me or show affection to me. This other person seems to understand. This other person is affectionate toward me. I'll just spend a little more time with this person in order to get this need for understanding and love met in my life. I won't leave my spouse. In fact, I'll make sure my spouse never knows—and even so my need will be met. Surely God doesn't want me to go without someone who truly values me."

And so it goes. Eve's rebellion was calculated and measured. She knew she was acting in disobedience to God, but she convinced herself that her rebellion would be valuable to her in the end. Potential for good and promise of pleasure are very powerful when they are linked to possibility.

BYPASSING GOD TO GET WHAT WE WANT

Eve perceived that the fruit would give her an edge—that it would make her wise, more knowledgeable, smarter, more experienced, more enlightened, more capable. We must recognize that Eve did not eat first and then discover that the fruit made her wise. To the contrary, she concluded that the fruit would give her God's wisdom before she ever took a bite.

Eve was bypassing God. God had all the wisdom Eve ever needed, and God was entirely willing to impart to Eve the answer to every question she could ever ask. God put no limits on the wisdom that He made available to Eve. He never once told her, or Adam, that they could be only so wise, so satisfied, so fulfilled. There was no degree established on what God had offered to them of Himself.

Eve saw the fruit as an alternative path to God Himself. She saw the fruit as a way to wisdom apart from her relationship with God.

How many times do we face that temptation in our lives? How prevalent is this lie in our world today? How many people truly believe in their hearts that they can become wise without God, rich without God, joyful without God, satisfied without God? How many people have bought the lie that they can experience peace and inner satisfaction without a relationship with God? How many methods have been concocted in an attempt to meet needs totally apart from God's presence?

Eve intended to meet her own need for wisdom in her own way in her own timing. She was taking her life into her own hands. She had not consulted God or even factored God into her decision. And neither does any person who gives in to Satan's temptation. Every person who yields to the allure of sin has concluded at some level, "I don't need to talk this over with God. I can do this on my own. I can make my own judgments, my own decisions, my own evaluations. I can know what is best for me—not only now but in the future. I am capable of determining what will be for my good."

Surely if Eve had bought in to the lie that God was withholding things from her, there is no end to what she might have imagined was being withheld. Eve had convinced herself that God had been withholding something interesting that would make her wise. It is no great leap to conclude that God might have been holding something that would make her more healthy, more wealthy, more interesting to Adam, more sexually appealing, more vivacious, more valuable. It wouldn't take much for Eve to imagine that God might have a whole world outside the Garden of Eden that would be interesting for her to explore and experience. Was God withholding that from her?

We do precisely the same thing when we assume a "God is keeping something from me" perspective. We question within ourselves, What fun is God withholding from me? What relationships and experiences am I being denied? What material blessings is God keeping from me?

The truth is that God is not keeping anything from you that is for your good. Anything that is for your eternal good, God makes available to you. James wrote, "Do not be deceived, my beloved brethren. Every good gift and every perfect gift is from above, and comes down from the Father of lights, with whom there is no variation or shadow of turning" (James 1:16–17).

God is the source of all truly good things. What the Father gives us is for our perfection. He does not play favorites. He does not hold out something to us and then snatch it back at the last minute. God does not play games with His blessings or His rewards.

God may withhold some things from us at a particular time or in a particular season of our lives in order to work out something in our characters or in our spiritual development, but ultimately everything our hearts truly desire is possible for us to experience and to attain. It is a lie of Satan that God has a vast storehouse of both internal and external blessings that is locked and inaccessible to us.

THE ALLURE OF THINKING WE CAN HANDLE IT

When we have a general feeling of neediness in our lives—an inner restlessness, frustration, dissatisfaction—too often we begin to reason, "Something out there will satisfy this longing in my heart. I just can't see it right now. I sense that it is there, but I don't quite know what it is." We search for the missing element according to our reasoning and intuition. Some people even justify this behavior to themselves by saying, "Well, God gave me a good mind, so surely He expects me to figure this out. God gave me common sense, so I will follow my nose and see where it leads me."

To a certain extent, that was what Eve did. She might very well have reasoned, "God gave me the insight to see this tree for what it is. I was immature before, but now I am mature. I now have the good sense to know that this won't harm me. It is something that will benefit me. It will energize me, enlighten me, empower me."

Too many people seem to reason within themselves, "Well, this might have been wrong for me when I was a child or a teenager, but now that I'm an adult, I can engage in this behavior. Surely it is acceptable now." Or they say to themselves, "Only a person who is very naive and very innocent hasn't experienced this. Surely God doesn't expect me to be a stupid person whom others might ridicule or look down upon. I need to have this experience, so I can say, 'I tried that and it didn't work.'"

A man told me that he had experimented with drugs as a teenager after having followed precisely that line of reasoning. All of his friends were making fun of him for not having smoked marijuana, so he finally smoked a joint of marijuana, telling himself all the time, "Now I can say to my friends, 'I tried pot and I didn't see any big deal in it. Jesus is more satisfying.'" The trouble was, the marijuana temporarily was very pleasing to his senses. He liked the high that he felt. The second time marijuana was offered to him he said, "Well, maybe I didn't give pot a good try the first time. Maybe there's more to it than I experienced that first time. I should know the *full* effects of this before I tell my friends that it's a waste of time and money."

The trouble with that line of reasoning was that there was no sure out for the young man. There never is. The justification that he used for trying marijuana became the same justification that he used for trying cocaine and a wide variety of pills and substances. "I'll just try it, and then out of my experience with it, I'll tell others not to do it or tell them the negative side effects."

I have met a few Christians who seem to think that they need to experience some sin in their lives in order to have a more dramatic testimony about God's power to deliver from sin. This is a twisted, warped line of reasoning, but there are those who buy into the lie, "Those who sin have a more powerful witness about God's delivering and saving power." The truth is, those who do not sin have the more potent witness. Theirs is a testimony that assures the unbeliever that God truly can keep people from sinning once they trust Him with their lives.

What hope is there for the people who are not born again to think that they will continue to be in the grip of sin after they accept Jesus Christ, but that Jesus will bail them out repeatedly when they sin? There is so much more hope and comfort in the truth that once people are born again, the indwelling power of the Holy Spirit can help them keep from sinning and therefore keep them from ever experiencing the negative consequences of sin.

Eve believed that in some strange way, she was doing the mature thing for herself in acting by herself. She had determined that her independence from God was a good thing, a noble attribute, and even something that God might have desired or planned for her all along. Nothing could have been farther from the truth for her, and nothing is farther from the truth for us. God desires that we depend upon Him and trust Him for all things. The deeper the relationship a person has with God, the more reliant that person will be upon the Father for all provision, all wisdom, all esteem, all love, all security.

THE CRASHING REALITY OF SIN

In the end, Satan was wrong. Absolutely and completely wrong.
Adam and Eve did die.
God's word was absolute.
God was not keeping anything good from Eve and Adam.
The end did not justify the means.
The fruit was not beneficial to mankind.
Adam and Eve were not above the requirement of obedience.

Eve was absolutely and completely wrong in her reasoning. The fruit was not suitable food for her, however available it might have been. The fruit was not pleasant in its effects, even though it might have been beautiful in its appearance. The fruit did not make her wise or in any other way bring benefit to her.

Adam was wrong too. Absolutely and completely wrong. Just because someone he loved, trusted, and counted as his own flesh had partaken of something God had forbidden, he did not need to partake of it.

Adam and Eve lost *everything* in their false assumption that life after disobedience to God's command could possibly be better than life before disobedience.

Friend, God will never allow any choice we make for our security or provision to replace Himself. He made Himself to be our source of total supply and identity. Nothing else will ever replace Him.

God alone is eternal. Nothing else we may choose in God's place will last into eternity.

God alone is all-loving. No one else we may choose will love us as vastly or as unconditionally as our heavenly Father.

God alone is omniscient. No one else can know us as completely as God knows us or can see into the past and the future with the clarity that God sees.

God alone is always present. Every other person we may choose in God's place will eventually leave us, either through the normal circumstances of life or through death.

God alone is always forgiving. Every other means of forgiveness that we seek apart from the love of Jesus Christ is rooted in works and will eventually fail because none of us can do enough works to match the gift of Jesus' shed blood on the cross.

The only thing we can do when we realize that we have yielded to temptation, that we have sinned before God, and that our need is related to our sin is to ask for God's forgiveness. No amount of self-justification will work. No amount of making amends or doing penance will compensate for our sin. We must come to God and humbly confess our sin, ask Him to forgive us and to free us from the guilt of our sin, and ask Him to help us not to sin again. And then we must begin again, determined that we will neither listen to Satan nor ponder the things that God has forbidden us to experience.

· 11 ·

Ten Reasons We Experience a Delay

Why might God delay in meeting our needs?

In Philippians 4:12, Paul stated, "I know how to be abased, and I know how to abound. Everywhere and in all things I have learned both to be full and to be hungry, both to abound and to suffer need." Paul knew what it meant to experience God's full supply, but he also knew what it meant to suffer need—which is being needy to the point of suffering. Why would God allow such a great servant as Paul to suffer? What is the purpose of God in our experiencing need?

There are at least ten reasons why God delays in meeting our needs. Any one of these reasons is sufficient in itself to keep God from meeting a need, but these reasons often work in combination.

1. DELAY CAUSED BY OUR DISOBEDIENCE

Psalm 81 tells of God's past provision for the children of Israel and how God desires to meet the needs of those who love and serve Him. In Psalm 81:10–12, we have a clear indication of both God's desire to meet needs and one of the reasons God delays in meeting needs:

I am the LORD your God,
Who brought you out of the land of Egypt;
Open your mouth wide, and I will fill it.
But My people would not heed My voice,

149

And Israel would have none of Me.
So I gave them over to their own stubborn heart,
To walk in their own counsels.

Clearly God desired to meet their needs—He wanted them to be in a position of opening their mouths wide and then being filled. This is a picture of God's desire to meet their need for food, and beyond that, His desire to meet all of their inner needs.

What kept them from having their needs met? Their rejection of God and their failure to obey His voice.

God said,

He would have fed them also with the finest of wheat;
And with honey from the rock I would have satisfied you. (Ps. 81:16)

God wanted them to have the very best. But they cut off the supply lines by their behavior. They not only failed to receive God's best in their lives, but they also ended up stubbornly wallowing in their own ideas and plans. What a terrible place to end up!

If you have a need, or needs, in your life, consider whether you are willfully disobeying what God has said to you.

I once met a man who bemoaned the fact that he was experiencing some serious financial problems. He said, "I keep praying and asking God to meet my needs, but I get no answer. Why doesn't God help me? Surely He can see that I am struggling greatly. Surely He can see that I am in serious trouble."

Yes. God knew all about that man's struggles and financial problems. But God also knew that the man was no longer tithing. He had stopped tithing years ago.

"But what," you may ask, "does tithing have to do with God's meeting a person's financial need?"

It has a great deal to do with obedience and God's conditional promise regarding financial need. Let me remind you of God's Word in Malachi 3:8–10,

"Will a man rob God?
Yet you have robbed Me!

But you say,
'In what way have we robbed You?'
In tithes and offerings.
You are cursed with a curse,
For you have robbed Me,
Even this whole nation.
Bring all the tithes into the storehouse,
That there may be food in My house,
And try Me now in this,"
Says the LORD *of hosts,*
"If I will not open for you the windows of heaven
And pour out for you such blessing
That there will not be room enough to receive it."

God's promise of abundant, overflowing blessing is directly linked to obedience in giving tithes and offerings to Him.

To ask God to supply your financial needs even when you deliberately withhold tithes and offerings as an act of your worship is to be foolish. To ask God to bless you financially even though you are in disobedience to His commandments is to ask God to overlook His own laws and statutes and to deny the truthfulness of His Word. God will not do that. Our role is to obey God in all matters, including our giving of tithes and offerings. This is not an area of negotiation. Even a schoolboy or -girl can understand God's command regarding giving and receiving in Malachi 3:8–10. We must never expect God to turn His back on His Word for the sake of meeting our personal needs.

2. DELAY CAUSED BY OUR DOUBT

James 1:5–8 gives us a major principle of God regarding the meeting of our needs:

If any of you lacks wisdom, let him ask of God, who gives to all liberally
and without reproach, and it will be given to him. But let him ask in
faith, with no doubting, for he who doubts is like a wave of the sea driven
and tossed by the wind. For let not that man suppose that he will receive

anything from the Lord; he is a double-minded man, unstable in all his ways.

Although this passage specifically addresses the need for wisdom, virtually any need can be named in place of the word *wisdom* in this passage because the principle of God is so clearly stated: the person who asks anything of God without faith is not going to receive what he requests.

I know countless people who make their petitions to God by saying, "God, I know You are all-powerful and all-wise and You can meet all my needs, but . . ." That *but* clause is usually a statement of doubt, not faith. It is a "but in this case" instance of doubt. Many people believe God *can,* but they have doubts that God *will.* They recite to God all of their inadequacies, unworthiness, shame, and inability. God says if you come to Him with that attitude, don't waste your time praying.

Jesus had something very crucial to say about the impact of belief and doubt upon one's prayers:

> *Have faith in God. For assuredly, I say to you, whoever says to this mountain, "Be removed and be cast into the sea," and does not doubt in his heart, but believes that those things he says will be done, he will have whatever he says. Therefore I say to you, whatever things you ask when you pray, believe that you receive them, and you will have them. (Mark 11:22–24)*

How many people do we know who come to God with a request and then they add statements of doubt to it?

- "Oh, God, I know that You can meet all my needs and that You promised to meet all my needs. This is a need in my life, but, Lord, I'll understand if You don't meet it at this time."
- "God, I know in Your Word that You said I could ask anything in Your name, but did You really mean for me to ask for this?"
- "God, this is what I want, but perhaps I'm wrong in wanting this need to be met."

But . . . but . . . but. A shadow of doubt is cast against the petition. And with that doubt, the petition actually becomes null and void. Jesus said that we have our needs met when we pray and ask God, *believing* that we will receive what we need.

WHY DO WE DOUBT GOD?

Why do we doubt almighty God, who has created all things, has control over all things, loves us with an infinite love, and has made such awesome promises to us in His Word?

The real reason, I believe, is that we don't really know God. We may know a great deal *about* God, but that is not the same as *knowing* God. You can know a great deal about the person who lives next door—his name and the name of his wife, how many children he has, what kind of pet lives in the backyard, what kind of car he drives. You may know where he works, where he attends church, and many of his likes and dislikes, ranging from the kind of pizza he has delivered to his home to the type of lawn mower he chose to buy. But all of that is not the same as knowing your neighbor. It is not the same level of information and understanding as you would receive from spending time with your neighbor over the weeks, months, and years that you live next door to each other, talking and laughing and sharing life's important occasions, including both those that are joyful and those that are sorrowful. Knowing your neighbor is not remotely the same as knowing some things about your neighbor. And so it is with our relationship with God.

Paul said to the Philippians, "*My* God." He was in relationship with God. He knew that God knew all about him, Paul, and all about his situation. He also knew God. Out of his knowing God intimately, Paul knew God would neither abandon him nor sell him short. God would supply what he needed.

Again, let's refer to your relationship with your neighbor. You may know that your neighbor is capable of helping you out in many ways—in financial or practical matters. You may know that he has a particular tool or appliance that he could loan to you. You may know that, given his job title and place of employment, he is likely to be able to contribute to worthy causes. You may even surmise that because your neighbor has helped others you know, he will also help you. But knowing that your neighbor *can* help you and may be inclined to help you is not at all the same as knowing that your neighbor *will* help *you*.

The assurance that your neighbor will help you comes only if you know your neighbor. If your neighbor has become a very close friend, then you are likely to have a much greater assurance that your neighbor will come to your aid when you have need. Again, this is true of our relationship with God. Knowing that God can help is not the same as knowing with certainty in one's heart that God will help.

3. Delay Caused by Our Attempts at Manipulation

To manipulate is to take matters into our hands and try to get what we desire through our own efforts at controlling others. At times we even try to control or manipulate God, justifying our actions all the way.

A biblical example can be found in the book of 1 Samuel. When the prophet and high priest Samuel anointed Saul to be the first king of Israel, he made very clear to Saul the limitations of his office. Making sacrifices to the Lord was to continue to be the privilege and responsibility of Samuel, the high priest. However, after Saul had been king for a little more than two years, he chose three thousand men as soldiers under his and his son Jonathan's command, and he went to battle against the Philistines. The Philistines responded to the attack against one of their garrisons by gathering together thirty thousand chariots and six thousand horsemen and countless foot soldiers. The Israelites were vastly outnumbered, and the Bible tells us they followed Saul to Gilgal "trembling." Saul had apparently summoned Samuel to Gilgal so that he might make a sacrifice to the Lord and consult God's will in the matter, but after seven days, Samuel still hadn't arrived. The soldiers, increasingly afraid for their lives, began to question Saul's command. The longer Samuel delayed in coming to Gilgal, the more uneasy the soldiers became.

At that point, Saul took matters into his own hands:

Saul said, "Bring a burnt offering and peace offerings here to me." And he offered the burnt offering. Now it happened, as soon as he had finished presenting the burnt offering, that Samuel came; and Saul went out to meet him, that he might greet him. (1 Sam. 13:9–10)

That act of disobedience before God brought about the loss of the throne for Saul. Even though it was more than two decades before the throne passed to David, Saul no longer was God's choice as king from that moment on. The prophet Samuel said to Saul,

> *You have done foolishly. You have not kept the commandment of the LORD your God, which He commanded you. For now the LORD would have established your kingdom over Israel forever. But now your kingdom shall not continue. The LORD has sought for Himself a man after His own heart, and the LORD has commanded him to be commander over His people, because you have not kept what the LORD commanded you.* (1 Sam. 13:13–14)

Up to that point of disobedience in engaging in battle and offering a sacrifice apart from God's leading and provision, Saul had been the greatest, most powerful, and most admired man in all of Israel. But no more. Saul lost everything that was important to him through his disobedience. Not only did he lose personal favor with God, but he lost all possibility of passing on his throne to one of his heirs. To a great extent, he lost his alliance and fellowship with Samuel. And as events showed in the years ahead, Saul lost much of his sanity and certainly his peace of heart.

Saul couldn't wait for God to supply his need in God's timing. Many people today get in trouble for precisely the same reason—they will not wait for either God's timing or God's method. They are so consumed with the problem of their need that they act ahead of God or instead of God. They manipulate circumstances, people, and events on their own, seeking to resolve their need according to their own timing and cunning schemes.

Acting apart from God, they have compounded their need. Not only do they have their original need, but now they also have the need that arises from being disobedient.

Consider those who steal from others. They can't wait for God to meet their need. They refuse to be obedient to God's commandments. They choose not to trust God to provide according to His means and methods. They act on their own, seeking the solution right now and their way.

Consider those who engage in sexual behavior prior to marriage. They can't wait for God's right timing for satisfaction of their sexual needs.

They choose not to trust God to provide for this need according to His methods and plans. They choose to disobey. They act on their own, sometimes seeking immediate sexual gratification from the nearest available person.

Consider those who are so desirous of getting a promotion at work that they resort to lies about coworkers and dishonesty in reports and procedures. They can't wait for God to bring about the recognition and rewards that are desired. They act in contradiction to God's statutes. They seek what they want *right now*, according to their own methods.

Take any sin in any place at any time, and you are going to find a great deal of manipulation at work—people acting in their own timing and according to their own plans, both of which are acts of disobedience before God.

The end result is never entirely good. Oh, the immediate result may seem good. But not for long. The end result will always be heavily marred by disappointment, dissatisfaction, lack of fulfillment, and diminished success. The disobedience will result in more need, not less, because the overall need of the person will include needs associated with the consequences of sin.

Nobody can circumvent God to meet needs and come out ahead. How much better to wait upon God to meet our needs in His way and in His timing.

4. Delay Caused by Wrong Motivation

A person can have the right need but the wrong motivation. This, too, will cause a delay in receiving God's solution to a need. In James 4:3, we read, "You ask and do not receive, because you ask amiss, that you may spend it on your pleasures."

The thing that is requested may not be wrong in God's eyes, but if the purpose is totally self-centered or tinged with evil intent, then the request is wrong and God will not respond to it.

Let's say, for example, that you desire to send your child to a private Christian school. I have nothing against private schools or home-schooling. Neither do I condemn all public schools. Each parent has a responsibility before God to provide the very best education possible for his child. Such a decision needs to be made after careful research and much prayer. If a parent considers all options, feels God's clear leading, and then makes a decision to send a child to a private school, there is nothing wrong with that decision in God's eyes.

Let us further suppose that you have made this decision regarding the schooling that is best for your child, but you do not have the finances necessary to pay the tuition and fees at the private school of your choice. You have a need in this area. Again, such a need, especially if it is associated with a decision that you clearly believe is part of God's plan for your child and your family, is a legitimate and good need before God. Your need for more money is real, genuine, and vital.

But let us further suppose that deep down inside, the main reason you desire for your child to attend this private school is that everybody else's children in your neighborhood attend this school. Your primary concern is not really with the quality of education or God's leading; you are motivated by a strong desire that your child come up to the social standard of the other children in the neighborhood. Your desire is that you as a family might conform to your peers and that your children might be socially acceptable to their peers.

What is really at work here?

Pride. Plain and simple. Deep-seated, hard-core pride that we must have what others have or have *more*, do what others do or do *more*, and be like or be better than others.

We can all be deceived so easily—in a thousand ways, in a thousand situations—when it comes to our inner drives and motivations. It is so easy to justify our need before God and to fail to recognize our motives that are not in line with God's Word.

We feel a need for more expensive clothes because we believe they are a necessary part of getting ahead on the job. Why do we need to get ahead? We need a promotion at work in order to have more money to provide for our families. Why do we need more money? We need more money to provide for our families because our needs have outstripped our budgets. Why do we want more things? Because we want more and more prestige. We want more prestige so that we can have more recognition, approval, value, and love. And so we go out and buy ourselves the new suit or the new dress we can't afford, all the while claiming to ourselves and to God, "I *need* this."

We feel a need for a different car because we believe it is important to have reliable transportation to get to work on time every day. We need a safe car. But what happens when we get to the car lot? Suddenly we need a car that is a little shinier, a little sportier, with a little more horse-power, and several more options because we need a car that will give us increased status and put us one step ahead of our rivals. We plunge our-selves into car payments that are over our heads because we claim to our-selves and to God, "I *need* this."

We often fail to get our needs met because our motivations are wrong. They are rooted in pride, self-centeredness, greed, or a desire to meet our lusts.

5. Delay Caused by Our Lack of Responsibility

There are times when God does not meet a need because we have ignored or refused to shoulder our responsibility in a particular mat-ter.

A man told me that he was out of work and needed a job. I asked him what he was doing about his situation. He replied, "I'm trusting God." I said, "Great. What else are you doing?" He looked at me as if I were asking a totally irrelevant question.

If a person needs a job and all he does is sit at home and wait for some executive at a major corporation to look up his name and phone number and call him, he may be waiting a very long time!

In Proverbs 19:15, we read,

Laziness casts one into a deep sleep,
And an idle person will suffer hunger.

If a person is lazy or negligent in conducting his general business affairs, God cannot be expected to compensate. I have yet to see a pay-check to anyone that is signed by the angel Gabriel.

We live in a practical, material world, and God expects us to function in this world in a practical way. Nobody is exempt from the responsibil-ity to work, to contribute, to function, to act, or to expend effort and energy on behalf of others.

In Proverbs 20:4, we read,

The lazy man will not plow because of winter;
He will beg during harvest and have nothing.

I'm all for helping people who cannot help themselves, but throughout the Scriptures, we find a condemnation on those who do not do what they are capable of doing. God will not contribute to laziness.

Consider the student who says, "Well, I guess I'm not going to be able to come back to school next semester." A concerned friend might ask, "Why not? What happened?" To which the student replies, "Well, my folks can't afford to pay the tuition."

My response to such a statement would be, "Have you considered working to put yourself through school?" Countless people have done just that and have emerged from the experience not only strong in self-esteem, but stronger in faith from having trusted God to help them juggle a job and schooling, more disciplined in their use of time and resources, and with greater job skills. Furthermore, they already have job experience and a track record of working as they prepare to go out into the career of their choice.

So many people today seem to expect others to provide for them when the responsibility for their provision rests with themselves.

Younger people always hate it when the older generation says, "Back in my day . . ." I think one of the reasons younger people hate these comments is that there's truth in what is being spoken to them about laziness. Even so, let me reflect for a moment. When I was in college, I once had a job washing glasses in a cafeteria for $0.60 an hour. Four hours a day, $0.60 an hour, $2.40 a day. I would have done any kind of legitimate work to pay my way through college, and at the time, that was the best job I could find. I was glad to do it. I needed the money to pay basic living expenses, I didn't expect anybody else to give me a handout, and I didn't seek a loan that had to be paid back with interest.

If you are facing a need today, ask yourself, What is *my* role in meeting this need? What can I do? What does God expect me to do? In nearly every case, a person has some role to play in meeting a need in his life. Don't shirk that responsibility.

6. Delay Caused by an Illegitimate Need

We have raised an entire generation of children in our society who believe that they somehow have a right to grow up with their own private color television set, a car of their own, and designer clothes. They feel a need for these things. In reality, nobody needs a television set, a car, or designer clothes to be healthy physically, emotionally, or spiritually; have good relationships with other people; praise and worship God; grow in faith; produce honest work; or engage in ministry outreach to others.

Take another look at your need. Is it really a need in your life, or is it something that you have come to expect through habit? Is it something that somebody else told you that you should need, or is it a true and genuine need in your life?

Through the media and through peers, we are told countless times in a week about products and services that we need. Need for what purpose? The answer is likely to lie in a motivation that is not one that God will honor or respect.

What we nearly always discover when we realize that we are asking God for provision to meet a need that is not really a need is this: an underlying emotional or spiritual need that is far more important than the need we thought we had.

"Dear God," a woman might pray, "give me a new house." When the woman faces up to the fact that she doesn't really need a new house, and she begins to address the question, Why did I think this was a genuine and legitimate need in my life? she comes face-to-face with her real emotional and spiritual needs.

"I need to have a drink to calm my nerves," a man might say. When the man faces up to the fact that the need is not the lack of a drink but the stress and anxiety he is feeling, he is in a position to discover his real needs.

Needs that aren't true needs tend to mask genuine needs. Don't continue to live in denial of your real needs. Don't continue to push them down and ignore them. God desires to meet all of your needs.

7. Delay Caused by Rejecting God's Method

A significant number of people fail to receive God's provision for their need because they reject the method that God chooses for meeting their need.

Let me give you an example. Let's say that someone has wronged you, no question about it. And furthermore, let's assume that you are facing a financial need. What would be your response if the person who had wronged you offered to help you with your financial need? Perhaps you would say, "Thank you, but no thank you. I can handle it." You are too angry, too upset, or too proud to accept the solution to your need because you don't like the person who is offering the gift.

This is an instance of pride. It never dawns on you that perhaps God has convicted that person of his sin in wronging you and has told the person to offer you help as a means of bringing about forgiveness and restitution of your relationship. Stubborn pride can keep needs from being met in many areas of life.

We must be very certain that we don't shut down God's chosen channel for meeting our needs. Too often, people turn away from knowledge or wise counsel that is offered by others. Too often, they turn away from an offer of time, skill, or effort. They choose instead to be self-sufficient, perhaps saying all the while, "I'm going to trust God."

An old and widely circulated story illustrates this attitude. A woman found her home in danger of being flooded as a nearby river crested over its banks. A man from the county Corps of Engineers came by her home and advised her to evacuate. She replied, "Oh, I'm going to trust God to take care of me."

As the waters began to lap at her front door, a neighbor came by in a rowboat and offered to take her to safety. Again, she replied, "No thank you. I'm going to trust God to take care of me."

The waters continued to rise, and soon she found herself standing by a second-story window as yet another rowboat came by. "Come with us!" the rescuers urged. "Let us take you to higher ground." But again the woman said, "Thank you, but I'm trusting God to take care of me."

As night fell, the woman could be seen on the roof of her home, the waters still rising. A helicopter flew overhead and let down a rope. The woman called up to her would-be rescuers, "Thank you, but I'm going to trust God to take care of me."

Before dawn, the house was completely underwater and the woman drowned. As she entered paradise, she asked the Lord, "Why didn't You rescue me? I was trusting You with all my heart."

And the Lord replied, "What do you mean? I sent you a warning, two rowboats, and a helicopter!"

Don't turn away the help that comes your way. Avail yourself of all opportunities to learn, to grow, to receive, and to be helped or assisted along good paths.

Don't turn away a means of supply because it doesn't fit your criteria.

Don't turn away a provision because the person offering you assistance intimidates you.

Don't turn away a provision because it doesn't come up to your standard.

A woman offered to buy her grandson four new tires for his car. Even though he was in need of new tires, he rejected his grandmother's offer because he wanted fancy wheels, not just ordinary tires. He continued to experience need until one day a tire blew out while he was driving on a highway. He narrowly missed serious injury.

Had God sent provision to the young man? Surely. But it hadn't been the provision that he thought he deserved.

There was a time in my life when I wrecked an automobile, and as I was being transported to the hospital, the Lord spoke very strongly in my spirit, "Don't buy another car right away."

I needed a car. I knew that the Lord knew that. After about a week, my family asked me why I wasn't looking for a car—I think out of fear that I might use one of their cars. I didn't have a release in my spirit from the Lord to go car shopping. I managed for nearly three months to survive quite nicely without a car.

Then one day a man offered to give me a car. I felt very blessed by his offer. I accepted his gift of a car and drove it with thankfulness. It was an older model, a bit of a gas guzzler, but nevertheless, I knew it was the Lord's provision for meeting my need for transportation.

People asked me, "When are you going to get a new car?" I'd reply, "I don't feel any directive from the Lord to do that right now." I knew that in their hearts they were thinking, *Surely the pastor should be driving a car different from this one.* But why? To make a better appearance? To come up to the standards of others?

Rejecting the offer of the car would have hurt the feelings of my friend, and it would also have meant that I missed God's provision for my need. God knew precisely what I needed. He knew precisely what He was doing in the heart of the man who gave me the car. He knew exactly what the reward would be to each of us for our obedience in giving and receiving. Too often we think that we are to be obedient to God only in our giving. We also are to be obedient to God in our receiving.

If you reject provision that might solve your problem because you don't like the channel, the quality, or the method of delivery, ask yourself, *Why not?* What is standing in my way of receiving what God is making available to me? Is it pride? Is it anger or hatred? Is it distrust? The thing that is keeping you from receiving in obedience to God may very well be the deeper need that God is seeking to address in your life.

PERFECT METHODS DON'T EXIST

In my conversations with young men and women, they have described for me their ideal mates. Some of these young people have lists of qualities and characteristics that are so long and so perfect that once they get through telling me about the person they are trusting God to bring into their lives, I have a sick knowing in my spirit that no such person has ever lived, is alive today, or ever will live on this earth. They ask for perfection that doesn't exist.

What is the right prayer to pray to get a marriage partner? It is this: "God, give me what I need, not what I want."

I don't believe God will ignore that prayer. His purpose is to produce in us greater and greater conformity to the image of Christ Jesus. If we genuinely want what God believes that we need, then I believe God will act to give us what we need.

Too often we reject even the opportunity to get to know another person because the person isn't handsome or beautiful enough, isn't rich enough, doesn't come from the right kind of family, or doesn't have the right color of hair or the right laugh.

Be open to what God has for you. His choice will be the right one. It will be based not upon what you think would be appealing or satisfying, but upon what He knows will be the best for you.

8. Delay Caused by God's Redirection

God doesn't always meet our needs immediately or in a way that is completely satisfying to us because He is in the process of redirecting us or preparing us for something new.

The life of Joseph in the Old Testament is a perfect example. Joseph had a need to be released from the pit into which his brothers had cast him. In Joseph's mind, he no doubt felt he had a need to be released so that he could go home. In God's plan for Joseph's life, however, the need was for Joseph to be released so that he could go to Egypt. God's provision for Joseph was found in a band of Ishmaelites who purchased Joseph as a slave they could later sell in Egypt.

Once in Egypt, Joseph had a need for security and provision. Joseph thought both had been given to him in the form of Potiphar, an officer of Pharaoh, for whom Joseph worked as a slave. Joseph had risen to the most trusted position in Potiphar's household—he was overseer of all that Potiphar possessed. Although still a slave, Joseph had all of his material and physical needs met. But God had another plan. He allowed Joseph to end up in a prison, falsely accused but nonetheless in a prison.

Joseph had a need to get out of prison. No doubt Joseph thought his need was to be out of prison and set free or, at the very least, set free to be a slave again to an Egyptian. God saw things differently. He allowed Joseph to remain in that prison until the right opportunity developed so that Joseph could interpret the dreams of Pharaoh. In a day, God took Joseph from being a prisoner to being the number two man in Egypt! The position was the one to which God had been directing Joseph's life all along. In that position Joseph was able to keep Egypt from suffering from the ravages of a great drought and famine. In that position Joseph was able to provide for his father and for his brothers and their families. In that position Joseph was able to give life-extending provision to people he loved. (See Gen. 37; 39–50.)

Did God meet Joseph's needs? Yes, most certainly He did. And in the process, He met the needs of Jacob and all of the other brothers who became the founders of the tribes of Israel. But along the way, Joseph no doubt felt at many times that God was silent and that he was left alone in his neediness.

Was Joseph faithful and true to God as a young man? Yes. Did he keep God's commandments? Yes. Did he do everything he knew to do to help himself in the midst of his need, willing to do his part in bringing about God's provision? Yes.

Why, then, did God delay so long in meeting the needs of Joseph? Why did he have to work for Potiphar? Why did he have to go to a prison? Why did he spend two years in that prison *after* his correct interpretation of the dreams of Pharaoh's butler and baker?

God delayed meeting Joseph's needs so that a greater purpose might be accomplished, the meeting of all the needs of Joseph's entire family. In like manner, sometimes God is in the process of redirecting our lives, and He delays meeting certain needs in our lives so that His greater plan for us—and for others—might be accomplished.

Be aware that if you are experiencing an unmet need today, it may not be time, on God's timetable, for your need to be met. The provision that God has for you is still under development. His plan is still unfolding. In such cases, there is nothing for you to do but to be patient and to continue to trust God to do what only God can do, which is to work all things together for your good. (See Rom. 8:28.)

9. Delay Caused by God's Desire to Teach Us

God often withholds certain things from us in order to teach us an important lesson. In numerous cases, the lesson is related to our ability to trust God.

Too many people do everything they can possibly do to meet the need in their lives until they collapse utterly exhausted at the foot of the cross and say, "Help me!" From God's perspective, they are finally in the position that He desired for them to be in all the time. God was just waiting for them to turn to Him and to learn to trust Him to be their total source of provision.

All of us will have needs all of our lives. Many needs repeat themselves regularly. We have a need for food, for example, and that need is met when we eat. Several hours later, we are hungry again. The need for food must be addressed again. No matter how wonderfully and miraculously

God may meet your need—even to the provision of manna in the wilderness for the children of Israel—the need is likely to recur, if not in exact form, in a similar form.

Our emotional needs appear again and again throughout our lives. If we need comfort from having been rejected in one instance, and God provides for that need, we still may be rejected again in our lives and feel our need for God's comfort again.

Our needs are never fully met for all time—at least not on this earth. Needs persist.

What can grow and develop throughout our lives is not an immunity to need but a relationship with God.

This is a critical concept for you to grasp. God desires to meet your needs, but His need-meeting is part of a greater process. God is always seeking to develop a closer and more intimate relationship with you. He is molding and fashioning you into the person with whom He desires to spend all eternity. He is seeking to draw you ever closer and closer to Himself.

Many of God's delays in meeting our needs are aimed at bringing us to a place where we will turn to God, trust in God, ask of God, and rely upon God. His purpose is to teach us what it means to be in fellowship with Him and to walk closely with Him day by day.

As the children of Israel walked through the wilderness for forty years, God did not give them a paved highway with blinking neon signs that said, "This way to Canaan." No. He gave them His presence in the form of a pillar of cloud by day and a pillar of fire by night. He said to them, "Trust Me. Follow Me. Rely upon Me." When the pillar of cloud and fire began to move, the children of Israel broke camp and moved to follow it. When the pillar of cloud and fire rested above the tabernacle, the children of Israel set up camp and remained where they were. Their needs for food and water continued day after day, year after year. But the deeper eternal needs in the children of Israel were being addressed over the years even as the temporal needs were addressed on a daily basis by the presence of God in their midst.

What were those deeper eternal needs? Their need for God's forgiveness, their need for reliance upon God, their need for restoration to and fellowship with God, their need to be a people that lived in obedience to God's plan, their need to trust God in all things.

Often God delays meeting our temporal and material needs so that we will focus on our spiritual and eternal needs. He delays meeting our needs so that we will turn to Him and learn to trust Him in all things and for all things.

The Scriptures contain multiple references to God as a jealous God. That is, God does not desire for any person or anything—including any career, any goal, any dream—to be raised to a higher position in our lives. God wants to be Number One. He wants us to look to Him first and foremost for all of our provision, security, and well-being. He wants us to look to Him always as *the* Source of our total supply. When we experience lack, want, or need, He wants to be the first One to whom we turn for counsel, comfort, and solutions.

Are you truly trusting God with all of your heart today to meet your need? Are you turning to Him as your first resort when need arises, or as your last resort?

10. Delay Caused by God's Desire to Bring Us to Repentance

God at times delays meeting our needs so that we will own up to our sin, confess it to God, and repent of it—which means to turn away from our sin and to turn toward God's righteousness.

We have a great example in the parable that Jesus told in Luke 15:11–31, the story known as the parable of the prodigal son or the parable of the loving father.

In this parable, a son asks his father to give him his portion of the family inheritance. The father complies. The son then takes his inheritance and journeys to a place that is as far away as possible from the culture, customs, religion, and life that the young man has known in his father's house. Over time, the son squanders his entire inheritance and eventually gives himself over to a citizen of that alien culture to be a bondservant. His new master gives him a job feeding swine. No position could possibly have been lower for this young Jewish man. He had once known total provision for his life. Now he is in a position of "no provision"— so hungry he would be willing to eat the pods that the pigs ate, and yet the story says, "No one gave him anything."

In this position of total depravity the son "comes to himself" and makes the decision to return to his father's house.

For many people, it seems, a delay in meeting their needs is required for them to come to their senses and face up to their sin and seek God's forgiveness. It is the necessary tool for them to come to the point where they are willing to do things God's way and to follow God's path rather than the one they had originally chosen for themselves.

How much better to confess our sinfulness to God, receive His forgiveness, and follow God's plan for our lives sooner rather than later. God does not desire to see us suffer. He longs to be in right relationship with us so that we can experience His full provision for all our needs. But God will allow us to suffer if that is what is necessary for us to turn to Him and confess our need of Him. God will allow us to experience the full consequence of our sin if that is what is necessary to bring us to repentance.

What happens when this young man in Jesus' story returns home? We have one of the most beautiful pictures of God in all the Bible. Jesus tells us that the father runs to meet his dirty, once-rebellious son, and he embraces his son and repeatedly kisses him. The father restores him fully to his place as a son in the household and orders a celebration to welcome his son home. What a wonderful picture of God's desire to forgive us completely and to enter into a loving Father-and-child relationship with us!

God does not delay meeting our needs because He delights in our struggle or in our suffering. No! God delays because He will not override our human will. He longs for us to make the right decision and to come to Him for forgiveness, restoration, and ongoing fellowship and provision. Once we do so, He runs to us with love and joy. He wraps us in His eternal arms and calls us His beloved children.

If you are in rebellion against God today as you are experiencing need, I encourage you to lay down your rebellion and turn to God. Confess to Him your need of forgiveness and your desire to experience His unconditional love. Do it now. Don't delay.

WHAT RESPONSE MUST WE MAKE?

As you have read through this chapter, you no doubt have felt convicted at one or more points, feeling in your heart, "That's my situation. That's what is keeping God from meeting my need."

Once you recognize the error that is causing a delay, don't try to justify your behavior. Own up to the reality of your life. Turn to God and ask Him to forgive you. Receive His forgiveness, and then ask Him to show you how to walk in obedience to His desires and plans for your life. Ask Him for the courage to follow Him in obedience and with complete trust. I believe God will answer your prayer and begin to move immediately to meet your need. The total provision may not be instantaneous, but the need has started to be met at that moment. The logjam will have been broken, and God's full provision will be on its way to you!

· 12 ·

Getting into the Right Position for Our Needs to Be Met

Faith born of a life of obedience to Christ is the key for us to receive what God has provided for us. And how is it that we act on our faith to claim God's promises? One of the greatest passages in the Bible related to need meeting is Matthew 7:7–8. In these two verses Jesus gave us the key for getting into the right faith position for our needs to be met: "Ask, and it will be given to you; seek, and you will find; knock, and it will be opened to you. For everyone who asks receives, and he who seeks finds, and to him who knocks it will be opened."

Jesus went on to give examples of how this principle works in our natural, human lives: "What man is there among you who, if his son asks for bread, will give him a stone? Or if he asks for a fish, will he give him a serpent?" (Matt. 7:9–10).

Then Jesus asked a critical question: "If you then, being evil, know how to give good gifts to your children, how much more will your Father who is in heaven give good things to those who ask Him!" (Matt. 7:11).

Jesus was saying, in effect, "Parents who are born with a sin nature know how to give good gifts to their children. How much more so our sinless Father in heaven!" Good gifts are the only kind that God can or will give.

How does a parent choose gifts for a child? Well, a good father would never give his two-year-old son a butcher knife to play with or a boa constrictor to have as a pet. A good mother would never give her eight-year-old daughter the keys to the family car and say, "Go out and drive for a while."

A good parent gives gifts that are appropriate to a child's development and maturity. A good parent gives gifts that will be a blessing to a child and will not cause the child harm. And so it is with God. He gives us the gifts that are appropriate for us according to our spiritual ability to handle the gifts in such a way that they are a blessing and not harmful.

Furthermore, this passage says that these gifts are given in response to *asking, seeking, knocking.*

Here in one simple and clear statement is the action God desires you to take when you perceive a need.

When you have a need, you are to ask God to meet it.

When you have a problem you can't solve or resolve, you are to seek God until He reveals the action you are to take.

When you feel shut off from the supply that you need, you are to keep pressing on in the Lord until you receive what you need for your wholeness.

ASKING

The purpose in bringing your needs to God is not to inform God about them. Long before you bring your needs to God, He knows about them. You can't inform an all-knowing God about anything. He already knows precisely what is going on in your life. He knows far more about what is going on in your life than you can ever know. He alone sees the beginning and the ending of your life and all of His plans and purposes for your life in between.

So why bring needs to God in prayer to ask of Him? The main purpose is to recognize your needs. Many times as you voice your needs to the Father, you come face-to-face with your needs for the first time. God desires for you to recognize, acknowledge, and confess each need. As is true in all cases, knowing the nature of a problem is the first step toward resolving that problem.

Second, God desires that you bring your needs to Him because in so doing, you acknowledge that you cannot meet your needs and He can. You honor Him as the Source of your total provision. You admit your total dependence upon Him.

ASK DIRECTLY AND SPECIFICALLY

Very often we think things, dream about things, or wish for things, but only when our thoughts, dreams, or wishes are voiced aloud do we truly face what we are requesting of God.

Consider this difference in these statements:

- "I wish I had all my bills paid."
- "I wish I had $11,250 to pay all my bills."

The first tends to leave the wishing in a rather wishy-washy, iffy state. It sounds like a nice dream, something unattainable.

The second statement sounds concrete. There is an element of reality to it. There is a recognition that $11,250 is a lot of money, a lot of debt. There is a call to confront how the debt mounted up. There is a mental challenge to plan a way to pay that debt—a way that doesn't involve wishing as nearly as much as it involves planning, reprioritizing, working, and all along the way, believing God to help one pay what is owed to others.

The same principle holds true in our prayers. If we say to God, "Please send me enough money to pay my bills" we are not being very specific in the request. Consider, instead, this prayer: "God, please give me the wisdom to refigure my budget so I can pay off my bills, and then help me to discipline myself so I can live within my budget. Lord, I would really like to pay off my bills in six months. Please show me where I can cut my spending and how I might earn more money. Please give me the health and strength and creativity and wisdom and opportunities to do this." In my experience, such a prayer is one the Lord is very likely to answer.

Before you go to God to ask for something, decide precisely what you are going to request.

Identify your need.

Make sure it is a need and not a desire.

Identify your part in meeting your need.

GOD EXPECTS YOU TO ASK

Numerous references in the Bible challenge mankind to ask God for very specific things that are needed by all of us at some time in our lives. Read through some of these familiar verses to remind yourself how important it is to *ask* God for the things you need. God expects you to ask!

At Gibeon the LORD appeared to Solomon in a dream by night; and God said, "Ask! What shall I give you?" (1 Kings 3:5)

They seek Me daily,
And delight to know My ways,
As a nation that did righteousness,
And did not forsake the ordinance of their God.
They ask of Me the ordinances of justice;
They take delight in approaching God. (Isa. 58:2)

Ask the LORD for rain
In the time of the latter rain.
The LORD will make flashing clouds;
He will give them showers of rain,
Grass in the field for everyone. (Zech. 10:1)

[Jesus said], "Again I say to you that if two of you agree on earth concerning anything that they ask, it will be done for them by My Father in heaven. For where two or three are gathered together in My name, I am there in the midst of them." (Matt. 18:19–20)

[Jesus said], "Whatever things you ask in prayer, believing, you will receive." (Matt. 21:22)

[Jesus said to His disciples], "Whatever you ask in My name, that I will do, that the Father may be glorified in the Son. If you ask anything in My name, I will do it." (John 14:13–14)

[Jesus said], "Until now you have asked nothing in My name. Ask, and you will receive, that your joy may be full." (John 16:24)

If any of you lacks wisdom, let him ask of God, who gives to all liberally and without reproach, and it will be given to him. But let him ask in faith, with no doubting, for he who doubts is like a wave of the sea driven and tossed by the wind. (James 1:5–6)

Whatever we ask we receive from Him, because we keep His command-ments and do those things that are pleasing in His sight. (1 John 3:22)

Now this is the confidence that we have in Him, that if we ask anything according to His will, He hears us. And if we know that He hears us, whatever we ask, we know that we have the petitions that we have asked of Him. (1 John 5:14–15)

If we were to summarize these verses, we would find some very clear and concise principles related to our asking:

- God wants us to ask Him to meet *all* of our needs.
- God delights in revealing to us His desires and His ways of doing things (in other words, His ordinances).
- We can ask God for all needs, including those that relate to the nat-ural world.
- We are wise to ask in agreement with others.
- We must always ask in faith and in the name of Jesus.
- We are to ask for things according to God's will.
- God will respond to our need not in a way that is contrary to His commandments, but in a way that is pleasing to Him and brings Him glory.
- We can be assured that whenever we ask God for something, He hears us and responds to us, giving us precisely what we need (which may not be what we think we need but is always what ben-efits us the most).

An excellent biblical example of asking is that of Hannah. Hannah was the wife of a man named Elkanah, but she was not his only wife. The other wife was Peninnah, and through the years, Peninnah bore sons and daughters to Elkanah, but Hannah was barren. It wasn't enough for Hannah that Elkanah loved her dearly. She longed for a baby of her own.

One year when the family went to Shiloh for the annual time of sacrifice, Peninnah began to tease Hannah about her barrenness. Hannah
arose from the feast and went to the doorway of the tabernacle, which
was the closest point she was allowed to go to the ark of the covenant
and God's presence. There in the doorway of the tabernacle she wept
and prayed to the Lord in great anguish. She made this vow:

*O LORD of hosts, if You will indeed look on the affliction of Your maid-
servant and remember me, and not forget Your maidservant but will
give Your maidservant a male child, then I will give him to the LORD all
the days of his life, and no razor shall come upon his head. (1 Sam. 1:11)*

The Lord heard Hannah's request and answered it. She bore a son
named Samuel, and when he was weaned from her, she took him to
Shiloh and he served God at the tabernacle. He became the high priest
and judge of all Israel. Would Samuel have been born if Hannah had not
asked God to give her a son? The Bible seems to give the answer, "No."
Samuel was born in direct response to Hannah's heartfelt request.

The Bible tells us, "You do not have because you do not ask" (James
4:2). For what things in your life have you failed to ask God?

SEEKING

Psalm 34:10 tells us how to get into a position both to know and to
receive God's good things: "Seek the LORD."

What does it mean to seek the Lord? It means that we put God first in
our lives. A relationship with Him becomes our priority and our foremost desire. No matter what happens to us or around us, we choose to
obey God, follow God, and have a daily and intimate relationship with
God. To seek the Lord means to want the Lord in your life. Those who
seek the Lord are in pursuit of the Lord. They talk to Him, listen to
Him, and are eager to consult Him at all times.

If we are truly seeking the Lord, we will be reading God's Word on a
regular basis. Over time, we will grow in our understanding of the fullness of God's plan and His desires for us. We will have an increasingly
clear definition of what God considers to be good and evil. The Bible is
filled with examples of those who experienced the consequences of

actions, relationships, and things that were good and evil. The meaning is clear in each instance, and the total picture of what God considers to be good and evil becomes more "in focus" the more we read and understand the whole of God's Word.

If we are truly seeking the Lord, we also will be asking the Holy Spirit to lead and guide our daily decisions. We will turn often to the Lord and ask, "Is this something You want me to have? Is this something that has Your stamp of approval on it? Is this something that is right for my life?"

Too many people automatically dismiss such questions by saying, "Oh, I can't know God's will in every instance." In my experience, these people use that line of reasoning as an excuse *not* to consult God when it comes to the things they desire. They will choose automatically to forge ahead with their plans, schemes, wishes, and dreams and then hope God might help them if they get in a jam.

EXPECT AN ANSWER

In my experience, and in the experience of a great many people I know, when I ask God specifically to let me know if something is right or wrong for me, He gives me an answer. And if I have no answer, then I assume that I need to do a little more investigating. I need to wait a while, ask more questions, delve a little deeper, do more research, or probe the situation a little more. Eventually I will come to a point where I *will* hear God's clear answer in my spirit: "Yes, this is something good for you," or "No, this is something to avoid."

A person who is truly seeking the Lord through daily, extensive reading of God's Word and through daily prayer and communication with the Lord—desiring to hear God's answer and to know God's definition of goodness—is going to desire and to ask God for the things that are good in His eyes. That's the automatic outcome of seeking God.

A person who seeks the Lord over months, years, and decades knows what God approves and stamps as good, and truly wants the things that are good. Such a person is in a strong position to ask for good things and to receive them.

Let me give you an example.

A number of years ago I felt impressed by the Lord that the time had come for the church I was pastoring to purchase a specific piece of property located adjacent to our church. The leading of the Lord was very clear.

People sometimes ask me, "How can you be sure that it was the Lord speaking to you?" My answer is a very simple one: "I'm familiar with His voice."

When I was a boy, I remember hearing my mother call me to dinner. That seemed to be the custom in our neighborhood. Mothers would stand on their doorsteps and call to their children. To my knowledge, no child ever went to the wrong house for supper! I knew my mother's voice. I would have known in an instant if a woman other than my mother had been calling my name. And so it is with the Lord. Jesus said,

He who enters by the door is the shepherd of the sheep. To him the door-keeper opens, and the sheep hear his voice; and he calls his own sheep by name and leads them out. And when he brings out his own sheep, he goes before them; and the sheep follow him, for they know his voice. (John 10:2–4)

Let me give you some background on these verses. In Bible times, and even today in some parts of the Middle East, shepherds name each of the sheep under their care. A lamb is given a name at birth, and from birth, a lamb knows the voice of its shepherd. Such sheep are kept for their wool, not to sell for meat, so a sheep might have many years of relationship with a shepherd.

For protection, the flocks of several shepherds might be kept in the same compound at night. These compounds are sometimes caves and sometimes areas that have been surrounded with high stone fences. At the entrance is a pile of thorny foliage, or in cases where no thorny foliage is available, a shepherd stands watch all night as the "door" to the sheep. By putting the flocks together in this way, only one person needs to stand guard at the entrance to the compound, which allows all the shepherds to get sufficient sleep in shifts.

In the morning, a very simple procedure is used to separate the flocks so that each flock will go with its own shepherd out to graze on the hillsides. The shepherd calls the name of each sheep in his flock, and the sheep comes to him when its name is called. The sheep are quick to follow the shepherd because they know and respond to his voice.

Now if sheep, who are among the most stupid of all mammals, can recognize and follow the voice of their shepherd, surely we can learn to recognize the voice of the Great Shepherd who has been with us from birth and who knows each of us by name. Any person who immerses himself daily in the Word of God and who is in an intimate relationship with the Lord, communicating daily with Him through prayer and meditating on His Word, will know when God speaks. He will know when God declares something to be good and when God says that something is to be avoided.

Now this piece of property adjacent to our church property had been for sale off and on through the years. At the time God directed me to buy this piece of property, it was not on the market. Nevertheless, we approached the owner with the idea of a purchase. The timing was precise. The owner had just reached the decision to sell, and for a price and terms that were very reasonable.

Had we been actively seeking to purchase the property? No. What we had been seeking as a church body had been God's direction about how we might expand our facilities to accommodate a growing number of people and a diverse number of needs in our church. God's answer to our seeking was specific direction about a piece of property, not only when to buy it but how to use it.

Those who truly seek the Lord will be led to those things that are good in God's eyes.

A single-minded pursuit of God. To seek God means to pursue God as one's only definitive and ultimate source for meaning and truth, for understanding and wisdom. It means to consult God first and foremost in all matters.

When we seek God, of course, we seek His commandments, His righteousness, His purity, His statutes—all of the attributes and manifestations of His being. God cannot be separated from His goodness, His justice, His provision. To seek God is to seek God's way for living a life that is pleasing to Him. It is to seek God as the fountain or wellspring of one's very life.

A powerful story in the Bible about seeking God's provision for a need is found in Daniel 2. King Nebuchadnezzar had a dream that troubled his spirit, and he called all of his magicians, astrologers, sorcerers, and Chaldean advisers to tell him his dream. The men said to the king, "Tell us your dream and we will give the interpretation." The king stunned them, however, when he replied,

> *If you do not make known the dream to me, and its interpretation, you shall be cut in pieces, and your houses shall be made an ash heap. However, if you tell the dream and its interpretation, you shall receive from me gifts, rewards, and great honor. Therefore tell me the dream and its interpretation. (Dan. 2:5–6)*

The king wanted the men to tell him what he had dreamed as well as its interpretation. In other words, the king couldn't remember his dream. He knew only that he had awakened deeply troubled, and he was certain he had had a bad dream foretelling great doom. He put the men under the penalty of not only their own deaths but also total destruction of their families if they failed at their impossible task.

The men replied,

> *There is not a man on earth who can tell the king's matter . . . no king, lord, or ruler has ever asked such things of any magician, astrologer, or Chaldean. It is a difficult thing that the king requests, and there is no other who can tell it to the king except the gods, whose dwelling is not with flesh. (Dan. 2:10–11)*

The king was furious at their reply. He immediately commanded that all of the wise men of Babylon be destroyed. The decree went out, and the captain of the king's guard began to execute the wise men.

Daniel was one of the wise men facing execution, even though the king had not directly consulted him. When Daniel heard about the decree, he immediately petitioned the king to ask for a little time so that he might discover the king's dream and its interpretation. The king agreed.

Then Daniel went to his house and called together his companions, Hananiah, Mishael, and Azariah (whom we often call Shadrach, Meshach, and Abed-Nego). He and his companions purposed in their hearts to "seek mercies from the God of heaven concerning this secret" (Dan. 2:18). They shut themselves away with God, turning to Him as their sole source of supply in this matter. Their total reliance was upon God.

To seek God means to go to God and stay with Him until God alone gives His opinion or answer on the need at hand. To seek God is to look to God and God alone. A person cannot seek out two people at the same time, follow two opinions at the same time, or pursue two avenues of thinking at the same time. To seek is to set one's face in one direction and to pursue that direction until an answer is discovered, a solution is found, or an explanation or decision is revealed.

God gave Daniel the secret to the king's dream in a night vision. And Daniel's response was immediately to bless God. His praise to God holds an important truth about seeking God:

> *Blessed be the name of God forever and ever,*
> *For wisdom and might are His.*
> *And He changes the times and the seasons;*
> *He removes kings and raises up kings;*
> *He gives wisdom to the wise*
> *And knowledge to those who have understanding.*
> *He reveals deep and secret things;*
> *He knows what is in the darkness,*
> *And light dwells with Him. (Dan. 2:20–22)*

Notice especially the statement, "He gives wisdom to the wise and knowledge to those who have understanding" (v. 21).

Whatever wisdom you have, you got from God. Only God can truly reveal how to apply knowledge and understanding to the practical issues of life. Furthermore, whatever knowledge you are able to take in and assimilate into your life is made possible because of the ability God has given you to discern, perceive, and understand.

We do not think in a vacuum. Ideas may seem to come out of nowhere, but in truth, they have a source—either God or the enemy of our souls working in the imagination and lustful desires. Feelings may seem to erupt spontaneously, but in truth, they have a source—the heart, which is turned toward or away from God. It is critically important for each of us to recognize as we seek God that He is the Giver of wisdom and the One who gives the ability to understand and to take in knowledge. Acknowledge your abilities as God-given abilities.

Furthermore, Daniel was saying that the wise are those who will continue to pursue wisdom and, therefore, will continue to grow in wisdom and become even wiser. We never know it all. We never find God completely in our seeking. We are always to seek God's immediate and eternal answers to needs. The wise person knows that he doesn't know it all and that he depends upon God to impart to him greater and greater wisdom.

The same is true for knowledge and understanding. The person who is smart, said Daniel, will continue to take in more knowledge and cause his understanding to grow. Again, the process is cyclical. The more a person knows, the more a person knows what he *doesn't* know, and how essential it is to look to God to reveal what is important to know in facing any particular need.

REWARDS GO TO THOSE WHO SEEK

As you read through the following verses, note especially that blessing and righteousness are the rewards of those who seek God with a humble and repentant heart:

> *[Jehu the prophet said to King Jehoshaphat), "Nevertheless good things are found in you, in that you have removed the wooden images from the land, and have prepared your heart to seek God." (2 Chron. 19:3)*

> *But as for me, I would seek God,*
> *And to God I would commit my cause. (Job 5:8)*

> *The LORD looks down from heaven upon the children of men,*
> *To see if there are any who understand, who seek God. (Ps. 14:2)*

> *He shall receive blessing from the LORD,*
> *And righteousness from the God of his salvation . . .*
> *The generation of those who seek Him,*
> *Who seek Your face. (Ps. 24:5–6)*

> *One thing I have desired of the LORD,*
> *That will I seek:*

That I may dwell in the house of the LORD
All the days of my life,
To behold the beauty of the LORD,
And to inquire in His temple. (Ps. 27:4)

When You said, "Seek My face,"
My heart said to You, "Your face, LORD, *I will seek." (Ps. 27:8)*

O God, You are my God;
Early will I seek You;
My soul thirsts for You;
My flesh longs for You
In a dry and thirsty land
Where there is no water.
So I have looked for You in the sanctuary,
To see Your power and Your glory. (Ps. 63:1–2)

You who seek God, your hearts shall live. (Ps. 69:32)

I love those who love me,
And those who seek me diligently will find me. (Prov. 8:17)

With my soul I have desired You in the night,
Yes, by my spirit within me I will seek You early;
For when Your judgments are in the earth,
The inhabitants of the world will learn righteousness. (Isa. 26:9)

[Daniel said], "Then I set my face toward the Lord God to make request by prayer and supplications, with fasting, sackcloth, and ashes. And I prayed to the LORD *my God, and made confession, and said, 'O Lord, great and awesome God, who keeps His covenant and mercy with those who love Him, and with those who keep His commandments, we have sinned and committed iniquity, we have done wickedly and rebelled, even by departing from Your precepts and Your judgments. Neither have we heeded Your servants the prophets, who spoke in Your name to our kings and our princes, to our fathers and all the people of the land. O Lord, righteousness belongs to You, but to us shame of face, as it is this day.'"*
(Dan. 9:3–7)

Seek the LORD, *all you meek of the earth,*
Who have upheld His justice.
Seek righteousness, seek humility.
It may be that you will be hidden
In the day of the LORD's *anger. (Zeph. 2:3)*

[Jesus said], "Seek first the kingdom of God and His righteousness, and
all these things shall be added to you." (Matt. 6:33)

What are some truths we might summarize from these verses?

- When we seek the Lord, He makes Himself known to us. He is forever accessible and available to those who seek Him.
- We are wise to seek God anytime we have sinned, and to do so with prayer, fasting, and a genuinely humble heart.
- We are wise to seek God anytime we face danger.
- We must seek God with a humility of heart and with a desire to have a greater manifestation of righteousness in our hearts.
- We are always to seek God as our first priority.

Are you truly seeking God's opinion, God's method, God's way, God's timing, God's choices? That is what we are called to do!

KNOCKING

What does it mean to knock and have a door opened to us? In a broad sense, it means that God gives access to all of the things that currently seem to be inaccessible and unattainable. Barriers are removed. The things that keep us from having our needs met are swept out of the way.

How do we knock? Knocking is repeated and sometimes insistent. It is a continual asking and seeking *until the answer is received.*

A phrase that we find repeatedly in the Old Testament is this: "Inquire of the Lord." To inquire is to ask, and to continue to ask until an answer is received. We do this when we shut ourselves away with God and His Word, and as we read God's Word, we continually ask or inquire of the Lord, "What does this mean to me? How am I supposed to live in the light of what Your Word says?"

King Josiah said to the priest Hilkiah and others, "Go, inquire of the LORD for me, for the people and for all Judah, concerning the words of this book that has been found" (2 Kings 22:13). Josiah knew that his forefathers had not lived in obedience to the Word of God, and he was determined that he would do so. That same resolve must be our motivation for inquiring of the Lord, knocking and continuing to knock until we receive God's answer.

Perhaps no person in Scripture inquired of the Lord more than David. Consider these examples:

Therefore David inquired of the LORD, saying, "Shall I go and attack these Philistines?" And the LORD said to David, "Go and attack the Philistines, and save Keilah." But David's men said to him, "Look, we are afraid here in Judah. How much more then if we go to Keilah against the armies of the Philistines?" Then David inquired of the LORD once again. And the LORD answered him and said, "Arise, go down to Keilah. For I will deliver the Philistines into your hand." (1 Sam. 23:2–4)

David inquired of the LORD, saying, "Shall I pursue this troop? Shall I overtake them?" And He answered him, "Pursue, for you shall surely overtake them and without fail recover all." (1 Sam. 30:8)

It happened after this that David inquired of the LORD, saying, "Shall I go up to any of the cities of Judah?" And the LORD said to him, "Go up." David said, "Where shall I go up?" And He said, "To Hebron." (2 Sam. 2:1)

David inquired of the LORD, saying, "Shall I go up against the Philistines? Will You deliver them into my hand?" And the LORD said to David, "Go up, for I will doubtless deliver the Philistines into your hand." So David went to Baal Perazim, and David defeated them there. (2 Sam. 5:19–20)

David inquired of the LORD, and He said, "You shall not go up; circle around behind them, and come upon them in front of the mulberry trees. And it shall be, when you hear the sound of marching in the tops of the mulberry trees, then you shall advance quickly. For then the LORD will go out before you to strike the camp of the Philistines." And David did so, as the LORD commanded him; and he drove back the Philistines from Geba as far as Gezer. (2 Sam. 5:23–25)

Now there was a famine in the days of David for three years, year after year; and David inquired of the LORD. (2 Sam. 21:1)

David was totally reliant upon God for direction, not only about *what* he should do, but *how* he should proceed and *when* he should take action. He did not make the error of presuming that just because God had helped him defeat an enemy one time in one location, God would desire him to fight and defeat that enemy again in another time or another location. To knock on the door of God's plan for our lives is to recognize that God expects us always to be knocking, always inquiring, always trusting ·Him for daily guidance and for direction in every decision.

THE DOOR TO TOTAL SUPPLY

What door does God open to us when we knock repeatedly? It is the door of total provision for everything we need. When God opens to us the doors of His supply, the supply not only is for our today, but also is for our future. The work that we do will prosper; our sharing of the gospel will yield fruit; our relationships will flourish. The devil's work against us—which is to steal, kill, and destroy—will be rebuked by the Lord so that it is of no effect and no consequence. (See John 10:10.)

What drives a person to knock insistently on a closed door? Several things. A person who is being pursued by an enemy is likely to knock hard and long at a closed door in hopes of gaining *refuge*.

A person who is caught out in the elements, such as a blizzard or hurricane-strength winds, will knock insistently at a closed door in hopes of gaining *safety*.

A person who is weary and exhausted from a long or difficult journey will knock at a closed door in hopes of gaining *rest* and *renewal*.

A person who is extremely hungry or thirsty will knock at a door in hopes of gaining *provision* and *strength*.

A person who is lonely and miserable in his isolation will knock insistently at a door in hopes of finding *comfort* and an intimacy of *relationship*.

Many times we come to God with these same needs, seeking these same provisions—not only in the material and natural realm, but also in the emotional and spiritual realm.

We knock insistently because our need is great, and we must have relief from it. Our struggle with an enemy—human, demonic, or circumstantial—may cause us to knock at God's door.

The weariness of daily life may cause us to seek God's help. Spiritual exhaustion or great doubt, fear, or inner pain may cause us to come to God. An intense desire to know and understand more of God's Word may drive us to seek shelter in God's presence. Feelings of loneliness cause us to seek the warmth of God's embrace.

What we find when God opens more of Himself to us is precisely what we are seeking in the depths of our being:

- Refuge
- Safety
- Rest
- Renewal
- Provision
- Strength
- Comfort
- Relationship

God offers more and more of Himself to us as we come to rely increasingly upon Him and grow in our desire to know Him. He withholds nothing from us if we truly desire to develop a relationship with Him.

PERSISTENCE IN KNOCKING

We are to be persistent in our knocking. Jesus told a parable about the value of persisting in our desire for God's justice and provision:

There was in a certain city a judge who did not fear God nor regard man. Now there was a widow in that city; and she came to him, saying, "Get justice for me from my adversary." And he would not for a while; but afterward he said within himself, "Though I do not fear God nor regard man, yet because this widow troubles me I will avenge her, lest by her continual coming she weary me." (Luke 18:2–5)

The Lord then explained His parable, saying, "Hear what the unjust judge said. And shall God not avenge His own elect who cry out day and night to Him, though He bears long with them? I tell you that He will avenge them speedily" (Luke 18:6–8).

We are to persist in knocking until the door opens, until the need is met completely, and until we feel peace and rest in our souls.

When we begin to require God's blessings, choosing to knock insistently in our desire to receive from God's goodness and to enjoy the intimacy of His presence, we will find the answers to our questions, experience the provision for our need, and grow in our friendship with God our Creator.

An Ongoing Process

Each of the words in Matthew 7:7—*ask, seek, knock*—is in a tense that is perhaps better translated, "Ask and keep on asking," "seek and keep on seeking," "knock and keep on knocking." The more answers we are given, the more we are to ask even deeper, more penetrating questions. The more intimate our relationship with God becomes, the more we must desire to know God and to obey Him. The more God opens the doors of His storehouse to us, the more we must rely upon and trust Him to meet all of our needs.

Always Good Gifts

Jesus went on to conclude about our asking, seeking, and knocking,

What man is there among you who, if his son asks for bread, will give him a stone? Or if he asks for a fish, will he give him a serpent? If you then, being evil, know how to give good gifts to your children, how much more will your Father who is in heaven give good things to those who ask Him! Therefore, whatever you want men to do to you, do also to them, for this is the Law and the Prophets. (Matt. 7:9–12)

Of one thing we can be certain—our Father is the Giver of good gifts.

A Prayer to Claim a Promise of God

How might we claim a promise of God in faith and by prayer? Here is how I would pray with faith on the basis of the promise of God in Philippians 4:19—a promise that God will meet all my needs:

My God! You are omniscient. You are omnipotent. You are righteous, just, holy, loving, generous, abundant. You have forgiven me and accepted me into Your family. You are conforming me into the likeness of Jesus Christ. You want the best for me. You are my God! I praise and worship You today and thank You that You are able to supply abundantly and generously all the things I need.

I know and believe, Lord, that You will supply all of my needs—all of my emotional and spiritual needs, all of my physical and material needs, all of my relational needs, all of my financial needs. There isn't a need that I have that You won't supply and that You don't already know about. In fact, You have known about the needs that I have right now since before I was born, and You have already made a provision for meeting those needs. You have already looked ahead and planned for precisely what I need, when I need it, and the method for my receiving the solution to my need. I praise You right now for Your total and complete provision for me.

Make this prayer your own. Use your own words. God looks on the intent of our hearts, not at the language we use. Ask God boldly. Seek God intently. In faith, knock on God's door persistently. Begin to expect—and truly to *look for*—the good things that God has already provided for you!

· 13 ·

Confronting the Need to Belong

What is really happening in a society when twelve- and thirteen-year-old girls get pregnant? Stop to consider the situation for a moment. The young girl is looking for one main thing when she has sex with a boy—love, and by love I mean acceptance, worthiness, value, approval, unconditional favor. She is looking for something the boy can never provide for her, however—not fully and not forever.

In some cases, the girls are hoping to get pregnant because they think a baby will give them what they are looking for—love, acceptance, worthiness, value. They are looking for something a baby can never provide—again, not fully and not forever.

And what about the twelve- or thirteen-year-old boy who joins a gang and seems intent upon proving his manhood through acts of violence and treachery, even to the taking of another person's life? He is trying so hard to prove that he *is* somebody. What is that boy craving in his heart? The love of the gang—the acceptance, worthiness, value, approval, and unconditional love of others. He is looking for something the gang can never provide for him—not fully and not forever.

Young teenage girls and boys aren't the only ones who are caught up in this search for love. That same search is to be found in virtually everyone you meet, of every age, in every walk of life.

It is found in the person who joins committee after committee and becomes active to the point of neglecting his family and his personal devotional time with the Lord.

It is found in the person who feels driven to attend party after party, moving from one to the next until the wee hours of every morning.

The need to belong and to feel the love, value, and acceptance of a group is basic to our human experience. Every person I know has spent a great deal of time and energy looking for love, value, worthiness, acceptance, unconditional favor, and lasting approval from *somebody,* at least in some area of life.

OUR NEED TO BELONG

Where do we acquire this core inner need to belong? Often it arises because we have experienced rejection.

When a child grows up in a home in which Dad and Mom are too busy for personal attention and too self-absorbed to give personal affection, the child feels alienated from the family unit. It doesn't matter how much the parents claim to love the child or to be acting in the child's best interests. When attention and affection are withheld, the child feels adrift, alone, and alienated. These feelings are translated into feelings of being unloved and unwanted, and therefore unlovable and unworthy.

The need to belong, however, is so basic to our identity as human beings that we will continually seek to find someplace where we belong, and someone who will count us as lovable, desirable, and worthy. We will be restless in our hearts until we find that place for our hearts to call home.

A teen may look to the gang to be his family.

A young adult may seek friendship in parties and peer activities in an attempt to be accepted or to gain a reputation as being one of the group.

An adult may turn to group or club affiliations, even to an overactive church membership.

As a pastor, I rarely have the difficulty of a person desiring to do too much in support of the church, but it does occur. And what are my criteria for determining that a person is overly active? When a person tells me that he is too busy with church work to spend time with a spouse or children, or he is too busy for prayer, reading the Bible, or spending time in quiet meditation before the Lord, that person is too active! The Lord never calls us to church activity or ministry to the extent that our relationship with Him is neglected or our families are ignored.

When a child is wrapped up in the love, affection, and attention of the mother and the father, the child has a feeling of belonging. The child rarely turns to gangs or becomes overly concerned with peer approval. Certainly some concern with peer approval is going to be prevalent in each of us, but being overly concerned with what peers think or value is never healthy, for a teen or an adult.

Again, children perceive love and worthiness in two ways: attention and affection. There's an old saying that children spell *love* T-I-M-E. Attention translates not only into quality time but also into quantity of time. Children need for parents to be available when the children need the parents, not only when the parents think the children need them. A child who grows up believing that Mom or Dad is available at all times rarely has difficulty in grasping the concept that God is available at all times to hear the child's cries, to respond to the child's concerns, and to participate in the child's laughter.

Children also need lots of hugs and kisses and closeness with their parents. Pure expressions of love—not marred by a parent's desire for manipulation or desire for control, and not rooted in the parent's need for physical touch—are extremely important to a child's development of self-worth. The child who believes that Mom or Dad considers him untouchable is going to conclude, "Something is wrong with me. Mom and Dad don't want to be around me or be close to me. Something about me is unlovable."

Not only do children need physical expressions of affection, but they need to hear words of praise and encouragement that are translated by the children as terms of affection. They need to hear Mom and Dad speak well of them—both in the presence of others and in private moments—and to hear the words, "I love you."

The child who grows up experiencing affection from a parent has little difficulty believing that God loves him, God desires to be with him, and God takes pleasure in the fact of the child's very existence. This truly is the definition of unconditional love—regardless of a person's behavior, we love solely because the person has been created by God, and out of our love, we always desire God's best to be manifested in the person's life.

The person who has an adequate supply of attention and affection from parents, and who later receives this supply of attention and affection from the Lord, truly has a sense of belonging.

You may ask, "But, Dr. Stanley, are you talking about spiritual or emotional well-being?"

The two cannot be separated. We are emotional and spiritual beings simultaneously. Our spiritual well-being is expressed through our emotions. For example, when we feel deeply moved in our spirits, we often cry. When we feel God's great presence and power at work in our lives, we often find ourselves with a smile on our faces.

Especially in the life of a child, the things of God and the things of the family are inseparable. How a child feels about a parent and what a child feels from a parent nearly always translate 100 percent into how the child feels about God and what the child is capable of feeling from God. To a young child, Mom and Dad are such strong sources of love and such strong figures of authority that it is difficult for the child to distinguish between God and parent.

People have said to me, "Well, I wasn't able to spend that much time with my child when he was a baby, but he'll get over that separation we had between us in his early life."

No, he won't. That separation is a part of that child's inner emotional life. That feeling of not belonging, of being in some way unloved and unwanted, is going to lie at the core of that child's being until that need is fully met by God and wholeness is restored.

I know this not only from what people have told me to be true in their lives, but also from my personal experience.

Before I left home for college, I moved seventeen times. I was a child without the roots of a neighborhood community. My mother and I were on our own, without frequent or close family contact, after the death of my father when I was only nine months old until the time my mother married my stepfather a number of years later. My mother worked long hours, leaving me at home by myself and giving me the responsibility of fending for myself. I dressed myself, combed my hair, and fixed my breakfast before I left for school from the age of six onward. I know what it means to feel shortchanged in both attention and affection as a child.

I knew in my mind that my mother loved me and that she was doing her best to provide for me. But in my heart, I also knew that there were times when I ached for my mother's presence and she was not available; there were times when I needed her comfort and her hugs and she was not at home; there were times when I needed for her to tell me that she loved me and she did not speak those words, not because of the way she felt in her heart toward me but because she was too preoccupied with other concerns to express to me fully how she felt. I had a strong need to belong that was not met when I was a child, and I carried that need with me for many years, even decades, before I finally found that full sense of belonging in the Lord.

I came to this recognition of my need for belonging and received God's provision for this need long after I accepted Jesus Christ as my Savior—in fact, several decades after I accepted Christ. Coming to Christ is not the only step necessary for receiving the healing and wholeness that only Christ can give. Accepting the fact that one belongs to Christ and is fully loved and appreciated, valued, and counted as worthy by our heavenly Father is an act of faith and an act of receiving quite separate from accepting Christ.

WHAT MIGHT A NEGLECTFUL PARENT DO?

"What can I do now as a parent?" you may ask if you have been a neglectful parent.

You can always begin to show unqualified, unconditional love to your child. It is never too late to start expressing your unconditional love. You can seek ways of expressing approval, praise, and affection to your child, as well as ways of acknowledging the value and worthiness of your child before God. You can seek to spend more time with your child and to be available to your child *when your child needs you,* not when you need your child. And perhaps most important, you can express to your child your sorrow that you were not a wiser, more attentive, and more affectionate parent in your child's earlier years. You can ask your child's forgiveness for your neglect or your lack of expressed affection. You can pray for and with your child that God will heal this hurt and provide fully for this inner emotional need in your child.

All of these things can be highly beneficial, but only if you are consistent in doing these things in your child's life. You cannot do this once and consider that all of the past hurts are healed. You must remain faithful and enduring in your ongoing expressions of attention and affection.

You do well to continue to intercede for your child in a focused and consistent way, praying that your child will come to rely upon the Lord Jesus Christ for all of his sense of belonging and self-worth. Ultimately this need will be met in Christ Jesus. Through Him and His love, mercy, and forgiveness, a person becomes truly whole. Begin to trust God with all of your heart to do in your child's life what needs to be done to bring your child to this point of full acceptance of God's love.

WHY DID GOD CREATE IN US THIS NEED TO BELONG?

Why did God create in us the need for acceptance? So we would desire to belong to Him and to be part of the family of God.

God knew before you were born that there would be times when you would be rejected by the world. He knew that there would be times when you might give an opinion in a classroom that revealed your faith in Christ and subsequently be jeered by your classmates and even ridiculed by your teacher. He knew that there would be times when a colleague at work might put you down in the presence of others for your moral uprightness or the fact that you refuse to work overtime on Sundays. God knew that there would be times when even a close member of your family might rebel against the commandments of God that you seek to keep and might reject your faith in Christ as being out of it or extremist in light of what the culture as a whole proclaims as acceptable and right.

Furthermore, Jesus knows how rejection feels. Jesus knows what it means to be accepted by the Father. He also knows what it means not to feel acceptance.

At Jesus' arrest in Gethsemane, His followers rejected Him and fled. One of His closest and dearest disciples, Peter, denied knowing Him three times.

As Jesus hung on the cross and cried out to His Father, "My God, My God, why have You forsaken Me?" He was responding to feelings of not being accepted. (See Matt. 27:46.) As the full weight of the sins of all mankind fell upon Jesus, His taking on of those sins put Jesus for the first time in His entire existence apart from the Father. God the Father cannot coexist with sin. He does not remain in the presence of sin. Jesus had never known a moment of separation from the Father, nor had He ever known a moment of feeling unacceptable to His Father. He had always experienced the full approval and presence of the Father until that moment on the cross.

To feel a lack of acceptance was agony for Jesus. And it is agony for us. No need cuts quite as deep as our need to belong, especially our need to belong to our Creator, our heavenly Father.

How Are We to Respond to Rejection?

How, then, are you to respond when you experience times of rejection?

Are you to curl up in a dark corner someplace and engage in self-pity? Are you to withdraw from life and decide within yourself that you are never going to have friends or people who love you and accept you in Christ? No!

You are to do three very specific things when you feel an intense need to belong.

1. BELIEVE WHAT GOD SAYS ABOUT YOU

Down through the years, I have met a number of divorced or widowed people who have said to me, "I feel like a nobody." My response to them is, "That's not what God says about you."

God says that you are a somebody. You are a somebody who is so special and valuable to Him that He sent His Son, Jesus Christ, to die for your sins, and He made it possible for the Holy Spirit to come and dwell within you to remind you on a daily basis that you are a somebody in His eyes. You are valuable beyond measure to God!

"But I feel so all alone in the world," someone may say.

You aren't really alone. God is with you. He has promised to stay right by your side regardless of what happens to you, and even if everybody you know, and have ever known in the past, has rejected you, abandoned you, or left you, God will not leave you. That's a sure promise of God's Word!

God has fashioned our relationship with Him so that we can know, through our acceptance of Jesus' death on the cross and our belief in Him as our Savior, that we are forgiven of our sin nature and made a full member of God's immediate family. We can know that we belong to God. We are His children, never to be denied, rejected, or turned away from His presence.

In Romans 8:14–17 we read,

For as many as are led by the Spirit of God, these are sons of God. For you did not receive the spirit of bondage again to fear, but you received the Spirit of adoption by whom we cry out, "Abba, Father." The Spirit Himself bears witness with our spirit that we are children of God, and if children, then heirs—heirs of God and joint heirs with Christ, if indeed we suffer with Him, that we may also be glorified together.

Regardless of the circumstances of your birth or the experiences of your childhood; regardless of your human parents or your social status; regardless of your race, sex, cultural background, or physical appearance; regardless of what others say about you or how they treat you; regardless of anything external or historical about you; you can know that you belong fully to God's family. You are His child!

In Ephesians 1:5–6, Paul wrote that we have been predestined to "adoption as sons by Jesus Christ to Himself, according to the good pleasure of His will, to the praise of the glory of His grace, by which He made us accepted in the Beloved."

I want you to note three things in these two verses of Scripture:

First, as a believer in Christ Jesus, you are an adopted child of God. In the time that Paul was writing, adoption of a child was a very serious step. A parent might disown a natural-born child, but a parent could never disown or disavow an adopted child for any reason. A parent might cut a natural-born child out of his will, but an adopted child could never be refused part of the adoptive parent's estate. To be adopted meant that a child had full legal and financial rights related to the parent, and that those rights could not be denied. When you and I accept Jesus Christ as our Savior, we are adopted as children of God and are heirs to all of God's provision. We are heirs with Christ of all that God the Father has made available to His Son.

Second, God adopts you solely on the basis of the "good pleasure of His will." Your part involves believing in and accepting Jesus Christ as Savior. No other works need to be performed. No other good deeds must be accrued. Jesus has paid the price in full for your salvation and your adoption as a child of God. You are accepted on the basis of what Jesus did and on the fact that the heavenly Father desires and takes pleasure in your acceptance of Christ. Nothing that you ever do can undo the good pleasure of God's will in this matter. Just as you cannot earn your salvation or your adoption, neither can you lose your salvation or your adoption through your actions.

Third, God fully accepts you in the Beloved. You do not need to do anything to earn the status of *accepted* or *included* in the body of Christ. Regardless of what human beings may say or do, God requires nothing but your belief for you to be fully accepted. We human beings often have long lists of works that must be performed, accomplishments that must be earned, or rituals that must be completed before we accept one another into our clubs and organizations. Even on an informal basis, we often set up certain criteria for those we will accept into our clique group or social set. Not so with God! You are fully accepted in the Beloved the moment you accept Jesus Christ as your Savior.

Acceptance is a step beyond adoption when it comes to how we feel. Adoption can be perceived as a cold, hard, legal fact. But acceptance is a warm, intimate fact of the heart. Adoption can be regarded as something objective and outward. But acceptance is totally subjective and inward. God not only adopts you; He also accepts you. He guarantees you all of the privileges of being His child, and He extends to you the genuine fellowship of His presence and invites you to enter into a deep and intimate relationship with Him.

What good news this is! We do not have to do anything to win our way into the arms of our heavenly Father. We do not have to achieve anything before we enter His presence. He makes Himself totally and completely available to us.

In recent years, I have noted the vast number of contests that seem to have provision for instant winners. While our faith is certainly not a contest or something to be trivialized, we are instant winners of the fullness of God's love and presence the very moment we believe in Jesus Christ as providing our atonement for sin.

2. SEEK GOD'S ACCEPTANCE FIRST

A woman who had recently been divorced by her husband confessed to me, "I feel as if I have been torn from my roots. My life has been ripped apart. I don't feel as if I belong anyplace anymore."

This woman felt the deep separation from her husband, to whom she had given her life and with whom she had built a life, and she felt separated from everything that she knew as a routine, a relationship, an association. She felt disjointed because she no longer had the responsibilities and daily chores that she once had. She felt that all of her friendships were out of harmony because her friendships had always included her former husband or were friendships she and her former husband had established together. Even her relationships with her children and other members of the family were affected. She no longer had the same feeling of relationship with her former in-laws. She felt herself a stranger in the church she had attended with her husband, even though church members were loving toward her and continued to include her in their invitations. Church services just didn't seem the same to her since she had faithfully attended the same church with her husband for most of the years of their marriage.

Divorce is devastating because it destroys a person's sense of belonging. It creates an even greater need to belong, a need that isn't felt as keenly or as deeply when a person is happily married.

"What can I do?" this woman asked me.

"Go to Christ," I said. "He has promised to be a husband to the widow, and as far as you are concerned before the Lord, you are just as a woman whose husband has died. He has left you just as completely as if he had died. Trust the Lord to be the One who provides for you, who gives you your identity, and who comforts you in your loneliness. Trust Him to direct your paths and to give you the responsibilities and daily chores that *He* desires for you to do in service to Him. Trust God to be the One who shelters you from evil, who teaches you and upholds you, who guides you on a daily basis. Trust Him with the whole of your life and surrender yourself completely to Him."

Have you accepted God's acceptance? Are you counting His acceptance of you as being far more important than the acceptance by any other person or group? Or are you still setting up obstacles to this acceptance in your heart?

"But what about . . . ?"

"Except perhaps . . ."

"As soon as . . ."

"If you only knew about . . ."

Are you still trying to come up with excuses for why God can't accept you fully into the Beloved? Are you still downgrading God's acceptance?

Give it up! If God chooses to adopt you and to accept you fully into the Beloved as the result of the good pleasure of His will, then that is God's choice, and there is absolutely nothing that you can do to undo God's plan and God's acceptance. You can balk against it, refuse to accept God's acceptance, and resist the warmth of His spiritual embrace, but you cannot negate or change His acceptance and adoption of you.

I watched a young child stand in obstinate rebellion against the outstretched arms of her father. Her father wanted his little daughter to come to him and receive his hug, and she had decided that she wanted to be by herself and ignore her father. The father waited patiently, his arms outstretched as he gently called her name. She did everything in her power to ignore her father. She tried very hard to preoccupy herself with other things and to go about her business of playing with various toys. But eventually she looked at her daddy. And when she saw the love in his eyes, she forgot all about her agenda. She raced to him and allowed him to scoop her up and hug and kiss her. She not only giggled in delight at his embrace but also genuinely hugged him back. It was a tender moment.

Oh, how our heavenly Father longs to have you run to His arms, to accept His acceptance, and to enjoy His presence. You have been given the ability and prerogative to ignore Him, continue on your own way, and rebel against His desire for your close presence. But why not look at Him fully and see the love He has for you? Why not give in and yield to His tender and compassionate embrace? Why not receive all that the Father longs to give you? Why not choose to be the recipient of His love and to accept His acceptance?

3. RECOGNIZE THAT GOD WILL NEVER REJECT YOU

Perhaps you are reluctant to believe God accepts you fully because you are afraid that you might one day lose His acceptance and love. Nothing, my friend—absolutely nothing—can destroy your acceptance by God or diminish His love extended to you. Not now, not ever.

When my grandson was very young, the first thing he would do when he came to my house was to demand that he be brought to me, and then once in my presence, he would demand that I pick him up and hold him on my lap. On more than one occasion, I was at my computer working on a sermon or notes for a Bible study when my grandson came to visit. Even so, he was content to sit on my lap and watch me push the keys on the keyboard and see the words appear on the screen. Nothing needed to be said between us. The truth is, at his young age he wasn't exactly speaking my language yet. The only message that he truly understood, and the only message that was truly important that he understand, was that his grandfather loved him, wanted to be close to him, and delighted in his physical presence. He understood through my holding him on my lap that I loved him.

I can tell you precisely what was attractive to my grandson about sitting on my lap. It was the warmth of my presence, the acceptance of my touch, and the fact that I loved my grandson for just who he is and I was delighted to have him on my lap. He intuitively and emotionally felt my acceptance and love, which fulfilled part of his need for belonging. When he was with me, he had a sense—rightly so—that there was no other person I would rather have been with in that moment.

Friend, that's the way God feels about you and me. When we come to Him, whether we are aware of it or not, He picks us up, holds us on His divine lap, and loves us. He delights in being with us. He enjoys watching us enjoy the world around us. He holds us tenderly. And there is no other person in the world He would rather be with. The amazing truth about our infinite God is that He is capable of holding you and me at the same time and expressing to us all of His love and attention so that each of us is the sole object of His concern. In our finite minds we cannot grasp that, and we cannot do what God alone can do. But in God's great and infinite love, He can meet all of my need for belonging just as surely as He can meet all of your need for belonging, and He satisfies our need with His loving presence.

The greatest intimacy occurs when two people are deeply in love, and they don't need to say anything to each other. Each knows that the other is 100 percent contented, comfortable, and adored. Such silence is rich and meaningful, soothing and healing. And very often, our need for belonging is met fully when we come to sit in the Lord's presence in silence, not saying anything to God but absorbing in our spirits all that God desires to give to us of His love, compassion, and tender concern.

When you come to the Lord to have Him meet your need for intimate belonging, come to Him with a heart open to receive all that He gives you. Come with a desire to just sit for a while in the close presence of the

Lord. Come with a willingness to be held tenderly in His everlasting arms. Allow yourself to relax in His presence.

If a sin comes to your mind, confess it to Him and receive His forgiveness. If a thought comes to your mind, express it to Him. If a word of praise fills your heart, voice it softly as if whispering it into His ear.

This is not a time for you to attempt to justify yourself, apologize for your actions or feelings, or feel guilty for your lack of responsiveness to God in the past. This is a time for you to accept the fact that Jesus has justified you before the Father, Jesus has freed you to receive the Father's forgiveness and love, and Jesus has taken away all guilt from your life. This is a time for experiencing the gentle warmth of God's Holy Spirit as it flows around you, in you, and through you.

As my grandson, Jonathan felt he belonged in my lap.

As a child of God, a person who has received Jesus Christ as your Savior, you belong in God's presence. You are 100 percent welcome there. You are desired there. He longs for you to be there.

THE FAMILY AND THE CHURCH ARE TO BE PLACES OF BELONGING

God intends for us to have places on this earth where we feel completely secure and accepted. That is the Lord's desire for us in our families. He desires for each person in a family to have a sense of belonging, regardless of personality quirks or unusual traits.

The Lord also desires for each person who is part of a church to have a sense of belonging. The church is to be a place where people of many spiritual gifts and practical talents can find opportunities to be of service to Christ and can work together to bring about the furtherance of God's kingdom on this earth. The church is to be a place of loving acceptance—not acceptance of sin, but certainly acceptance of sinners. It is to be a place where a person can be appreciated for being a child of God and a special creation of God. Belonging to a church should run far deeper than simply signing a membership roll or attending regularly. Belonging should be a feeling of caring and of serving and of acceptance.

CONFRONTING THE INSTIGATORS OF A NEED TO BELONG

God does not hate divorced people, but God does hate divorce because it so completely devastates the people He loves.

God does not hate children who rebel and run away, physically or emotionally, from their parents, but God does hate rebellion because rebellion inevitably produces forms of hatred and rejection.

God hates all of the causes that deepen our need to belong because the deeper the need, the greater the healing that must take place in our lives. The things and the people that cause us to feel a greater need to belong are not of God. They act as enemies and as countermeasures to God's purposes.

There are times when we need to take a firm stand and say no to those who would attempt to destroy us. We must say no to those who sin against us. We must say,

"No, you will not destroy me."

"No, you will not influence my life for evil."

"No, you will not cause me to move away from my commitment to the Lord Jesus Christ."

"No, you will not abuse me any longer."

At the same time we say no to things that alienate, estrange, and produce rejection, we must say yes to things that unite, bridge, and bring us together as genuine believers in Christ Jesus.

"Yes, I will let you help me."

"Yes, I will join hands with you."

"Yes, you may join my group."

God calls His children to be one in the Spirit. As we unite with other believers for the purposes of praise, worship, ministry, and evangelism, God's kingdom on this earth is advanced. The body of Christ is expanded. And the body to which we belong becomes ever more accessible to us.

GIVING A SENSE OF BELONGING TO OTHERS

Part of what allows us to accept God's acceptance of us is for others to accept us. As Christians, we grow in our ability to accept ourselves when other Christians accept us. What are some practical ways we might show our acceptance of others?

First, I encourage you to greet others in the name of the Lord with a hearty handshake, a clasp on the shoulder, or even a hug if that is appropriate to your relationship with the person. Men in the church should feel free to hug other men in the church—don't let the world's warped views influence you in this. If your love is pure, you can hug folks and have that hug be pure! Acceptance is felt by children and adults alike through physical touch.

We should be sensitive about how others might perceive and receive physical touch. If you sense at all that another person is uncomfortable with your physical closeness or a hug, don't force your presence on that person. Too often, however, we err at the opposite end of the spectrum. People are starving for expressions of physical concern and closeness, and we withhold our touch.

Second, tell other believers that you love them in the Lord. Don't let the world's continual overtones of sex confuse the issue or keep you from saying that you love others. Nothing is finer than an expression of pure and godly love between two followers of our Lord Jesus Christ. To say to a Christian friend, "I love you," is to say to that person, "You belong and I belong. I accept you; I value you; I care about you as God cares about you."

Third, be free in your compliments and praise of others. Build up others. Not in a fake or artificial way. Not with a fawning attitude or a manipulative undercurrent. False flattery can always be detected. Be genuine. Something can be praised or complimented in every person. Find it. Be generous in saying to a person, "Your smile always brightens my day," or "The sight of you always warms my heart." An expression of praise for God's gifts in another person's life is always welcome. It is a reminder to that person that he is, indeed, special to God and that he is God's unique and beloved creation.

Fourth, when you hear of a need and there is something practical that you can do to meet that need, get involved. Visit the hospital. Go to the funeral. Take a gift of food or flowers to the home of the person who is experiencing a hard time. Stop by to visit and say a prayer with the person who is struggling. When you extend a gift of your time, presence, talents, and resources, you say to another person, "I'm in this with you. You and I are part of the same body of Christ."

"But," you may say, "I have this need for acceptance in my life. How can I get my need for acceptance met?"

The very same way!

Greet others in a loving way, just as you would like to be greeted. As you greet them, you will receive their greeting in return.

Be free and bold in telling others you love them. You'll hear loving words in return. Accept them!

Give genuine compliments to others. Their thanksgiving and appreciation will form a bond between you.

Be quick to serve others. In giving, you will receive.

There's an old but true phrase, "To make a friend, be a friend." To give acceptance to others is to receive acceptance. To widen your circle of friends to include others is to be included in the broader circles of their lives.

Jesus taught, "Give, and it will be given to you" (Luke 6:38). When you give to others a sense of belonging, you feel a greater sense of belonging.

· 14 ·

Confronting the Need to Feel Competent

"What do you do?"

How many times have you been asked that question by a stranger? So often the first thing we ask about a person we meet, after we have exchanged names, is a question related to a job or a position in a company. Our sense of work is tied to the deep need we have to feel competent. We have a deep inner need to feel that we are capable of doing something that contributes and that matters.

I have met a number of people through the years who have been told from their childhood, "You'll never amount to anything." What a terrible message regarding a person's worthiness or value.

The truth of God is what that person needs to hear! God says you *do* amount to something. You are so valuable that God desires to live with you forever. He desires to transform your sin nature into the very nature of Christ Jesus. He has a plan and purpose for your life, and He desires to help you fulfill that plan and purpose by giving you the Holy Spirit to help you in every way that you need help.

Paul wrote these encouraging words to the Ephesians: "We are His workmanship, created in Christ Jesus for good works, which God prepared beforehand that we should walk in them" (Eph. 2:10).

God created you to be competent. He created you to be able to do good works. Furthermore, God already had the good works in mind for you to do before He created you.

Think for a moment about a carpenter who is getting ready to build a house. He has the blueprints in hand. He has acquired all of the materials necessary, including all of the lumber. He looks at his tools and says, "For this particular job, I need a hammer." And he pulls out a hammer and begins to use it. In a similar fashion, God had a job in mind that needed to be done this year, in your particular area of the world. He created you to be His tool, His instrument, His vessel in getting that job done. He made you from your birth to be fully equipped, fashioned, and prepared for doing the job He had planned. All of your life He has been developing in you the competency required so that as you yield yourself to His Spirit—placing yourself in His hands as the Master Craftsman of the ages—His purposes can and will be accomplished.

It is up to you, then, to discover what you were created to do, to develop your talents to the highest performance level possible, and then to employ your talents in a way that will bring glory to God.

Suppose someone asks you, "Why did God make me? Why am I here?" You can answer that person with wisdom: "God made you to be here. He gave you specific talents and abilities for you to use in fulfilling His plan and purposes for the ages. He made you to bring glory to Himself. He made you to have fellowship with Him and to be in a close, intimate relationship with Him."

I can think of no higher purpose than for a person to be a close personal friend of God and to use the talents that God has given him to the best of his ability all the days of his life. It is to this life we are called. It is for this purpose that the Holy Spirit helps and guides us on a daily basis.

A SENSE OF COMPETENCE

Competence is a feeling that we are capable of doing something that matters or that makes a difference in our lives and in the lives of others. Competence is knowing how and then actually doing something that renders a service to mankind. Competence is the development of God-given talents and abilities through study, practice, and experience. It is the acquisition of skill and ability.

Every person has a built-in need to feel that he is good at something. It is an "I can" and "I'm capable" attitude.

I overheard a father say to his son in a sporting goods store, "I'm not going to buy you a tennis racket. You can't play tennis." My question for that father was, "How do you know? He doesn't have a racket, so how can you know if he can play tennis?"

Never tell another person, especially a child, that he *can't* do something. It is far better to say, "Let's see what you *can* do." Set up your child for success at tasks, not failure. Give him a mind-set of trying and exploring as he discovers and develops God-given talents.

A mother was so totally convinced that neither of her children could sing that she bypassed an opportunity to enroll her children in a children's choir at church. She based her understanding of her children's ability on the fact that she had very little musical talent and couldn't carry a tune. A wise Sunday school teacher overheard the two children singing choruses in a Sunday school class and told the children's choir director about them. He called them to his office at the church for an audition and discovered that both of them were exceptionally talented. They became part of their local church choir and eventually part of a citywide choir. One of the children then went on to sing in a national boys' choir.

Let your child experiment with his talents in a positive way. Not every experience is good for a child to have, but experiences that allow a child to discover his talents are generally good ones. One can usually find a group situation in which a child can explore his talents, such as a school band, orchestra, or choir; a cooperative team activity in sports, such as soccer; a school club that focuses on a particular interest or skill, a group ballet or gymnastics class, and so forth. Let your child know in advance that you are not requiring him to become the best in the world at his choice of activity, but you do want your child to try his best, all in the perspective of discovery. If your child finds that he has little or no aptitude for the activity, don't belittle his efforts. Help your child conclude, "This just isn't my thing. It's nice to know that early in life. Let's see what else I might enjoy." Don't give up too soon, however, in concluding that your child has no ability in a certain area. One or two lessons are not going to reveal virtuosity.

Also recognize that some activities are fun even if a person is not highly skilled at the activity or does not have great talent in it. Many people enjoy playing sports or singing even if they are never going to have careers in sports or music. Competence is not exclusive to those who are experts at a task or skill. It also includes those who are good enough at a task or skill to enjoy the activity.

COMPETENCY VS. COMPETITION

Never push your child to be number one. Encourage your child's best, but your child's best may not be *the* best in a group. To push a child to be number one is to move beyond competence into competition. A fiercely competitive spirit can kill many godly traits. It can also lead to frustration, anxiety, and poor interpersonal skills. Competition is inevitable in our society without a parent having to push a child to be competitive.

DISCOVER ALL YOUR GIFTS

God has gifted each of us in one or more areas of life. Every person ever born has had at least one talent. We all have the ability to be good at something, and often at two or more things. Most people I know have the ability to do more than they presently are doing. Most children I meet have abilities that neither they nor their parents have yet uncovered.

Furthermore, God always encourages the development and use of the gifts He has given us. In truth, He has given us our gifts so that we will develop and use them. God, however, has not gifted any person to be able to do everything. Experts in this area have estimated that most people have two to five strong gifts or talents, and that very few people have five or more talents. Most people have two or three prominent areas of giftedness, and these areas have been resident in them from birth.

Competence lies in knowing not only what you are good at doing, but also what you are *not* good at doing. If someone required me to teach a calculus class tomorrow morning, I'd probably choose to call in sick. And I would be sick because I have absolutely no aptitude for calculus and never have had any aptitude for that subject. I did not excel in math in school, and had no interest in math, and God did not call me to a career that involves extensive math. Math is not my gift. I know that, and I trust others to be the mathematicians in our world. My gifts lie elsewhere.

I am not the least bit embarrassed to admit to you that I would be a failure as a calculus teacher or as a mathematician. Neither should you be embarrassed about an area that is not your gift, even if you are in the presence of someone who has that gift. Each of us has been crafted uniquely and specifically by God for His divine plan. To each of us, He has given talents and gifts that are important to the accomplishment of His purposes, and no one area of talent or giftedness is superior to others when the talent is developed to the highest level possible and is used for the glory of God.

Neither should you be ashamed of your talents and gifts. Embrace them. Develop them. Become an expert at what you are innately good at doing. And above all, do what God has gifted you to do with good, consistent effort. As you work at your skill, you will develop your skill. As you apply your skills to help others, you will be a success in God's eyes, and in all likelihood, you will also experience success in the practical and material areas of life.

ENCOURAGE THE TALENTS OF OTHERS

Be an encourager of the gifts of others. There is plenty of opportunity for every person to become excellent in his use of his gifts. One person excelling in one area does not mean that another person might not excel in the same area or a different area.

Can you imagine how the disciples must have felt when they saw Jesus at work? They no doubt thought, *I'd love to be like Jesus, but I could never do the things He does.* Jesus didn't share that opinion. Read what Jesus said to His disciples on the night of the Last Supper: "Most assuredly, I say to you, he who believes in Me, the works that I do he will do also; and greater works than these he will do, because I go to My Father" (John 14:12).

Many people I know have a strong desire to be better than others, and they resent those who are equally talented or who seem to have superior talent. They are jealous of people who do more or better work than they do. Jesus didn't suffer from that complex. He wanted His disciples to accomplish even greater things than He had accomplished in His three years of active ministry. Certainly none of the disciples were going to be required to be the definitive sacrifice for the sins of all mankind—none of them had been chosen from before their birth for that task. The apostles were not called to be the Savior. But they didn't have to be! Jesus filled that role. Each of the apostles was called to give his life in the service of the Lord in a different way.

Jesus affirmed that when He met with the disciples after His resurrection. Jesus said to Peter, "Most assuredly, I say to you, when you were younger, you girded yourself and walked where you wished; but when you are old, you will stretch out your hands, and another will gird you and carry you where you do not wish" (John 21:18). Jesus was telling Peter how Peter would die for the glory of God, and then He said to Peter one more time, "Follow Me."

Peter then asked Jesus, "What about this man?"—referring to the apostle John. And Jesus replied, "If I will that he remain till I come, what is that to you? You follow Me." (See John 21:21–22.)

John went on to say in his Gospel account that Jesus said that *not* because John would remain alive until Jesus returned, but that what Jesus did in John's life was the business only of Jesus and John. It was to be none of Peter's concern.

We must have that attitude. The Lord has a plan for each of us, and it is our responsibility to live out that plan in obedience and faithfulness. What the Lord plans for another person's life—and how that other person lives out God's plan—is the business only of the Lord and that person. It is not our responsibility. We are to encourage and help others as they fulfill God's plan in their lives, but we are not the creator, originator, manipulator, or policeman of that plan and purpose. God is fully capable of dealing with each person individually, and our role is to trust Him completely with our lives and with the lives of those we love.

Parents so often desire to instill talents and traits into their children that God has not placed there. They attempt to play God in the lives of their children. We all have heard parents say, "My son is going to be a doctor," or "My daughter is going to be the first female president of the United States." Maybe so, maybe not. That is up to God and the son or daughter in question. He has a plan for each life, and His plan may not be remotely what the parent desires or attempts to manipulate.

More often than not, parents seem to be the last to know what God has called their children to be and do. They are so intent on seeing that their children fulfill their own desires for them, they fail to see objectively the unique talents and gifts that God has placed in their children, or be aware of the unique calling that God has placed on the use of those talents and gifts. Choose to see your children as God sees them. Choose to encourage in your children the development of the talents God has given them.

WE CANNOT LIVE IN OUR OWN STRENGTH

We are not equipped to fulfill God's plan for our lives in our own strength. God has given us talents and abilities, and He has given us the Holy Spirit to enable and empower us to use our talents and abilities effectively. The Holy Spirit is the One who guides us into all truth (John 16:12). He is our Helper in all things (John 15:26).

As competent as we may become in our own strength, we are never as fully competent by ourselves as we can be if we will allow the Holy Spirit to work in us and through us to accomplish God's will for us. Our competency may be great, but it is never complete until we allow the Holy Spirit to enlarge, enhance, multiply, and bless our efforts.

Indeed, there are some things in which we seem to fail, but God works the failures for a good purpose. This is one of the messages of Romans 8:28: "We know that all things work together for good to those who love God, to those who are the called according to His purpose."

There have been times when I have not seen an immediate result from my preaching or teaching of God's Word. I knew in my spirit that hearts should have responded but had not responded as God desired in a particular congregation of people to whom I preached. Did I consider my efforts in preaching to be a failure? No. I knew that God had given me the message I preached, that I had done my best in delivering the message. Therefore, I felt confident that the *consequences* of my preaching were up to God. He is the One who moves on the heart to respond to the gospel of Jesus Christ. My sermon was, at the very least, one more Christ-honoring seed in the life of the person God was calling to Himself.

Anytime we engage in ministry efforts, we are likely to conclude that we have been incompetent if others do not respond in the way we think they should respond. That may not be the case at all. A deep inner work may be put into motion in the life of another person without any visible, outward sign. The results of what we do are in God's hands. He can take anything that we do or give in love, with a right motive, and turn it into something effective and purposeful in the lives of others.

In 2 Corinthians 3:5–6, Paul wrote about our proper attitude toward competency: "Not that we are sufficient of ourselves to think of anything as being from ourselves, but our sufficiency is from God, who also made us sufficient as ministers of the new covenant." What good news that God is the One who makes us competent and that He is the One who makes all of our ministry efforts "sufficient."

Can you fail in witnessing to others about Christ? Not if you give your witness to the best of your ability and with a heart motivated by love.

Can you fail in praying for others in the name of Jesus? Not if you pray the way God leads you to pray and with a heart motivated by love.

Can you fail in doing a work of ministry that is designed to help others? Not if you are acting as God has led you to act and you offer your services with a heart motivated by love.

Certainly we benefit at all times by receiving wise instruction from human mentors and the wise counsel of the Holy Spirit. Certainly we benefit from practice and from life experiences that make us more humanly competent. But in the end, God is the One who is responsible for bringing about the consequences of our efforts.

Trust God with the Consequences

Consider the doctor who prescribes medications or performs surgery. He does what he is skilled to do, to the best of his ability, and with a desire to see a person made well physically. But can that doctor heal a person? Can he make the medicines work? Can he force the healing of the tissues that have undergone surgery? No. God heals.

Consider the preacher who prays for a person's healing. He does what he is trained to do, to the best of his ability, and with a heart filled with faith and love. But can that preacher cause healing to occur? No. God heals.

We do what we do—with as much human competency as possible—and then we must trust God to do what only He can do in our lives and in the lives of others.

Paul wrote to the Philippians, "I can do all things through Christ who strengthens me" (Phil. 4:13). Does that mean that Paul could do all things? Was he talented in every area of life? No. Paul was the first to admit his weaknesses and failures. But Paul could do *all things through Christ who strengthened him.* Paul could do whatever the Lord empowered and enabled him to do. He was completely reliant upon the Lord to do the Lord's work in him and through him.

You, too, can do whatever the Lord leads you to do if you trust in the Lord to give you the ability and the power to do it. Nothing is beyond the realm of possibility if you trust God to help you fulfill His plan for your life. When God gives us a destination point, He gives us the road to travel. When God orders something done, He gives the provision to accomplish the job.

WE GROW IN COMPETENCY

Competency is developed over time. As we develop our God-given skills and traits, the Holy Spirit enhances the abilities at every stage of development. The Holy Spirit, however, never skips a developmental stage or allows us to become an expert overnight.

The Holy Spirit could do that since the Spirit of truth knows all things. But for us to have instant success or to become an instant expert would not be in our best interests because we would not have developed the patience, discipline, and other character traits necessary for us to know how to use and apply our skills in the best ways.

Competency can be a dangerous thing if it is separated from wisdom, which is the ability to know when and where to act so that God's full purposes are realized. A highly skilled or knowledgeable person can miss God's perfect timing or fail to apply skills and knowledge when and how they are needed, and the results can be devastating, even though the competency is evident.

So often we desire too much too soon. This is true in our desire to become highly competent and in our desire for material success, career success, and family success. Competency takes time for full development. The acquisition of wisdom happens over time. Character is built slowly.

David knew about the development of competency over time. David was anointed to be the king of Israel fairly early in his life, probably when he was a teenager. Yet David did not automatically become king.

In the military realm, few people experienced as much success as David did. We must remember, however, that David slew a bear and a lion long before he encountered Goliath. God was working in David while he was a shepherd, giving him experiences that would instill courage in him. David, for his part, no doubt spent countless hours practicing with a slingshot while tending his father's flocks. He also grew in his reliance upon God. When David recalled his shepherding experiences for King Saul, he was quick to say, "The LORD, who delivered me from the paw of the lion and from the paw of the bear, He will deliver me from the hand of this Philistine" (1 Sam. 17:37). David's faith was based upon the Lord's presence in his life during past experiences. And so it is with our competency. The Lord works through our competency, at whatever stage we have developed certain skills, and the Lord makes us effective and successful.

When King Saul tried to give young David his armor, including his helmet and his coat of mail, David could not even walk in the king's armor. David said to Saul, "I cannot walk with these, for I have not tested them" (1 Sam. 17:39). David was not competent as a soldier when fully armed in the armor of Saul. His skills were with a sling and a handful of stones.

Very often we attempt to rely upon certain equipment or possessions to give us the competency we otherwise lack. Equipment can enhance competency, but it never makes up for an absence of competency. I enjoy taking photographs, and over the years, I have learned a great deal about photographs and have taken literally thousands of photographs around the world in all kinds of conditions. A fine camera is a wonderful tool to have as a photographer. I know that having the right gear, and having top-quality gear, can make a significant difference in the quality of the photographs I take. And yet I also know that a good photographer can take a good photograph with an old box camera. The eye that is necessary for a photographer to have—the ability to see a good shot and to capture it well—is a skill that can and must be developed quite apart from having state-of-the-art equipment. The very best equipment in the hands of a person who doesn't know how to use it or who hasn't developed the skills necessary to compose a good shot is equipment wasted.

So it is with all skills and abilities. Good equipment can be of help, but only if you know how to use that equipment to full advantage.

David did not go from being a favorite person in the king's court to being king. The Lord allowed David to be in exile for more than a decade, all the while refining certain leadership skills in him. In exile, David wrote many of the psalms that we have in our Bibles today. In exile, David learned to trust God in all circumstances, regardless of his personal feelings. Those years of being on the run from Saul, often fearful for his very life, were years that the Lord used to refine certain competencies in David—to make him an excellent statesman and military commander as well as a compassionate leader and provider for his followers.

Ask God to Reveal Your Talents to You

If you are not fully aware today of the unique talents and gifts that God has given to you—and that have been present in you from your birth—ask God to reveal those gifts to you.

Once God reveals your unique talents, ask Him to help you develop them. Be sensitive to ways in which you might receive further training in your area of talent. Avail yourself of learning opportunities. Discipline yourself to practice regularly your craft, skill, or ability.

As you develop your talents, ask God to reveal ways in which you can use your talents for His glory. Don't wait until you are an expert. Part of the way to become an expert is to start using your talents for God's purposes when your talents are at the beginner stage. God will use you to the degree and in the capacity that are right for your stage of development.

And always praise God for your giftedness. God has given talents to you. What you do with the talents becomes your gift to God!

· 15 ·

Confronting the Need to Feel Worthy

While our most basic spiritual need is to receive forgiveness from God, our most basic emotional need is to have self-worth. We have a great need for worthiness. We have a built-in need to be able to say,

"I'm worth something."

"I'm worth having around."

"I'm worthy to be noticed and appreciated."

"I'm worth having as a friend."

"I'm worthy of this job."

By self-worth, I am not referring to a cocky, self-centered attitude that cries, "Hey, look at me. I'm special." Such an attitude is nearly always a mask for deeper feelings of inadequacy and lack of self-worth. Neither am I referring to a pride born of years of bad teaching that conveys the attitude, "I'm worthy because I'm born into this special family, nation, tribe, or race." Such an attitude is rooted in bigotry, and deep within, a person who makes such a claim often has serious doubts about the truth of his claim. No, I'm talking about a genuine, heartfelt feeling of value and self-worth.

THE NEED TO FEEL WE ARE WORTHY

Self-worth is simply what it says. A person has a feeling that he is worth something—worth knowing, worth having around, worth conversing with, worth touching, worth calling a friend, worth dating, worth laughing with, worth loving. Self-worth is having a feeling of being valuable.

What is the source of self-worth? How do we acquire self-worth?

The opinions of value that are offered by parents who love unconditionally do a great deal to create in a child a feeling of self-worth, and often this feeling forms a foundation of self-value that lasts a lifetime, long after the parents have died.

The opinions of grandparents, aunts and uncles, teachers, pastors, and other valued adults and friends can contribute immeasurably to self-worth.

The greatest source for building up self-worth in a person is God Himself. His is the foremost opinion that we must come to believe. We must see that God considers us to be valuable and worthy—that He delights in having created us and that He loves us unconditionally.

In the end, it is love—and especially the infinite, unconditional, forgiving love of God our heavenly Father—that creates in us a feeling of value and worth. If Jesus, God's Son, went to the cross for us, surely we are worthy. If Christ died so that we might live with God forever in a heavenly home, surely we have value. If God created us, redeemed us, and desires to call us His children forever, surely we are of great importance to Him.

The answer to feelings of unworthiness is love. An always-and-forever kind of love. A love that is based not upon what a person does, but upon who a person is—a beloved child of almighty God.

Ultimately, however, the person must believe inside himself, *I am worthy. I am valuable.* The person must come to believe what others have said and are saying about him. The person must agree with those who say, "You are a likable, lovable, cherished person who has tremendous value and worth on this earth." And the person must come to accept with assurance, *I am loved by God. I am counted as worthy and valuable in God's eyes. I am God's child.*

A Pervasive Lack of Self-Worthiness

On the surface, you may have concluded that just about everybody in our society today has a tremendous sense of self-worth. So much bravado and self-confident behavior are shown on television and voiced on radio that you may think, *I'm the only person who feels lowly and unworthy in this entire nation.* Not so.

In my experience, the majority of people have low self-worth. How do I know that? Because I have the opportunity to meet a lot of people and to shake hands with many of those I meet. It is the rare exception, not the rule, for me to meet a person who will look me right in the eye and carry on a conversation. It is the exception, not the rule, for me to meet a person who will give me a hearty, firm handshake instead of a limp, dishrag handshake.

"But," you may be saying, "that's because you're Dr. Stanley, and they are nervous about meeting you because they have seen you on television or they know you are a preacher."

Perhaps to a degree that is the reason. But the real reason, I believe, goes far deeper than that. The real reason lies in the fact that they do not feel worthy in God's presence.

When I meet a person who looks me in the eye and gives me a firm handshake, I nearly always discover in the course of our conversation that the person has a sure, ongoing, and growing relationship with the Lord. The person knows that he has been forgiven, has a daily walking-and-talking relationship with the Holy Spirit, and truly feels loved by God and by others.

I have met millionaires and heads of corporations and founders of highly successful businesses who could not look me in the eye when the talk turned to anything personal, emotional, or spiritual. I have met people who have been happily married for several decades yet could not look me in the eye when the subject of our conversation turned to their early childhood or their relationship with God. I have met people who have earned significant awards or achieved major accomplishments but suddenly seemed to go limp inside when the conversation turned to personal relationships or issues that involved emotions.

It is not possible to project and to sustain a projection of self-value if a person's worthiness is not derived from knowing the forgiveness and love of God. And in my experience, the majority of people, including a high percentage of Christians I meet, have not truly received God's forgiveness and love. They believe God has forgiven them. They know in their minds that God loves them because the Bible says so, but they have not received in their souls the forgiveness and love of God.

I can relate to them. I've been there. I lived for years believing in, and even preaching, the forgiveness and love of God without having a personal emotional experience related to God's love. It was not until I opened myself fully to God's love and allowed myself to receive His healing for the wounded part of me suffering from rejection and loneliness early in life that I truly became able to feel worthy in God's presence.

THREE ROOT CAUSES OF LOW SELF-WORTH

I believe three primary reasons are at the root of low self-worth: (1) abusive neglect, (2) repeated failures, and (3) sin.

1. ABUSIVE NEGLECT LEADS TO FEELING UNIMPORTANT

Perhaps the foremost reason for low self-worth is some form of abusive neglect that a person experienced as a child. That abuse is not necessarily the type associated with abandonment and physical neglect. When it comes to neediness of the inner person, one of the worst forms of abuse occurs when a child is made to feel unwanted.

Consider the child who comes into a room wanting to ask Dad or Mom a question or to spend time with Dad or Mom, but the parent says, "I'm too busy now." The message is perceived by the child, *To Dad, I'm not as important as the newspaper he is reading. To Mom, I'm not worth as much as her soap opera on television.*

Children rarely want to spend much time in conversation. They ask questions, get answers, and then move on to the next thing that captures their attention. They sit close a while, perhaps give or receive a hug, and then they are off. If you are a parent, I encourage you to take time for your child when your child needs a moment. Most chores can be postponed for a few seconds or minutes. Most activities can be interrupted without your suffering harm or losing out on important information. If you must delay your response to your child for a minute or two, call your child to your side and put your arm around him so that you convey the message, *I want you close to me. I like being with you. I'm not rejecting you, merely delaying my response to your question for a few moments.*

Other forms of abuse also send a message to children that might be summed up, *What I want is vastly more important than whatever pain I cause you.* Again, the message is internalized as a lack of self-worth.

Although I do not believe that home-schooling is necessarily right for every child or every parent, I see one great benefit in it—a benefit that is rarely the reason that parents decide to home-school their children. Children who are home-schooled always seem to convey to me a very strong sense of self-identity and self-worth. I believe that is directly linked to the hours that the child's parents spend with him. The child has an intuitive sense, *I am important to my parents. I am so important that they want the very best for me, including the very best education they believe they can give to me. I am so important that they are willing to give their time and energies to be with me. My parents believe I have the ability to learn this material, and therefore, I must be able to learn it.*

I have little doubt that the high achievement scores that are attributed to many home-schooled students are directly related to the home-schooled child's self-confidence and feelings of self-worth. A cycle is created: the child feels worthy, the child gives an even better effort to learning as a result of the feelings of self-worth, the child achieves more and learns more, the child has an enhanced feeling of self-worth through his accomplishments and the resulting praise from the parents, and the cycle goes round again.

Many people tell me that the quantity of time spent with a child doesn't matter as long as it is quality time. I heartily disagree. Children who do not feel they have access to their parents when they need access feel ignored, shunned, and of diminished worth. Such children inevitably have problems with their self-worth later in life.

2. REPEATED FAILURES SABOTAGE SUCCESS

A second key reason for low self-worth is related to failure.

If you take an objective look at people who have succeeded greatly in their careers or their talents, you likely are going to find people who have also failed on a number of occasions. Babe Ruth, for example, was the home-run king. He was also the strikeout king. Thomas Edison made a number of important discoveries and inventions. He also had thousands of failures in the course of his career, including thousands of failures related only to the inventing of the electric lightbulb. Michael Jordan is perhaps the most outstanding basketball player ever to have played the game to date. Jordan did not make his high school varsity basketball team the first year he tried out for it. More than a few people we consider to be stars had numerous flops in their early endeavors.

This is not only true in our world today. It was also true in Bible times. Some of the greatest heroes of the Bible experienced times of failure. Moses, for example, had a speech problem. He was not an Egyptian, although he lived in the home of one of Pharaoh's daughters. As a young adult, Moses killed an abusive Egyptian and ran from the consequences. He began living among a foreign people in a distant place to hide out from Pharaoh, who sought his life in retribution. He had been a shepherd in Midian for nearly forty years when God called him to deliver the Israelite people from Egyptian slavery. From a human standpoint, Moses was perhaps the least likely person to be chosen as a spokesman for his people in the court of Pharaoh. His life was largely a failure up to that point.

The difference between those who have succeeded in spite of their failures and those who have allowed their failures to create low self-worth is this: those who have succeeded have not internalized their failures. They have not thought less of themselves personally for having failed. They have refused to think of themselves as failures or worthless. Failure is something they have done but not something they are. This is a huge difference. In some cases, failures have spurred them on to try harder or to explore new avenues. Those who allow failure to be internalized often give up in their failures and refuse to take the risk of failing again.

One of the most important lessons you can ever learn is this: failure is something you *do*, not something you *are*. If you did not learn that lesson as a child, begin to learn it now!

3. UNFORGIVEN SIN LEADS TO GUILT

A third root cause of low self-worth is sin.

Sin operates in our lives like termites. It erodes or eats away at our sense of value deep inside. A person cannot help having a degree of guilt over sin, and guilt eats away at self-worth.

The person who has unconfessed sin and an unforgiven sin nature will find it very difficult to forgive others freely or to accept admiration, love, or forgiveness from others. Those who marry with deep guilt feelings have a need for love that no spouse can ever fill in their lives, no matter what the spouse may do or say.

Something that often happens in the lives of those with unconfessed sins is that they destroy or sabotage their successes. In part, this happens because they do not feel worthy of what they seemingly have achieved. They undermine their efforts. At times the actions they take seem bizarre or even laughable—it's as if they are lashing out to destroy the very thing they have worked so hard to create. They do not feel they deserve the reputation that goes with achievement.

I have seen businessmen get to a high level in their businesses and then make an unwise decision that sets them back significantly. That can happen to anyone, but these businessmen generally manage to rise to that high level again, only to make a similar unwise decision that sets them back again. The cycle is repeated several times. It's as if something in them cries out, "You don't deserve what you have accomplished."

That failure to maintain success may be rooted in a parent saying to a child early in life, "You'll never amount to anything. You'll never succeed." But it also is rooted at times in a person having unconfessed sin, and the guilt of the sin cries out, "Those who sin as you have sinned do not deserve this kind of reward in life."

At times the sin is not a person's sin but the sin of others. A child may be the true victim of a parent's sin, yet the child assumes guilt related to that sin. At times the guilt associated with the sin of a sibling or a close relative other than a parent can be guilt that a person transfers to himself. Even though such guilt is false guilt—guilt that is not deserved and should never be internalized—the result is the same: a demeaning, self-deprecating spirit of unworthiness.

At times the sin is a person's own sin. The person might have committed the sin years ago, even decades ago, but the sin has never been confessed and released to God. The person has never received in his spirit the forgiveness of God. And thus, the guilt remains and continues to fester deep within.

Guilt does not evaporate over time. It does not disappear through denial. It does not go away when a person becomes an adult. It does not stop gnawing at a person just because the person says, "I'm not going to think about that any longer," or "I'm not going to let that bother me." Rather, guilt continues to bore a hole in the soul of a person and eventually comes roaring to the surface where it results in behavior that is always harmful to the person and sometimes harmful to others.

If a person does not deal with past sin and guilt, the person will be reluctant to believe that others genuinely love him or forgive him. It is nearly impossible to perceive that others can love deeply without having an ulterior motive.

The only way to deal definitively with guilt is to confess the sin associated with it. A person must go to God and say, "I acknowledge this sin, and I own up to it before You, God. I ask You to forgive me for my sin and to wash this sin from my conscience and from my soul."

If you have uneasy, needy feelings in your life, I encourage you to examine your past and to face any unconfessed sin. Allow God to forgive you and to free you. In receiving God's forgiveness, you are also receiving God's love, which declares you to be worthy of His forgiveness and love. Only in Christ Jesus can genuine worthiness be found.

THREE TRAPS THAT BESET PEOPLE WITH LOW SELF-WORTH

The feelings associated with low self-worth are pervasive. The person feels rejected, discouraged, and at times invisible, as if he is truly a nobody.

When a person does not have a healthy sense of self-worth, he will always have an inner feeling of something lacking. He will have an abiding feeling of neediness, of feeling on the outside, of feeling like an observer, of feeling hungry and dissatisfied for something more in life.

It won't matter how much money, property, or rewards the person acquires. It won't matter how great the title or the status achieved. It won't matter how many or what types of relationships the person has. If the inner feeling of being valuable and worthy is not intact, the person will have a pervasive and a prevailing sense of neediness deep within.

When a person has such feelings of low self-worth, he is much more inclined to fall into one of three traps that often beset those with low self-worth. These traps are enticements to take action to overcome the feelings of unworthiness. They are traps that create an aura of worthiness: (1) the trap of appearance, (2) the trap of perfect performance, and (3) the trap of status.

1. THE TRAP OF APPEARANCE

Very often people who are completely wrapped up in their appearance feel unworthy deep in their spirits. They hold to the conviction that they must look their best at all times in order to have others think well of them. What a trap this is! Eventually everybody has a day when he does not look great. What happens then? The person becomes depressed and feels even more unworthy. Of even greater consequences is the aging process. What happens when the person wakes up one day and discovers that he no longer looks as handsome as he did in the past? The realization can be devastating to a person of low self-worth.

I have met women, and a few men, who are so devastated at their loss of beauty that they do not desire to be around people they once considered close friends. This happens especially if they become ill with any type of degenerative or wasting disease. They don't want anybody to see them in their condition, and they turn their backs on those who would like to visit them and bring them words of encouragement, pray for them, or help them in practical ways.

God does not desire that we create any form of false security. That can mean putting trust in things. It also can mean putting trust in appearance or in one's reputation with others.

I once heard about a woman who had worked for years to meet the need for approval in her life. She had changed virtually everything about her physical body. She had gone through more than a dozen surgeries to have various features of her physical self altered, lifted, augmented, diminished, or straightened.

She went through twenty-three years of professional counseling from therapists who didn't know Jesus Christ as their Savior and Lord. She read hundreds of books in an attempt to improve herself, and along the way, she earned a doctorate and took cooking lessons at one of the finest chef schools in the world. She did everything she knew to do to make herself more intellectually stimulating and therefore appealing to others.

She tried meditation, travel to distant monasteries, self-deprivation for inner enlightenment to make herself more emotionally appealing to others.

She got involved in all sorts of good works and charitable efforts to win approval from others. She worked her way to the top of a corporation to win the praise of those she counted as important. And in the end, she *still* felt a need deep within for validation and worthiness and self-identity.

It was only when she confessed her sinful nature to God and accepted the death of Jesus Christ on the cross as being the full atonement for her sin that she experienced the approval of God. She was completely and gloriously immersed in His forgiveness and love. And everything else she had attempted to do on her own paled in comparison. None of it truly mattered. God had loved her all along, just the way she was. God had valued her as His beloved child from the moment she was conceived in her mother's womb—and even before. He had allowed her to go through many self-improvement attempts, but none of the attempts had increased or decreased His opinion of her, His love for her, or His compassion for her. And she knew it.

The woman did not allow herself to degrade herself or condemn herself for the false paths she had followed. Rather, she focused on what God said about her, what God had done for her through Jesus Christ, and what God desired to do in her and through her by the power of the Holy Spirit. She is on the path today of trusting God with more and more of her life, and she is becoming a truly outstanding witness to God's love—not through anything she is *doing* to win approval, but through what she is *allowing* God to do in her heart and mind.

Does she have the approval of God? She does! Having His approval is all that matters to her.

Does she have the approval of other people? To a very great extent, she does—not because she is seeking it, but because others are experiencing the love she pours out to them, others are being led to Christ through her friendship, and others are being helped through her generosity toward them. They are approving the right things in her—the God-produced character, the godly traits, the God-centered focus.

Does she feel approval? Yes. And she is humbled by it. She delights in the awesome fact that God loves her and has forgiven her and is preparing her to live with Him forever. She also feels the acceptance and appreciation of others, but she doesn't rely on them. She is grateful for their acts of love and kindness toward her, but people are no longer her source for approval. God is.

The good news I hold out to you today is this: what God has done and is doing in this woman's life, He desires to do in your life. He longs for you to accept His approval through accepting His Son's death and desiring the Holy Spirit's presence in you. He longs for you to look to Him for approval rather than to others. And when you do, He will give you vastly more than you have ever imagined or hoped.

Material possessions never satisfy. Consider the young woman who grows up being taught repeatedly by her mother that appearance is everything—it's the key to being liked, to getting married, to being considered acceptable in society, to getting a good grade in a class or a good job. This young woman does everything possible to make herself presentable and attractive. And yet her efforts don't seem to be enough. She still doesn't seem to have many friends. She still isn't married. She still doesn't get invited to what she perceives to be the "best" parties. She concludes that she must have more expensive clothing and jewelry and accessories. She decides that she must go to the most expensive salons, and once there, she opts for the most thorough makeovers. When these efforts don't produce the results she desires, she buys still more expensive possessions to give her the appearance she believes is so vital. Eventually she is deeply in debt.

What is this woman's need? Well, from the surface it may seem to be debt because she has far exceeded her means in obtaining all of the possessions and beauty-related services she has desired. Others might say, "This woman is materialistic and superficially hooked on things." Others might say, "She suffers from vanity and pride."

But what is truly at the root of this woman's feelings of neediness? An unfilled need to feel worthy enough to be loved or liked. Her mother couldn't accept her just as she was. This woman, as a young girl, internalized the belief that she had to look a certain way and present a certain appearance to others in order for her mommy to love her. Love was conditionally granted based on appearance. And the little girl has been searching for that love ever since.

Material things will never satisfy this young woman. They will never lead her to what she truly desires. The more material possessions she acquires in her quest for acceptance based upon physical beauty and appearance, the more her material possessions will disappoint her. Furthermore, her preoccupation with her physical appearance is very likely to consume her time, energy, and talents to the point that she turns away from the Lord and the establishment of a relationship with Him.

The person who is obsessed with what others will think very often tries to keep his relationship with Christ a secret from peers, colleagues, and even family members who do not follow Christ. Such a person is afraid that being perceived as a Christian could cause him to be seen in a negative light, and thus, a Christian witness becomes counterproductive to the quest for acceptance.

Jesus taught very plainly that we cannot pursue the material things of this world and at the same time pursue the things of the Spirit (Matt. 6:24).

2. THE TRAP OF PERFECT PERFORMANCE

Those with low self-worth also attempt to perform with perfection. They cannot bear for others to see them slip up or fail to any degree in any task or skill. Anything less than an A+ grade is a cause to hide their faces. A trip on a stair is a devastating embarrassment. A burned slice of toast is counted as a failure.

Perfect performance isn't possible in this life. God most certainly does not require it. When self-worth is based upon performance, anxiety and frustration are nearly always present.

A sad reality is that those who associate perfect performance with worthiness often expect perfect performance from their children. I have heard parents belittle their children for making a B on a test. Any person overhearing their remarks would have thought the children had failed the test, committed a major crime in the process, and brought shame upon the family for the next several generations. I have had parents tell me later, "He could have done better. He just didn't try. He has to try if he's going to succeed as an adult. I am criticizing him for his own good to encourage him to try harder."

One look at the child's face tells me that isn't so. In the first place, the child isn't encouraged to do better. He may be afraid to do the same or worse, but he isn't genuinely encouraged to do better. In the second place, the child is injured by the parent's public belittling far more than the child is helped in any way. And in the third place, the child might have given the test his best effort. What happens when a best effort isn't good enough? In most cases, the issue is not the child's performance at all, but the way the parent feels about the performance. The child hasn't performed to perfection, and the parent feels that the child must be perfect so that perfection can reflect upon the parent.

I heard a parent at a Little League game shout with great anger and frustration at his son for not making a hit. The young man was a very fine ballplayer. He had one of the highest batting averages on the team. But on that one occasion he struck out. From listening to the parent, you would have thought that the child had never made a hit in his entire life and that he had absolutely no talent for the game. Who was the failure in this instance? Why, the parent, of course. That father very likely has his reputation and self-image totally wrapped up in his son's performance. When the son fails to be perfect, the father internalizes that failure as his own. What a sad trap!

Sooner or later, we all fall short of our own best. We all come in second, third, or even last place. We all have moments when we don't achieve to the level we would like to achieve, when we fail to prepare as thoroughly as we could, or when we don't perform as well as we have at other times. That's part of being human. God does not require perfect performance from us at all times, and we are unwise to require it of ourselves or our children.

I have also met a few people who require perfection of their spouses—men who believe their wives must always look perfectly dressed and keep a perfectly clean and beautiful home, women who believe their husbands must always look perfectly groomed and drive a spotless vehicle and win the top awards at work every month. Such people are likely suffering from personal feelings of unworthiness. Deep inside, they believe their only hope for being considered worthy of the praise of others, and ultimately the praise of God, is that the spouse is perfect and that perfection reflects upon them.

3. THE TRAP OF SOCIAL STATUS

Many people feel they must rate in the eyes of others in order to have worth. They ascribe to others the defining opinion that belongs to God alone.

If a neighbor buys a new car, they must buy one.

If a colleague at work gets a raise, they feel the need to demand a raise for themselves.

If a friend gets a date with a pretty girl, they feel compelled to find an even prettier girl to date.

The trouble with status is that no person ever has enough of it. The bar keeps raising as the competition gets greater. The person who is in hot pursuit of status will move to a new and more expensive neighborhood, only to find that he must have more and more signs of personal wealth in order to feel worthy in that neighborhood. Once he has achieved a sense of being accepted in that neighborhood, he finds reason to move on to an even more expensive lifestyle.

When is enough status acquired? Never, to the person who is caught in this trap. The opinion of an even more important person will always be required and desired.

In the end, the only opinion that truly counts is God's opinion.

THESE TRAPS REQUIRE CONSTANT EFFORT

Continual, sustained effort is required from a person who is caught in any of these three traps. If the trap is status, the person must continually strive to maintain status or achieve higher status. If the trap is performance, the person must continually maintain perfect performance or strive to improve performance to the perfection level. If the trap is appearance, the person must continually work at looking good.

A great deal of money is required, which also is almost always related to effort. Usually one must work even harder to afford the material things that have become associated with status. One must spend considerable sums on clothing, jewelry, spa treatments, plastic surgery, and so forth if appearance is to remain at a perfection level. One must spend countless overtime hours and engage in countless community service activities if one is to be perceived as perfect in performance at all times.

God never intended for us to spend all of our time, energy, and material substance on these things in an effort to feel worthy of the respect and admiration of others, and ultimately His respect and admiration. To strive for these things is to be totally caught up in the doing of works in an effort to please God and even to impress God.

Works don't cut it with God. God responds to humility, faith, and expressions of thanksgiving and praise. God isn't impressed with what you accomplish, earn, or acquire, be it money, things, fame, or beauty. God wants a relationship with you, and in order for that relationship to be established and to grow, you must come to Him in humility and ask Him to forgive your past sin nature, to change your nature so that you will no longer desire to sin, and to help you live the life He desires for you, not the life you map out for yourself.

God wants a walking-and-talking relationship with you. Your appearance, your status before others, and your performance matter little to God. He is concerned about the state of your heart and your innermost desires for eternal things.

You can wear yourself out trying to achieve an external appearance of worthiness. You also are likely to wear out others as well, including your spouse or your children. And for what end?

THE FUTILITY OF SELF-STRIVING

Your striving to live in your own strength to achieve a semblance of worthiness based upon the opinions of others is futile for several reasons:

First, it is a life that cannot be sustained by any person for all of that person's life. No matter how high you fly, how much you achieve, how excellently you perform, and how perfect you may be in performance, the day will come when you will *not* be able to sustain that level.

Second, people are fickle and standards change. The very people you are trying to impress may still not like you or think well of you. Or if they like you one day, they may not like you the next. No person, no matter how fine a performer, how beautiful, or how famous, sustains admiration in the public eye for long periods of time. Our cultural definitions of beauty change. Those who won beauty contests fifty years ago may not even be in the race today. Our cultural definitions regarding the things that are "in" change rapidly. Today's fashions last for today; the "in" looks are likely to be very different a year from now. Our cultural definitions regarding performance also change. Records are broken every season. The times that won races fifteen years ago may not even be qualifying times in today's races. Those who made $50,000 a year were considered wealthy fifty years ago, but today the standard has moved much higher.

Third, most people eventually see through the efforts of a person to achieve status and beauty as a means of gaining self-worth. People as a whole don't admire status, performance, or appearance nearly as much as they admire character and heroic acts of service to others. Your reputation is not the result of how good you looked at the last party, what car you drove to the party, or how hard and how smart you worked in order to be able to buy that car. Your reputation is going to be based on the way in which you treated other people once you were in their presence, the quality of topics you discussed and the ideas you expressed, the manners and the kindness you extended, and the way in which you spoke with honesty, integrity, and morality.

Fourth, God does not accept us, love us, or forgive us on the basis of performance criteria. He does not love the beautiful more than the ugly. He does not love the high achiever more than the low achiever. He does not love the rich, famous, and others of high social status more than the poor, unknown, and those of low social status. Nothing you can do regarding status, performance, or appearance will elevate you one inch in God's eyes. He accepts you because you come to Him believing in Jesus Christ as the One who has taken upon Himself the full consequences of your sin. He loves you because He created you and has chosen to love you from the moment He first thought of you. He forgives you because you have faced up to your sin nature and have opened your heart to receive His forgiveness.

A STRIVING FOR PERFECTION

Striving for perfection is the ultimate form of self-striving. It can occur in striving for appearance, performance, or status, but it generally is more pervasive to cover all areas of one's life. Anytime you show me a person who is consumed with having everything in his life honed to absolute, down-to-the-detail perfection, I will show you a person with a very deep-seated lack of self-worthiness.

I'm not talking here about a person who tries to do his best or encourages the best from others. I'm talking about a person who will not settle for anything other than being the best in any given group of people, continually is obsessed with having the best, performing the best, and accomplishing the best regardless of the task. He will require that every person with whom he is associated perform at 100 percent output without error.

At the root of perfectionism is *not* a desire to do one's best, as a perfectionist often claims. Rather, it is a desire to be acceptable and ultimately to prove oneself acceptable to God.

One of the easiest ways to determine whether a person is a perfectionist is this: Can the person laugh at his foibles and innocent mistakes? I'm not talking about deliberate or rebellious errors, but innocent human "goofs" that we all make from time to time and that are a part of being human. Can a person laugh at those things and go on, or does he seem to withdraw into himself in embarrassment or even express anger at himself or others? Is the laughter genuine and lighthearted, or is it cover-up laughter that is really a sign of embarrassment and shame? The perfectionist will tend to internalize every mistake and to think about his mistakes repeatedly, each time with a sense of shame. The nonperfectionist will be able to leave the incident behind.

During the early years of my ministry as a pastor, I was a perfectionist. I drove myself to do everything I knew to do as a young pastor, and then I sought to do more. No effort was ever quite good enough. I always had a feeling that I could preach better, counsel better, have things in better order, study the Bible more, pray more. I spent every waking hour improving my performance so that I might be pleasing to those whom I pastored. In truth, I was striving very hard to please God because I was never really sure that He was 100 percent happy with me or my efforts. At the same time I drove myself toward perfection, I drove those who worked with me toward perfection. I expected everything to be in tip-top order at every moment, and I had a very low tolerance for error.

I covered my perfectionism, as most perfectionists do, by stating that I simply wanted to do my very best and that God deserved my best. Now there is nothing wrong with doing one's best, and certainly God deserves our best effort, but there was a very big problem in the way I defined *best*. Best was being better than anybody else. Best was being better than anyone with whom I might be compared. Best was coming out number one. God does not require that of us. It's impossible for everybody to be number one in any given area of life, and it's impossible for any one person to be number one all the time. God expects us to work hard, but not twenty-four hours a day. God expects us to live as a witness to Christ, but our witness is measured not by our efforts but by our relationship with Christ.

Most perfectionists are trying to win approval of others and ultimately of God. They have not faced the reality that God does not judge us on our performance. He judges us according to what we have done about

Jesus Christ. Have we believed in Christ Jesus as our Savior? Are we in relationship with Christ Jesus as our Lord? Have we received the Holy Spirit into our lives, and are we listening to the Holy Spirit's guidance as He speaks the truth to us on a daily basis?

God rewards us for our obedience in doing the things He calls us to do. His rewards are for our obedience, not necessarily our success! Our accomplishments in the kingdom of God are actually the Lord's accomplishments. No person ever saved a soul. No person ever healed another person. No person ever delivered another person from evil. The Lord does those works. Our part is to share the gospel, pray in the name of Jesus, and believe God to work on our behalf. We are tools, or instruments, in His hand, but the workmanship is His.

How did I get over my perfectionism? Two things happened. I realized that in my trying to do it all and be it all, I was leaving no room for the Holy Spirit to work in me or through me, and I was leaving little room for the Holy Spirit to work in and through other people. I finally reached the end of myself and said to the Lord, "Lord, this is *Your* church, *Your* ministry. My life is *Yours*." I began to give responsibility and authority over various areas of church activity to others, trusting God to deal with them directly and to do His work in their lives and in their ministries to others.

I also came to the place where I accepted that the Lord loves me, Charles Stanley, as He has made me to be and continues to make me to be in the image of Christ Jesus. It is not my job to make myself; I am to yield to His creative work in my life. We've all heard this comment: "He is a self-made man." While that may have a ring of truth to it in the area of business or education, it is never something that can be true in the spiritual realm. What we are in the spirit is what our heavenly Father makes us to be through the power of His Holy Spirit at work in our lives. We are His workmanship, His creation, His masterpiece.

Our lives are in process. The apostle Paul wrote of this in Romans 8:29–30 when he said,

> *For whom He foreknew, He also predestined to be conformed to the image of His Son, that He might be the firstborn among many brethren. Moreover whom He predestined, these He also called; whom He called, these He also justified; and whom He justified, these He also glorified.*

From the very beginning, God has had a plan to conform you and me into the image of His Son. He has called you to that process. The moment you accepted Jesus Christ as your personal Savior and began to follow Him as your Lord, He began a process of conforming and justifying you—conforming you into the character of Christ and justifying all of your actions so that they line up with His divine plan and purpose. The more you are and do what He created you to be and do, the more glory you bring to Christ Jesus, and thus, the greater Christ's glory will be reflected in your life now and forever.

You cannot predestine yourself, no matter how hard you try.

You did not call yourself to come to the place where you confessed your sins before God and received Jesus as your Savior.

You cannot conform yourself into the full likeness of Jesus Christ and His character, no matter how much you may strive to do so.

You cannot engineer all of the work and accomplishments of your life totally on your own in a way that is pleasing to God, no matter how many long-range plans and lists you make and how diligently you attempt to turn your plans into success.

You cannot bring lasting glory to yourself, no matter how much you may achieve in human accolades, rewards, and honors.

To strive for perfection is futile.

"Well, should I just give up trying?" you may ask.

Trying to do your best? No, never give up on that.

Trying to *be* the best at all times? Trying to live an error-free life? Yes. Give it up.

Trying to do it in your own strength and power? Trying to force others to serve you and make you number one? Yes. Give it up.

Trying to live your life without God's help? Most definitely, yes, give it up.

One evening I found myself ready to walk out onto the platform at church to perform a wedding, and I looked down at my feet to discover that I was wearing one black shoe and one dark brown shoe. They were of the same style, and in my haste at getting to the church on time, I had failed to notice that I pulled two different colored shoes from my closet. In my perfectionist days, that discovery would have put me off balance. I would have been embarrassed at such a mistake and angry with myself. In the process, I likely would have had less than a joyful attitude in conducting the wedding. I would have been concerned that others might notice my mismatched shoes and ridicule me for such a mistake, or that the bride and groom might think less of me for making their wedding less than perfect in all details.

On that particular night, however, I just smiled at myself. It was a silly mistake, and I took it as such and laughed it off. I feel quite certain that nobody at the wedding noticed, and if someone did, I didn't care then and don't care now what conclusions the person might have reached about my mistake. If his opinion of me as a person and as a child of God was diminished because I wore shoes of different color, then he didn't think very highly of me in the first place, or he was looking for an excuse to think less of me. A hundred years from now, nobody will know or remember that Charles Stanley wore one black shoe and one dark brown shoe while performing a wedding. I am a human being, and I made a human mistake that hurt nobody and had no eternal consequences. And so it is with most of our mistakes. They are a part of our human condition.

Our self-worth does not lie in our being perfect and in living lives that are completely "nailed down" and error free. Our self-worth lies in our relationship with Jesus Christ. In the end, nothing else matters but that.

OUR PART IN HELPING THE PERSON WITH LOW SELF-WORTH

People with a low sense of self-worth would like to be able to look another person in the eye, accept a genuine compliment, give a firm handshake, or respond with a sense of humor about themselves. Those with low self-worth do not choose or desire to have low self-worth. They desire the very opposite.

How can we help such a person? Not by letting go of his limp handshake as quickly as possible, but by grasping his hand with both hands and holding his hand until he grips our hands in return. Not by moving quickly on to the next person but by continuing to talk to the person until he does look us in the eye. Not by letting the compliment go ignored or diverted but by saying again with even greater sincerity and intensity, "I don't think you realize that I truly meant what I said. I think you did great."

We don't help the perfectionist by laughing at him, in hopes he will laugh at himself. We help by admitting our own foibles with a laugh, perhaps saying, "You know, I've made that same mistake myself. I laugh about it every time I think of it." At times you may want to share a similar moment of error or embarrassment in your life to show the person that every person makes mistakes and that innocent mistakes and shortcomings are not a cause for shame.

Self-worth, however, can never be acquired solely through the praise and recognition of others. It doesn't matter how many compliments a person receives, how many trophies or plaques are put on the person's shelves, or how many supportive friends a person may have. The kind words of praise and appreciation from others will have a hollow ring to him unless he believes with the most basic of beliefs that God approves, God loves, God forgives, and God considers him to be valuable and worthy.

The best thing we can do for a person with low self-worth is to pray for that person and to remind him often of how valuable he is to God.

How Can We Acquire More Self-Worth in Ourselves?

If we lack in personal self-worthiness and we recognize this need, how can we increase our feelings of self-worthiness?

By truly accepting Jesus Christ as our personal Savior and Lord, and by accepting that what Jesus Christ did on the cross—dying for our sinful nature as the one definitive and substitutionary sacrifice of God the Father—was for us personally, specifically and individually.

How does someone know that he is valuable?

The answer is to be found when one looks at the Cross. When a person comes face-to-face with the Cross and confronts the fullness of its reality, a person comes face-to-face with his own value.

How much are you worth?

You are worth so much that God sent Jesus to die in your place on the cross.

A person comes to grips with the issue of self-worth when he reasons within himself, "If God sent His only begotten Son, Jesus Christ, to die on that cross for *my* sins, surely I am valuable to God. If God considered me to be worthy of the shed blood of Jesus, who was without sin and yet went to the cross to die for me, a sinner, then surely I am worthy in His eyes."

How many sinners were required before God required Jesus to die on the cross as the perfect, substitutionary sacrifice for sin?

One.

Jesus didn't go to the cross because millions and millions of sinners—born and as yet unborn—were in need of salvation. He went to the cross because the heart of man was sinful. Even if only one person had been ruled by a sinful heart, Jesus would have died on his behalf.

That is the stark, shattering, and yet utterly affirming fact of the Cross!

Jesus died for *me*. He died for *you*. He died so that you and I might live in the presence of God the Father forever, forgiven and made whole spiritually by God's great love and redemptive power.

We do not acquire feelings of self-worth by standing in front of a mirror and repeating to ourselves, "I am worthy, I am worthy, I am worthy." We acquire feelings of self-worth when we stand in front of the cross and come to the realization of the greatest truth of all time, "I am worthy because God says I am worthy. I am worthy because Jesus died in my place for my sins so that I might live in eternity with God."

Are we worth something on the basis of our talents, abilities, gifts, or accomplishments?

No. We are worth something because our worth was purchased with the ultimate price: the blood of Jesus.

A human being may consider that you are worth dying for, but how many people truly die on behalf of others willfully and for their sin nature? Nobody I know.

God did not only say that you are worthy of the death of Jesus Christ on the cross. He actually sent Jesus to the cross to die on your behalf. God followed through on what He said about your worthiness. Jesus actually died in your place so that you might believe on Him and live with our heavenly Father forever. God believed in your worth to the point of sacrificing His only begotten Son (John 3:16).

Friend, you are worthy. God says you are. He sent His Son to die for you because He considered you worthy of saving and worthy of living with Him for all eternity.

You are competent because God makes you competent. He sends His Holy Spirit to help you do anything He calls you to do.

You belong because God brings you into full fellowship with Himself through Jesus Christ. You are His child now and forever once you accept Jesus Christ as your Savior.

What a wonderful sense of self-worth comes when a person believes and then says to himself and to others, "God and I are in agreement. He is in me and I am in Him."

Christ in me is the ultimate proclamation of self-value!

The person who has a deep and abiding sense of self-worth can hear all kinds of criticism and cutting remarks from other people and let the negative comments slide off him like water off the back of a duck. He can go on about his life's work with joy because he has an inner smile on the soul that says, "So much for your opinion. I know *God* loves me, and His opinion of my value never diminishes, never changes, and is the only opinion that truly counts." Your critics, your detractors, and your enemies have no hold on you when you draw your identity, your help, and your sense of worth from God Himself.

God will never change His attitude about you. He will always love you and desire your best. Only God truly can produce in a person eternal self-worth. Turn to Him today, and receive all the love and acceptance He offers.

· 16 ·

The Key to Loving

Until we have genuine feelings of belonging, competency, and self-worth we cannot begin to address the other emotional needs that we feel in our lives. These are the bottom line when it comes to emotional neediness, especially the need for worthiness. Until that level of neediness is met, all efforts to meet other emotional needs will fall short.

Consider for a brief moment the rather gruesome picture of a person whose arm has been broken and the bone has ripped through the skin. You can place all kinds of bandages on that wound, using entire bottles of disinfectant and a round of injections to keep infection from developing in the wound, and perhaps, with a little shifting of the bone, you might get the surface wound on the skin to heal. In the end, however, that arm will remain useless and the problem will never be fully resolved until the broken bone is set and allowed to mend.

The same is true for belonging and worthiness needs. Bandaging efforts may work to a degree. But genuine wholeness and an ability to function well with others require deep inner healing. As long as a person remains needy in the deep emotional area of his life, that person's ability to reach out to others, accept them, and love them as God desires is limited. Our ability to minister to others is directly related to the degree to which we are whole in emotions and spirit.

LEARNING TO LOVE OTHERS AS WE LOVE OURSELVES

Jesus taught that we are to love our neighbors *as we love ourselves.* (See Matt. 22:39.) Even so, many of us Christians have been taught from an early age that we should *not* love ourselves—that to do so would be self-centered, egotistical, or prideful.

When we love our neighbors as we love ourselves, we are to love our neighbors as God loves them just as we love ourselves as God loves us. When we factor God's love into the equation, everything becomes crystal clear! To love others in a genuine, sacrificial, and pure way, we must know what it means to be loved.

We see the evidence of such love best in the life and death of Jesus Christ. Jesus genuinely loved those who followed Him. He gave His life so that others could experience God's forgiveness. His love was pure, vast, and eternal. Jesus' love was unconditional. It is only as we receive such love into our lives and acknowledge the importance that God places upon us as individuals beloved by Him that we truly can give such love to others and fully appreciate the importance that God places upon them.

SELF-RESPECT IS THE HIGHEST FORM OF SELF-LOVE

God has given us a healthy way to love ourselves. The word that most readily comes to mind is *respect.* Respect yourself. That is what it means to have good self-value or self-worth. Regard yourself as God regards you—a unique, irreplaceable, and beloved creation with a divine and eternal plan and purpose.

Don't allow what others say to drag you down.

Don't put yourself down.

Hold your head up and face the world with the knowledge that you are a child of God and your Father is the King of the universe!

Respect your body and the way God made you. Don't abuse your physical body by putting harmful substances into it.

Respect your mind and the purposes God has for it. Don't feed your mind the trash of this world. Give your mind only the most noble and uplifting ideas.

Respect your emotions and the role God intends for them to play in your life. Don't engage in activities that eventually dull your conscience. Don't negate your emotions or deny their existence. Don't continue friendships or career associations that bring emotional heartache on a continual basis. It is not God's desire that your emotions be constantly abused or trampled.

I have met people through the years who believe that in some perverse way God wants them to suffer emotionally. Some people have said to me, "I'm not worthy of being loved by others," or "God seems to allow my heart to be broken again and again so this must be His will for my life."

No, an ongoing broken heart is not God's will for you. It is not His will for you to be without the love of other people. You are worthy of being loved. God sent His only Son to die on a cross for you because He considered you to be worthy of His love and forgiveness. God desires for you to be in loving and giving relationships with other people and for your heart to know the fullness of what it means to give and receive love. Don't buy this lie of the enemy another day! God loves you and He desires love *for* you. He wants you to be the object of great love from others who rely upon Him also as their supreme source of love.

Respect yourself enough to hold out for God's best and highest in your life. Refuse to engage in evil. Refuse to give in to temptation. Refuse to negotiate away your integrity or to make compromises in your character.

Respect yourself enough to say no to anything that would diminish, destroy, negate, or deny you the full privileges of being God's beloved child.

LET GOD DEFINE WHO YOU ARE

Suppose you are shut out of a particular social circle.

Suppose you lose your job.

Suppose you are in an accident that results in deep scars on your face or body.

If your worthiness is rooted in your status, performance, or appearance, you are likely to come apart at the seams when tragedy strikes. You are likely to be swallowed up by shame. You may seek to move to another community so that nobody will know what happened to you. You may try to shut yourself off from people.

Is that God's desire for anyone? Absolutely not.

Furthermore, if the person who struggles with unworthiness is honest with himself, he doesn't like associating with people whom he perceives to be down and out. He doesn't like to be near anybody he considers to be a loser who doesn't come up to his standards.

Is that God's desire for a Christian or for a church? Absolutely not.

God's desire for us is that we seek Him first and foremost. Our definition of character and all matters pertaining to the human heart are to be derived from looking at Jesus and seeking to become like Him.

God's desire is that we have inner strength based upon our faith and our relationship with Him. Then when storms strike, everything around us and even our own health and well-being may take a hit, but our spirits remain vibrant, hopeful, and strong.

God's desire is that we reach out to others regardless of their status, level of performance, or appearance. We treat winners and losers alike. We are gracious and kind to all we encounter without any regard for their appearance.

Those who have deep feelings of unworthiness can rarely extend worthiness to others in this way unless God does a healing work in their inner souls. Those who feel worthy before God, on the basis of what God has done for them and who God proclaims them to be, are men and women who are capable of making others feel worthy and of accepting others as they are, even as they encourage others to accept the love and forgiveness of our heavenly Father.

A PRACTICAL MEANS OF LOVING OTHERS

Love is far more than an attitude or a feeling. It is behavior. As one person has said, "An attitude in action." Jesus was very practical in His definition of who our neighbor is and how we are to love our neighbors. Jesus taught:

You have heard that it was said, "You shall love your neighbor and hate your enemy." But I say to you, love your enemies, bless those who curse you, do good to those who hate you, and pray for those who spitefully use you and persecute you, that you may be sons of your Father in heaven . . . For if you love those who love you, what reward have you? Do not even the tax collectors do the same? And if you greet your brethren only, what do you do more than others? Do not even the tax collectors do so? (Matt. 5:43–47)

It is easy for most of us to extend love to those we like or those who are close to us. However, Jesus taught here, as well as in other places, that our neighbor is not only the person who attends church with us, lives in our neighborhood, or is a person who is like us, but our neighbor is every person who crosses our path.

James reminded us that "if you show partiality, you commit sin, and are convicted by the law as transgressors" (James 2:9). He wrote this specifically in reference to what he called the "royal law according to the Scripture, 'You shall love your neighbor as yourself'" (James 2:8). Every person with whom we have contact is our neighbor, even our enemy.

And how are we to express love for our neighbors, those who are enemies as well as those who are friends or family members? We are to bless them, do good to them, and pray for them.

BLESSING OTHERS

To bless people means genuinely to desire that God's best come into their lives. God's best, of course, is God's forgiveness and love. To bless people is to desire that they come to know Jesus Christ as their Savior.

DOING GOOD TO OTHERS

To do good to people is to extend practical and tangible acts of kindness toward them—to speak well of them and not evil, to help them rather than hinder them, to refrain from gossiping about them even if the story has truth in it, to be courteous and kind to them, and to point them toward others who may be helpful to them.

PRAYING FOR OTHERS

To pray for others is to ask God to push back all of the forces of evil that are at work in their lives, to ask the Lord to heal the deep emotional wounds in their lives, and to ask the Lord to send someone to them from whom they will be willing to receive the gospel of Jesus' death and resurrection on their behalf.

To love our neighbors is not some sort of ephemeral, otherworldly attitude toward others. It is a practical love.

Truly this is the way we are to love ourselves as well!

We are to desire God's best in our lives—God's highest and richest blessings. We are to receive God's forgiveness and love in an ongoing way in our lives and to diligently request and seek out all of the truly good things that God desires for us to have.

We are to extend kindness to ourselves—receiving the forgiveness of Jesus and then forgiving ourselves. We are not to beat ourselves up over the past sins of our lives. Rather, we are to receive the forgiveness that Jesus extends to us and then forgive ourselves and move forward in our lives. We are not to belittle ourselves or to criticize ourselves before others from a motivation of trying to appear humble, saying, "Oh, I really don't deserve that," or "I'm really not that great a person." Rather, we are to receive compliments with a grateful heart and view ourselves as Christ sees us: forgiven, beloved, and growing each day more and more into His likeness of character.

We are to pray that God will defeat the enemy at every turn and that He will keep us from evil influence and evil temptations. We are to pray that God will heal us and make us whole. We are to be open to the truth of God's Word at all times, eager to learn and to grow in our faith and in our understanding of the Scriptures.

Do you truly love yourself in this way—completely open to God's blessings, forgiving yourself and treating yourself kindly, and praying for yourself? Are you loving others in this threefold way: blessing them, doing good to them, and praying for them?

LOVING OTHERS IS A REFLECTION OF LOVING GOD

Our love for others is vitally connected to our ability to show love to God and receive love from God. Jesus addressed this issue clearly:

> *Then one of them [the Pharisees], a lawyer, asked Him a question, testing Him, and saying, "Teacher, which is the great commandment in the law?" Jesus said to him, "'You shall love the LORD your God with all your heart, with all your soul, and with all your mind.' This is the first and great commandment. And the second is like it: 'You shall love your neighbor as yourself.' On these two commandments hang all the Law and the Prophets." (Matt. 22:35–40)*

When we love God with all of the heart, soul, and mind, we must recognize as part of that very process that God has given us a heart, soul, and mind. We become aware of the eternal part of us, the deep emotional current that runs in us, and the will that has been given to us by God. When we become aware of these things in us—and value them—we become much more aware that God has made others with a heart, soul, and mind. We become more keenly attuned to the fact that God desires to spend eternity not only with us, but also with those we love as well as those who are strangers. We become more sensitive to the fact that others have deep emotions that may not be readily expressed and emotional needs that may not be met. We become aware that every person has a will and a decision-making capability, and thus, we are not and can never be the "savior" for another person. Only Jesus Christ can fill that role.

John wrote of this vital link between our love for God and our ability to love others: "If someone says, 'I love God,' and hates his brother, he is a liar; for he who does not love his brother whom he has seen, how can he love God whom he has not seen? And this commandment we have from Him: That he who loves God must love his brother also" (1 John 4:20–21).

Just as loving God with all our being is the way to have a right relationship with God, so loving our neighbors is the key to having right relations with other people.

To love God with all of the heart, soul, and mind is to love God with a right attitude and a right humility of heart. To love others as ourselves is to have a right attitude toward others and to live in humility toward them.

LOVING OTHERS IS A COMMANDMENT

Are you aware that you are commanded to love yourself as God loves you and to love your neighbor as God loves your neighbor? This teaching of Jesus that is directly related to your emotional need for worthiness is not optional. It is required of you.

Consider this statement of Jesus:

Now behold, one came and said to Him, "Good Teacher, what good thing shall I do that I may have eternal life?" So He said to him, "Why do you

call Me good? No one is good but One, that is, God. But if you want to
enter into life, keep the commandments." He said to Him, "Which ones?"
Jesus said, "'You shall not murder,' 'You shall not commit adultery,' 'You
shall not steal,' 'You shall not bear false witness,' 'Honor your father and
your mother,' and, 'You shall love your neighbor as yourself.'" (Matt.
19:16–19)

Jesus did not say, "Love others as you love yourself," as a nice idea about human relationships. His statement was not a suggestion; it was a commandment. In fact, Jesus was quoting a commandment given first to Moses. (See Lev. 19:18.) Jesus believed that commandment, kept it, embodied it, fulfilled it, and taught it. The commandment is no less in effect today than it has been in effect from God's perspective for thousands of years.

The command to love yourself must be kept before you can keep the command to love others. It is not possible to give to others a greater amount than you have received, not in any area of life. A basic law of transaction that God has set up in our world says we can give only from the supply that we have received. Yet an equal aspect of that law of transaction is that the more we give, the more we receive. To give love and a sense of self-worth to others, we first must receive love and have a sense of self-worth. And the good news is that we *can* receive love. John wrote it plainly: "We love Him because He first loved us" (1 John 4:19). In like manner, we love others because we have experienced God's love. Again, as John wrote, "Let us love one another, for love is of God" (1 John 4:7).

To Love Is to Refrain from Harm

I recently heard a man say, "I love my children."

A person interviewing the man on television responded by asking, "Then why did you kill their mother in their presence?"

He said, "I made a mistake. But I still love my children."

No, I don't believe he does. If that man had truly loved his children, he would not have hurt them by murdering their mother! Love does not act in a hurtful way, either to oneself or to others.

Every person who has ever loved another person, a spouse, or a child knows this to be true. We seek only good for those we love. We feel terrible when we accidentally hurt loved ones, and we feel indignant or angry when others hurt our loved ones.

God's command for us to love ourselves means, in part, that we are to do nothing that will bring harm to ourselves. We will take no substance into our bodies that is known to cause bodily harm or mental deficiency. We will engage in no activities that we know will bring detriment to us. We will forge no alliances or relationships that we know will be hurtful to us financially, materially, physically, or emotionally. God gave His law to mankind not to diminish man's fun or to put a damper on man's ability to experience life fully; rather, He gave the law so that man might avoid circumstances that would produce physical, material, emotional, or spiritual harm.

Every one of God's commands related to other people exists so that both you and the other person will be in a position to avoid harm. God's command, "You shall not commit adultery," was given so that *your* heart might not be broken, *your* marriage might not be destroyed, *your* reputation might not be damaged, *your* future might not be impaired, and *your* standing of innocence and purity before God might not be tainted. The commandment, when kept, yields a benefit to others and to society as a whole, but the primary beneficiary in keeping the commandment is the person who keeps it.

The commandment "You shall not murder" is of benefit to the other person, but the primary beneficiary is the person who keeps it. A person who keeps this commandment is spared the guilt of murder and all of the possible consequences that may come to pass in the life of a murderer: separation from family, imprisonment, a life on the run, lingering nightmares, hardness of heart, overwhelming remorse, or death.

Paul wrote to the Romans,

> *Owe no one anything except to love one another, for he who loves another has fulfilled the law. For the commandments, "You shall not commit adultery," "You shall not murder," "You shall not steal," "You shall not bear false witness," "You shall not covet," and if there is any other commandment, are all summed up in this saying, namely, "You shall love your neighbor as yourself." Love does no harm to a neighbor; therefore love is the fulfillment of the law. (Rom. 13:8–10)*

Consider these words of Paul: "For all the law is fulfilled in one word, even in this: 'You shall love your neighbor as yourself.' But if you bite and devour one another, beware lest you be consumed by one another!" (Gal. 5:14–15).

Sin breeds guilt and unworthiness inside us, and it puts us into a position to bring back upon ourselves the very sin that we inflict on others. Who is the person most likely to be murdered in an act of revenge? The person who has murdered. Who is the person most likely to have something stolen from him? The person who has stolen from others. As a simple, practical matter of living at peace with others in this world, it is wise to keep God's commandments. The benefits are great, outwardly in the material, physical, and natural realms of life, and inwardly in the emotional and spiritual realms.

Sin is also a way of harming oneself. Its consequences are always negative and eventually deadly. Sin kills from the inside out.

Show me a person today who is bent on destroying himself with alcohol, drugs, or an illicit love affair, or who harbors unchecked anger and bitterness in his heart, and I will show you a person who does not love himself. Such a person has no sense of worthiness. The undercurrent of that person's life is shame, guilt, and intense emotional need. Such a person is incapable of freely giving unconditional love to another person and of extending to another person great value and worthiness.

The person who genuinely loves will not harm either himself or others.

GOD DESIRES FOR YOU TO BE HIS AGENT OF MINISTRY

God desires to heal you in your inner self and to meet your needs, but His desire is with a purpose. He desires for you to be equipped and fully able to be His agent of love and ministry to others. Giving to others is part of the reason you were created and exist today. Giving to others is the only means by which you will feel fulfilled and satisfied that you have accomplished your purpose in life.

God stands ready, willing, and able—right now—to meet your needs for forgiveness, self-worth, belonging, and competency, and to complete the meeting of all other practical and material needs in your life if you will only turn to Him, seek His help, and be willing to live according to His plan.

Don't let anything keep you from receiving all that God desires to give to you through Christ Jesus.

I declare to you the same thing Paul declared to the believers in Philippi: "My God *shall* supply *all* your need according to His riches in glory by Christ Jesus."

Go to Christ Jesus today and receive the overflowing abundance of supply that He has for you. Your needs *can* be met!

Father, we honor and praise You today as our Need Meeter. Give us the courage and ability to see the deep inner needs that exist in ourselves and in others. And then give us the courage and direction to address these needs. Help us, Lord, to be honest with ourselves, with You, and with others.

Help us to trust You, heavenly Father, with our whole hearts and minds. Help us to look to You first and foremost as the One who is the source of all that we need. Give us discernment to see who and what means You are putting into our paths to help meet our needs, both internal and external. Give us the courage to accept what You so freely offer to us—Your love, Your acceptance, Your forgiveness, Your daily guidance and comfort, Your abiding presence and help. And then, Father, help us to love others as we grow in our ability to love ourselves. Use us for Your glory and for the building of Your kingdom.

We ask this in the name that is above all names, the name of Jesus Christ, our Savior and Lord. Amen!

About the Author

Dr. Charles Stanley is pastor of the 14,000-member First Baptist Church in Atlanta, Georgia. He is well known through his *In Touch* radio and television ministry to thousands internationally and is the author of many books, including *Enter His Gates, The Source of My Strength, The Reason for My Hope, The Glorious Journey, How to Listen to God,* and *How to Handle Adversity.*

Dr. Stanley received his bachelor of arts degree from the University of Richmond, his bachelor of divinity degree from Southwestern Theological Seminary, and his master's and doctor's degrees from Luther Rice Seminary. He has twice been elected president of the Southern Baptist Convention.

OTHER BEST-SELLING BOOKS BY CHARLES STANLEY

ENTER HIS GATES

Spiritual gates are much like the gates of a city. They are vital to your well-being as a Christian and, if not maintained, leave you open to attack by the enemy. *Enter His Gates* is a daily devotional that encourages you to build or strengthen a different spiritual gate each month.

0-7852-7546-0 • Hardcover • 400 Pages • Devotional

IN TOUCH WITH GOD

This unique gift book is filled with inspirational Scriptures as well as thoughts and prayers from Dr. Stanley. It will help you know God's heart on a variety of topics, including forgiveness, relationships, Spirit-filled living, Christian character, and God's plan for your life.

0-7852-7117-1 • Hardcover • 208 Pages • Gift/Devotional

THE POWER OF THE CROSS

Using inspirational Scriptures as well as personal insights and heartfelt prayers, Charles Stanley encourages you to see the transforming power of the Resurrection for salvation, victory over temptation, healing of emotional pain, and restoration with the heavenly Father.

0-7852-7065-5 • Hardcover • 208 Pages • Gift/Devotional

THE REASON FOR MY HOPE

Dr. Stanley reveals the promises and resources God provides His children, identifying nine key reasons for all believers to have unshakable hope.

0-8407-7765-5 • Hardcover • 256 Pages • Christian Living

Dunn Public Library
110 E. DIVINE ST.
DUNN, N.C. 28334